*To Robin W. Winks. A man who
knows a thing or two about empires.*

TABLE OF CONTENTS

PREFACE

EDUCATION OF AN INTERNATIONAL MANAGER

My arrival in Japan in 1987 coincided with the explosion of Japanese financial ambition internationally. As an outsider, skeptic, and market participant, I was both curious and interested. My sojourn in Japan provided an opportunity to observe and experience the actual operation of the Japanese financial institutions (JFIs). This book is an attempt to interpret that experience for the reader.

I was able to observe the JFIs' sudden emergence, their rise to prominence, and growing mystique, from the perspective of a participant in the international marketplace. From 1969 until 1987, I held a number of positions for Salomon Brothers in Boston, New York, London, Hong Kong, and Tokyo. My experience domestically covered fixed income, equities, derivatives, and capital markets. In February 1982, I was named manager of Salomon Hong Kong. At that time, Salomon's Asian operation was headquartered in Hong Kong, and Japanese clients were handled from there. The firm had only a representative office in Tokyo with a staff of four, and was applying for a branch license. However, the branch license application had been delayed at the Ministry of Finance (MOF) for a number of reasons.

At the time, I had very little professional knowledge of Japan and no great intellectual, personal, or business interest. Soon after arriving in Hong Kong, it was obvious to me that Japan would inevitably become a major financial center because of the sheer size of the assets controlled by the JFIs. My interest in Japan developed quickly. When the MOF finally announced that it would approve Salomon's branch license application effective September 1, 1982, the Salomon Hong Kong office was closed and moved to Japan. In terms of available resources and potential business, Tokyo demanded full attention. During my tenure in Tokyo, I had broad personal exposure to the MOF. I engaged in business that was purely domestic, in addition to handling cross-border activities. I had contact with every major JFI.

In 1987, I joined Morgan Stanley as a Managing Director, as head of their equity department in Tokyo. From 1989 to 1992, I advised a number of JFIs on their cross-border activities. In this role, I acquired additional insights into the internal operations of JFIs, especially in the U.S. and Japan.

My judgments on the Japanese financial system, therefore, are based on first-hand experience—and experiments—over a long period of time with a broad range of institutions, agencies, people, and markets. I met often and at length with clients and employees. Some meetings were conducted in English, others utilized interpreters. All usually yielded valuable insights. It is thanks to this continuous interaction with JFIs, the Japanese government, and my staff that I was able to develop an ability to move from the transactional to the conceptual plane in assessing the strengths, weaknesses, problems, and capabilities of JFIs.

I have also relied on secondary sources when relevant. I have critiqued many of the books and newspaper articles written about Japanese finance in an attempt to separate fashion from fact. Many of the journalists and authors in their haste tended to emphasize the sensational at the expense of a less interesting, but more accurate, account. At times, authors tended to overlook their previous interpretations which were off the mark. I have called attention to some of these cases so that there is a clear picture of what transpired in the 1980s and how this was interpreted for the public. I have tied together a lot of published material about Japan's financial institutions in order to highlight valid insights, as well as misconceptions. A better understanding of the myths about Japan in the 1980s, and how perceptions were created, should be gained by a review of these publications.

ACKNOWLEDGMENTS

I began writing this book after a decade's involvement with Japan. It is impossible to list the many people who have contributed to my understanding of Japan.

My contact with thousands of Japanese—salarymen and colleagues—provided the experience which led to my insights. They are, in effect, my interviewees. Many have urged me to write about the realities which they recognized. I am indebted to them for spending countless hours sharing their views.

I would like to acknowledge all those people, both Japanese and non-Japanese, who offered support and encouragement, but who did not want to be acknowledged because of either their Japanese client base or Japanese employer.

I would also like to thank Karen Patton for her sense of humor and for putting the manuscript into proper form.

I am very grateful to my agent, Jane Gelfman, who has been a great source of advice and support.

INTRODUCTION

BUSTED MUFFLER

I was walking to the subway station from my apartment in Tokyo on a Saturday morning in October 1987. It was a crisp, perfect, fall day. I was on my way to the office; as Saturday was an abbreviated work day, a time to think, to reflect and plan for the next week.

The serenity of my journey was abruptly shattered by a loud scraping noise. I instinctively stopped and looked towards the source of this offensive intrusion. I was amazed and embarrassed when I saw a white Cadillac whose muffler was dragging along the pavement. The sparks were flying, as this symbol of American industry limped along a side street in Tokyo. As we all know, mufflers pounding along the pavement produce a particularly irritating sound. An American car, in general, is an unusual sight in Tokyo. This spectacle was visual proof that American industry was inferior to Japanese, Inc. The image was powerful. Tangible failure was there. It was physical, not an abstraction.

I again reflexively scanned the area. I was hoping there were no Japanese witnesses. I somehow felt that I was associated with this farce. As an American, I could not avoid the linkage to America's decline. Worse yet, I was in Japan, a country whose automobile industry had just humbled GM, Ford, and Chrysler. Japanese just did not build cars with busted mufflers.

My pace involuntarily quickened, and I soon entered the Omote-Sando subway station, a spotless symbol of Japan's efficient public transportation system. I boarded the Chiyoda line—another reminder of Japanese planning, as subways in Tokyo actually have printed timetables that are very reliable. Japan's success and power were apparent. Its products were visible.

Yet, in the abstract world of finance, I knew that Japan was, in a sense, producing Cadillacs with busted mufflers. The metaphor applies, even though an abstraction, such as an overpriced bond, does not evoke the same response as a defective or obsolete physical product.

As I rode to the office, I thought about the paradox I observed everyday. The Japanese financial system was seriously flawed; yet the Japanese manufacturing sector appeared to be invincible.

CHAPTER 1

A GLORIOUS SUNRISE? THE ADVENT OF THE JAPANESE FINANCIAL INSTITUTIONS

"A Japanese empire is being born that will pose a fundamental challenge to American power in every sphere."[1]

—DANIEL BURSTEIN

THE SCOPE

Japanese Financial Institutions (JFIs) include all banks, securities firms, and life insurance companies, as well as other companies when their main activity is passive financial involvement. I will examine these institutions' overseas activities. Overseas activity includes operations abroad as well as international investments generated from Tokyo. We should remember that the international business serves as a window on the JFIs' domestic operations. I exclude, however, overseas business activity which existed exclusively to serve domestic clients.

There are several obvious advantages to focusing on the JFIs' overseas operations. For the purposes of analysis, overseas operations can be sepa-

---

[1] Burstein, Daniel, *Yen! Japan's New Financial Empire and Its Threat to America,* New York: Fawcett Columbine, 1988, p. 26.

1

---

rated from domestic activities on the basis of product, client base, and performance. The inherent competitive edge which the JFIs have at home is not present abroad, save for capital. Thus, business practices can be observed, if not in isolation from the domestic market then, at least, in sharp relief. Competitiveness can be assessed more accurately, and structural issues examined in a deregulated market. Most of the examples of overseas activities used will be drawn from the United States rather than Europe or Asia. The JFIs are equally poor performers around the world but, in Europe and Asia, their lending was almost exclusively to governments, quasi-governmental organizations, and transplanted domestic customers. Thus, there was less of a penalty for poor credit risk, and "success"— meaning visibility and market share—becomes largely a matter of price, which is to say, financial muscle.

By contrast, in the 1980s the JFIs were more active in the U.S. They had been there for a significant period of time. Many organizational departments were involved. They had access to far more public information on which to evaluate business opportunities. Thus, their ability to identify what information was relevant, gather and analyze that information, and then make necessary judgments, can all be studied more effectively within the context of their U.S. activities.

" JFIs . . . Their employees come from the same cultural, educational, and family backgrounds. This produces a workforce that is hard-working, well-educated, loyal, self-sacrificing, group-oriented, and singleminded in the pursuit of corporate goals. But does such uniformity have a darker side . . . ?"

I pay particular attention to issues of organization and management. JFIs, like all Japanese corporations, have common management systems. Their employees come from the same cultural, educational, and family backgrounds. This produces a workforce that is hard-working, well-educated, loyal, self-sacrificing, group-oriented, and singleminded in the pursuit of corporate goals. But does such uniformity have a darker side, at least for the JFIs, that is not well understood?

I seek to put the JFIs in the context of the Japanese economic system and business environment. It considers such questions as: Do the Japanese manufacturing companies have a background similar to that of the Japanese financial institutions? What is the historical basis of Japanese financial companies' strength? Does the apparent success of Japanese manufacturing companies' overseas subsidiaries mean that Japanese financial companies will prosper outside of Japan?

Beyond this, I look at the structure and competitiveness of the JFIs.

■ Are JFIs structured properly for overseas business?

■ Have JFIs been successful overseas?

■ What have they built overseas?

■ What is the experience of JFIs in terms of localization of staff overseas?

■ Have they learned anything from their experience?

■ What are the results of the JFIs' joint ventures, acquisitions, and partnerships overseas?

■ How do the JFIs select foreign partners?

■ What is the influence of the Japanese practice of personnel rotation on overseas business?

■ What are the communication and coordination problems of the JFIs overseas?

■ How have the JFIs dealt with issues of analytical ability, creativity and assimilation capability overseas?

■ How does the Japanese Ministry of Finance (MOF) relate to the JFIs?

For purposes of comparative analysis, I briefly examine the strengths and weaknesses of Salomon Tokyo and Morgan Stanley Tokyo. The aim is to stimulate discussion about the problems and performance of any large financial institution operating offshore.

■ Do they have characteristics similar to JFIs?

■ To what extent do they lack focus?

- To what extent do they exhibit excessive (as opposed to generic) bureaucratic tendencies?

- Are the assimilation problems of Western financial institutions in other Western countries as difficult as those of the JFIs, e.g., does Deutsche Bank have the same difficulties as the JFIs in the U.S.?

- Are Western financial firms as concerned with publicity as the JFIs?

THE SETTING

Armed with seemingly endless capital, in the 1980s the Japanese Financial Institutions (JFIs) advanced upon foreign markets as never before. Until then the JFIs had been virtually anonymous outside of Japan, but by mid-decade they were conspicuous worldwide. They were the prime conduit for recycling the wealth accumulated by the Japanese as a result of their industrial success, high savings rate, ebullient stock and real estate markets, and Japan's easy money policies. The sums were too great to be employed solely in the domestic Japanese market, so the JFIs thrust themselves into overseas capital markets in a scramble for assets. The largest JFIs had been in Europe, North America, and Asia for years. But their presence in the 1980s was qualitatively different from their previous experience.

As Japanese manufacturing corporations accelerated their expansion overseas, JFIs followed to service their client base. The JFIs did not want to appear to lack international capabilities. Thus, JFI branches, subsidiaries, and offices sprouted outside of New York in such cities as Houston, Atlanta, Chicago, Los Angeles, and San Francisco. In Europe, London and Zurich were only part of a network that included most cities which were considered to have a financial presence. The JFIs wanted multiple beach-heads.

Japanese companies found the Euromarkets attractive for raising funds because their own domestic market was too archaic and restrictive. This was ironic because it meant the JFIs were essentially pursuing transplanted domestic business. Despite excess capital at home, Japanese companies went overseas to borrow.

Frequently, Japanese corporations used the proceeds of the borrowings to purchase financial assets such as fixed income securities or equities. Such investment was highly speculative—made without regard for credit risks or mismatched maturities. In its heyday, this practice of financial manipulation and asset accumulation was elevated to the financial equivalent

> **" Japanese companies found the Euromarkets attractive for raising funds because their own domestic market was too archaic and restrictive. "**

of high tech, "*zaitech*"—combining the Japanese word for finance with technology. When the bubble burst, *zaitech* became a pejorative term.

The JFIs' expansion overseas was done almost exclusively with Japanese rather than foreign staff. There was a huge demand for personnel to fill international positions. This phalanx of soberly-dressed Japanese added to the new sense of power the JFIs carried abroad.

JAPANESE PROJECT SOPHISTICATED IMAGE

From the outset, the sudden expansion of the JFIs in the 1980s was regarded differently by the international financial community from, say, the short-lived Arab financial glory a decade before. The Arabs were seen as primitive, unprofessional, and profligate. Arab wealth was viewed as a windfall, a lucky inheritance, not the result of honest hard work. The stereotypical spendthrift Arab playboy reinforced the prejudices.

The Japanese, by contrast, were found to be sophisticated, aggressive, hard-working, well-trained, and self-sacrificing. They had earned their wealth "the old fashioned way," despite the handicap of having no natural resources. The Japanese people were the country's "natural resource." The archetypal Japanese businessman was spartan, goal-oriented, and serious. Their dark suits, emotionless facade, formal manner, and conservative demeanor were all in stark visual contrast to the more flamboyant Arabs. Even the Japanese businessman's nightly entertainment rounds with his clients were judged to be a serious effort to promote business and facilitate communication, without connotation of frivolity or debauchery. Foreigners who witnessed this were astonished by the stamina of the Japanese, who could endure this nightly physical abuse and then undergo long, grueling days in the office.

The Japanese system was operating effectively in the manufacturing area. The JFIs were part of the same system. Foreigners immediately assumed that they were just as formidable competitors as the industrialists. Any unqualified analogy with the Arabs was ludicrous; the differences in behavior, attitude, and appearance were overwhelming. As the bestselling author, Burstein, stated, "any useful analogy to OPEC . . . must . . . (take) into account Japan's better set of circumstances for the maintenance and enhancement of its wealth."[2] If the Arabs in the 1970s evoked envy and contempt, the Japanese brought fear.

With fear came faith in the omnipotence of the Japanese, whatever might happen. Discounting the worst, Burstein, the popularizer, wrote:

> It is possible, even probable, that major unforeseen events will take place while this book is current . . . The Tokyo Stock Exchange might suffer a catastrophic drop, and Japanese investment abroad could be curtailed. All this would appear to seem at odds with the powerful image of Japan . . . presented here . . . But if these events come to pass, don't be fooled. Japan has survived many "shocks" to its system in the last two decades . . . the lesson is that even if Japan falls on hard times again, the gloom is likely to be short-lived. Unlike the Americans, the Japanese have evolved planning capabilities and procedures to carry out systematic structural economic readjustments to new conditions.[3]

Today, with Japan, Europe, and North America characterized by recession or modest growth, and the Japanese financial system in obvious disarray, the JFIs are no longer the vanguard of a new economic empire. They are no longer a threat nor the source of boundless capital. They are a drain on their own economy, their inefficiencies and spendthrift ways now subsidized by the Japanese people and Japanese manufacturers.

---

2 Burstein, *Yen!*, p. 42.
3 Burstein, *Yen!*, pp. 28-29.

REALITIES OF JFIs CONTRADICT MYTH OF JAPAN, INC.

In his most recent book, in a chapter entitled "The Japanese 'Plan' for a Post-2000 World," Paul Kennedy extols the virtues of Japan, Inc. as being more competitive than the rest of the world.[4] The myth of Japanese long-term planning and superiority is alive and well. Mr. Kennedy, an accomplished and eminent historian, has unfortunately probably never been inside a JFI. Otherwise, he would not have glossed over their loss of tens of billions of dollars overseas in bad loans and investments. Mr. Kennedy's understatement of their disastrous forays is difficult to comprehend, as he

> **" ... the JFIs are no longer the vanguard of a new economic empire. They are no longer a threat nor the source of boundless capital. They are a drain on their own economy, their inefficiencies and spendthrift ways now subsidized by the Japanese people and Japanese manufacturers."**

comments, ". . . Japan's aggressive spending on acquisitions across the globe, *some of which have yet to prove profitable*" (italics mine).[5] Mr. Kennedy used only secondary sources to support his theoretical structure, rather than build a credible thesis. Often these sources were unreliable.

Why is this professional historian citing the size of JFIs[6] without discussing the reason for their size and their abysmal record? He dragged out the usual statistics, ". . . seven out of ten of the world's largest banks in September, 1991 . . . were Japanese. Overall, twenty-nine of the world's hundred largest banks were Japanese."[7] So what! Japan has few banks and the world's second largest economy; hence, they have large banks. Unable to resist a comparison of the Japanese empire to the British empire, Mr. Kennedy saw ". . . a rising flood of Japanese businessmen, tourists, manu-

---

4 Kennedy, Paul, *Preparing for the Twenty-First Century*, New York: Random House, 1993.
5 Kennedy, *Preparing*, p. 145.
6 Kennedy, *Preparing*, p. 152.
7 Kennedy, *Preparing*, p. 152.

facturers, and capital penetrat(ing) most parts of the globe, in a manner
reminiscent of Britain's mid- to late-Victorian expansionism."[8] He naively
stated that ". . . the Japanese have found foreign countries and their assets
(from farmland to Impressionist paintings) relatively cheap."[9]

What does he mean by "relatively cheap"? The reality is quite different. The JFIs frittered away billions of dollars in losses and underperfor-
mance. Japan's economy has been constrained by a malfunctioning
financial system which is the product of overregulation without market accountability. JFIs were incompetent in their pursuit of overseas investments, loans, joint ventures, and acquisitions. Bureaucratic rot was the
cause of this failure. Japan's economic empire has very real limits. Lack of
skills and bureaucratic slough combined to humble the JFIs.

Even Japan's successful manufacturers boasted that the financial system played only a supporting role. They did not realize that allowing second-rate financial institutions to develop would be a costly mistake.

Foreigners and Japanese predicted that the JFIs would effectively and
quickly incorporate foreign ideas and expertise into their organizations.
This did not occur. Again, Mr. Kennedy succumbs to conventional wisdom, when he embraces the notion "When foreign experts declare Japan to
be deficient in a certain field (luxury cars, computer software, supercom-
puters), intense efforts are made to eliminate that deficiency."[10] JFIs spent
huge amounts of money for foreign firms and paid extravagant salaries to
foreigners without institutionally absorbing their knowledge. Simply put,
the JFIs overpaid for people and firms. Japanese xenophobia is common
knowledge, but the inability to assimilate foreigners within JFIs is not
given proper weight.

Often both Japanese and foreigners try to overlook JFI mistakes by
invoking the Japanese long-term mentality. We will see how the JFI internal practices force JFI employees to be quite short-term oriented.

Even the *keiretsu* (groups of companies) relationships have a dark side
which contributed to the JFIs' weakness. The *keiretsu* relationship removes
competition and thus ensures that bad practices will go unpunished. This
fosters the development of JFIs, which are insensitive to losses and performance—truly, second-rate institutions.

---

8 Kennedy, *Preparing*, p. 143.
9 Kennedy, *Preparing*, p. 142.
10 Kennedy, *Preparing*, p. 141.

All large organizations, both Japanese and non-Japanese, are plagued with excessive bureaucracy, but the Japanese are considered to be exempt. Their deliberate manner is deemed to be a thoughtful approach in attempting to gain consensus within their organization. Their slow reaction time is rationalized as their honorable and worthwhile attention to details and long-term planning.

The reality is, again, quite different. The consequences are even more

---

" **Foreigners and Japanese often attribute the JFIs' recent folly to the "bubble economy." In this scenario, judgment was suspended at the normally unerring JFIs from 1982 until 1992 because of arrogance induced by success and the availability of easy money. This view holds that the "bubble" was an aberration and that the JFIs will emerge triumphant from their brief hangover. This is false.** "

---

damaging than at Western firms because of the total absence of individual, departmental or firm accountability. The lack of concern with investor protection, assumption of an ever-rising domestic market in the 1980s, and arrogance all removed any checks within the system.

The use of Japan as a role model was fashionable. It was dangerous to consider JFIs as a positive role model. The lessons to be learned from the cozy, incestuous relationship between the JFIs and the Japanese MOF are primarily negative—fraud, manipulation, and tolerance of poor asset management performance. The current fantasy, held by some Americans, that public policy should be based on the alleged idyllic connection between JFIs and the MOF is naive.

Foreigners and Japanese often attibute the JFIs' recent folly to the "bubble economy." In this scenario, judgment was suspended at the normally unerring JFIs from 1982 until 1992 because of arrogance induced by success and the availability of easy money. This view holds that the "bubble" was an aberration and that the JFIs will emerge triumphant from their brief hangover. This is false. JFIs have structural weaknesses which severely restrict their ability to compete. Their problems are not temporary or superficial. The bubble made the structural faults surface in a very dramatic manner.

One of the strengths of JFIs is their inherited franchise, which has been granted by the MOF. As a result, JFIs have extensive capacity to distribute financial products. They manage an enormous amount of assets. This has been well-documented and well-publicized. They have shown no ability to properly select assets or manage money professionally. Actually, JFIs have had a disasterous record in their overseas investments and have been at the mercy of the Japanese economy in their domestic investment activities. They will not be a threat to conquer foreign markets, even though their asset base will remain significant.

Is it possible to reform Japan's flawed financial system? There has been no indication that the real problems have been identified, much less corrected. The vested interests of the JFIs and the MOF mitigate against meaningful reform of the financial system. Weaknesses are deeply imbedded structurally. Market forces are limited. The Japanese people have a seemingly infinite capacity for self-sacrifice. Peer pressure and hierarchy are still powerful forces. Change is made at the periphery. Publicity about reform, rather than actual reform, predominates. The JFIs simply were not able to compete abroad in a deregulated environment and are likely to remain second-rate internationally, because reform is not imminent.

Although this study focuses on the overseas activities of JFIs, the implications for their domestic activities is obvious. The same organizational issues that affect overseas activities are present domestically. The JFIs, although large, are prisoners of the system which gave them power.

The depth of Japan's financial institutional malaise is not understood. Meanwhile, Americans gloss over the realities of Japan, Inc.'s vulnerabilities. They prefer general fear to selective analysis. Pundits and journalists should be held accountable for their sensationalist approach to Japan, Inc., treating it as a threat.

CHAPTER 2

THE CREATION OF A MYTH: THE IMAGE OF JAPANESE FINANCIAL INSTITUTIONS IN THE 1980S

"The same sort of dominance (as the manufacturers) appeared in the field of finance. Well into the 1970s Japan's banks and financial markets were justifiably regarded as primitive . . . By the mid-1980s Tokyo challenged London and New York as an international financial center and, in sheer money power, overwhelmed both."[1]

—WILLIAM CHAPMAN

"Leading Japanese financial institutions border on the primitive."[2]

THE ECONOMIST

"As American business has ample reason to know, when the Japanese home in on a new market, they aim at the bull's-eye. In three short years, guided by strategic planning that subordinates quick profits to long-term

---

[1] Chapman, William, *Inventing Japan*, NY: Prentice Hall Press, 1991, p. 173.
[2] "Falling Apples," Japanese Finance Survey, *The Economist*, December 8, 1990, p. 3.

market growth, four major Japanese firms, Nomura,
Daiwa, Nikko, and Yamaichi, are well on their way to
becoming major players in U.S. financial markets . . ."[3]

EDITORIAL IN *BUSINESS WEEK*

No public relations firm could have done a better job. At the start of the
1980s, JFIs were regarded as primitive. Hidebound and inefficient, they
existed in the never-never land of a tightly regulated market. But by mid-
decade, the JFIs emerged as awesome global competitors and it was only
later, after the glitz of the media began to fade, that their true selves appeared again.

For much of the 1980s, journalists—both domestic and foreign—and
popular pundits such as Clyde Prestowitz and Daniel Burstein, spun a web
of myth around the JFIs. These, they said, were following in the same
tracks as the Japanese manufacturers. The strategy was familiar: co-opt
technology, acquire market share, then destroy the competition. The U.S.
watched Japanese manufacturers invade and conquer the automobile, consumer electronics, and semiconductor industries. Financial services, once
thought a U.S. preserve, would be the next.

NOTHING NEW: JAPAN'S ECONOMIC SYSTEM, AND ITS THREAT TO AMERICA, 1935

Articles warning of Japan's economic "advance" upon America were common in *The Saturday Evening Post* during the 1930s. Even before the
1980s, notions of Japanese economic superiority had permeated this icon of
American mass culture. The dean of the Harvard Business School, Wallace
B. Donham, described market share invasion vintage 1935:

> The Japanese slowly feel their way into a market learning local
> conditions as they progress. Then suddenly they flood it with rap-
> idly increasing quantities . . . The trend is ominous . . . her goods
> offered at prices well below ours, her stocks in bonded warehouses
> hang over the market and further disorganize our price structure.[4]

---

3 *Business Week*, September 7, 1987, p. 122.
4 Donham, Wallace B., "Japan Advances," *The Saturday Evening Post*, July 6, 1935, p.
    38.

Dumping circa 1935, Donham expresses admiration for Japan and the "great self-sacrifice" of the Japanese. The "Self-sacrifice" was required and imposed by the "Elder Statesmen," aka, the Japanese government officials.

The dean of the Harvard Business School spoke of our "national ignorance of Japan" and its goals. His confidence in the Japanese "Elder Statesmen's" ability to control the nation's destiny foreshadowed the beliefs of the Chrysanthemum brigade in the 1980s. His view of Japanese military aggression in the 1930s is significant—not because of his error. Simply, the importance lies in his extraordinary faith in the Japanese system:

> We resent it when Japan for what she considers vital national reasons, puts her own interpretations on international understandings about China and Manchuria . . . Japan is establishing a Monroe Doctrine for the Far East and at the same time absorbing territory of vital importance to her . . . Japan's principal home danger is that she may be driven too fast by the military group now in control . . . Militarization may yet bankrupt the nation . . . many Western observers expect this to happen . . . To me, this is wishful thinking . . . If necessary to maintain economic stability, Japan can at will slow down military and naval development.[5]

He "hazard(s) no moral judgments" and in a wonderfully vague statement avoids the issue:

> I look on her (Japan's) activities, particularly in China, with anxiety and regret, (although) I understand enough to both respect and admire her.[6]

Again, his views on Japan's incursions are not relevant. His certainty that Japan can adjust its course under a flexible system with the "Elder Statesmen" at the helm is a refrain which we will listen to fifty years later.

He was very explicit when stating that "there is a clash of Western and Eastern cultures, and this time the advantage is not to the West."[7] He warned that, "Our Western civilization is the target for an Eastern archer

---

5 Donham, *Japan Advances*, p. 10, 34.
6 Donham, *Japan Advances*, p. 11.
7 Donham, *Japan Advances*, p. 38.

whom we have taught, and the newly taught archer brings to his task both strength and skill."[8] We heard this repeatedly in the 1980s about the JFIs.

These were consistent themes in *The Saturday Evening Post*. Donham's style was decidedly academic, as he was lecturing to the American people. Other writers used invective and sarcasm to escalate the emotional level of the argument. One author described a fictitious boat trip from America to Japan. The boat is filled with American engineers and technicians who are selling their skills to the Japanese:

> We can't stand up against Japanese competition he (one of the engineers) assures you. "The combination of the cheapest labor and the most expensive machinery will close our factories. Something ought to be done about it." So after you have stopped laughing, you ask him (the engineer) where he is going. And he says Japan. And you ask him what he is going there for and he tells you he has a two-year contract to go over and install some machinery his company has invented and teach the Japanese how to operate it with the greatest efficiency and the lowest cost. "And when these factories get underway and start turning out goods, what will you do then?" And he says, "Oh, by that time my job will be finished and I will go home to America."[9]

The fear was not restricted to the industrial sphere of textile machinery. Another article entitled "Rising Sons—Japan's Bid for Athletic Supremacy," warned in its caption how "carefully the Japanese study the methods of athletes all over the world, copying the best features of each and win at the Olympics. They're coming along fast."[10] The author, Lawson Robertson, was the head coach of the American Olympic Team and track coach of the University of Pennsylvania. In rather typical *Saturday Evening Post* prose the article purported to describe a banquet hosted by Japanese for American athletes. The translator at the banquet, allegedly, made the following request:

8 Donham, *Japan Advances*, p. 38.
9 McEvoy, J.P., "The Traveling Salesman and the Farmer's Daughter," *The Saturday Evening Post*, August 28, 1937, p. 10.
10 Robertson, Lawson, "Rising Sons—Japan's Bid for Athletic Supremacy," *The Saturday Evening Post*, June 22, 1935, p. 10.

We're going to ask each of you (American athletes) to stand up and tell the secret of your supremacy in your particular event. How you train. How you get the best results in hurdling, sprinting, pole vaulting, or whatever your particular stunt may be.[11]

Many of the themes which we will encounter in the 1980s had already surfaced in American folklore and mass culture of the 1930s. The assumption of the superiority of Japanese systematic planning was evident. No distinction was made for industry segments or even sports, for that matter. The "Elder Statesmen," the officials of the MOF, were elevated to a status which we will observe in the 1980s. The success of Japanese market share strategy was already ingrained by the 1930s. Japanese ability to copy any method or invention was taken for granted. Japanese self-sacrifice was viewed as an unalloyed advantage, without any connotation of peer pressure and hierarchy. Nothing was mentioned about the unintended consequences or limits of the Japanese system.

Those popular articles add perspective. They should be remembered as the events of the 1980s are reviewed.

EXPERTS SPIN THE MYTH 1980s STYLE

Daniel Burstein's book, *Yen! Japan's New Financial Empire and Its Threat to America*, sensationalized the topic. His fictionalized scenario described the JFIs as "foremost among America's foreign bankers . . . who were just learning to use their massive capital surplus to sow the seeds of empire.[12] Another writer, Clyde Prestowitz did a better job capturing the spirit of inevitability in the new mythology:

The service industry idyll was blasted in November, 1986 when Nomura Securities announced that it had handled, entirely on its own, the placement of a major bond issue for General Electric Credit Corporation. Nomura was the first foreign company to do such a thing in the United States.[13]

---

11 Robertson, *Rising Sons*, p. 10.
12 Burstein, *Yen!* p. 15.
13 Prestowitz, Clyde, *Trading Places*, NY: Basic Books, Inc., 1988, pp. 11-12.

Although word of this coup was "buried in the back pages of *The New York Times*," according to Prestowitz, this was one of "several early tremors" showing a "major shift in the tectonic plates of the power structure of world finance." Prestowitz explained:

■ In 1980, a ranking of the world's ten largest banks had included two U.S. banks and one Japanese. In 1986, it included seven for Japan and one for the United States.

■ The Sumitomo Bank's purchase of a 15 percent interest in the Wall Street firm of Goldman, Sachs caused a stir of press comment in the summer of 1986. Few people knew, however, that Japanese banks had accumulated over 20 percent of the banking assets in California by acquiring four of its top ten banks. In the following year, a succession of Wall Street houses would announce partial sales of themselves to Japanese financial interests.

■ In January 1986, for the first time, Japan passed the United States in the share of international banking business held. It was predicted that "the Japanese now are on their way to becoming the world's banker."

■ In 1986, Japan's four largest investment banks accounted for virtually none of the trading on the New York Stock Exchange. By the end of 1987, they did nearly 10 percent of the trading, and the volume of Nomura Securities alone was approaching that of the giant Merrill Lynch, the largest U.S. trader.

"The process," Prestowitz warned ominously, "echoed what had happened in the manufacturing industries."

U.S. government officials paid homage to Prestowitz's all-encompassing theory of the effective alliance between Japanese government and business. Laura Tyson, the White House Chief Economist, said that, "Everything that I've seen has been consistent (with his account)."[14] In the same article U.S. Trade Representative Mickey Kantor acknowledges his indebtedness: "I talk to (Mr.) Prestowitz all the time."[15] The article attributes the success of Japanese industrial policy to government intervention. Prestowitz has applied his arguments about Japan's industrial conquests to

---

14 Davis, Bob, *The Wall Street Journal*, June 14, 1993, p. A-11.
15 Davis, *WSJ*, p. A-11.

the financial arena. U.S. officials are misinformed if they adopt Prestowitz's views without rigorous anaylsis—especially in the financial service "industry."

Surprisingly, even in the manufacturing sector, Japan's own senior government officials have begun to level some harsh criticisms of past policies. Mr. Noboru Hatakeyama, the Vice-Minister of MITI blasted Japan's high technology companies. "Up until now (1993), we never thought that some industries have lost competitiveness . . . But . . . we have to face up to it."[16] What has been the result of this government alliance? Certainly, it has not been unalloyed success. In the financial area, it is clear that the bargain between government and JFIs has been Faustian.

> " In the financial area, it is clear that the
> bargain between government and JFIs has
> been Faustian. "

Prestowitz is an astute, experienced and knowledgeable observer of Japan. His book, *Trading Places*, is about the manufacturing sector, yet reasons by analogy that the familiar pattern of Japanese domination would repeat itself in finance. The book looks for evidence that would suggest another Japanese victory and fit into his theory of Japanese dominance—and finds it.

ACADEMICS FOLLOW SUIT

By the late 1980s, the accepted wisdom about JFIs was pervasive. In 1988, even the historian Paul Kennedy writes in his book, *The Rise and Fall of The Great Powers*. "Not surprisingly," he wrote, "Japanese banks and securities firms are rapidly becoming the most successful in the world."[17]

Kennedy's book (which in translation according to the Japan *Times* has sold more copies in Japan than in the U.S.) described the paths which the Spanish, Dutch, British, and American empires followed in their ascendance and descendance. Validating Japanese views of their own ascen-

---

[16] Sanger, David E., *The New York Times*, March 11, 1993, p. D-7.
[17] Kennedy, Paul, *The Rise and Fall of the Great Powers*, New York: Random House, 1987, p. 466.

dancy, it mentioned the economic giant devoid of military power. Recognizing that Japan had joined the world's elite nations because of its economic prowess, Kennedy assumed that the JFIs, too, were destined to be successful overseas. Thus, the JFIs were incorporated into a projection of the new Japanese empire abroad.

In 1989, an article in the Harvard Business Review *reflected the prevailing notion of Japanese governmental prowess* when it recited the conventional truism, "The quality of Japan's financial regulators is unsurpassed; they are recruited from the top ranks of the best universities and they average decades of training and experience."[18] The article continues down the conventional path *by extolling the JFIs which "are the world's largest and, just as important, are conservatively managed and have high-quality assets."*[19] The *Harvard Business Review*, in this instance, had certainly succumbed to the myth of Japanese superiority.

By 1993, one former investment banker, at least, dared to ask what the Ministry of Finance was doing: "The question that has not yet been satisfactorily answered is, of course, where was the Ministry of Finance, the formidable all-controlling guardian of bank safety and soundness, when all this speculation (in the 1980s) was going on?"[20]

JAPANESE JOURNALISTS RESPOND JINGOISTICALLY

The Japanese press interpreted the activities of the JFIs overseas superficially, positively, and jingoistically. Accustomed to the success of Japanese manufacturers, the Japanese reporters had faith in the system and, therefore, considered the financial institutions just as invincible in the long run. Given their shared cultural and national assumptions, not to mention the nature of Japanese media, it is almost inconceivable that a reporter would do otherwise.

There is no tradition of objectivity in the Japanese press. Its task is to control or "manage" the news. A journalist who wrote a favorable article would gain further contacts in the business world. On the other hand, repri-

---

18 Murphy, R. Taggart, "Power Without Purpose: The Crisis of Japan's Global Financial Dominance," *Harvard Business Review*, March-April 1989, p. 74.

19 Murphy, "Power," p. 74.

20 Smith, Roy C., *Comeback: The Restoration of American Banking Power in the New World Economy*, Boston: Harvard Business School Press, 1993, p. 253.

sals or ostracism were real dangers for anyone who strayed too far from the established truth.

THE FOREIGN JOURNALISTS JOIN IN MYTH MAKING

The group most responsible for creating the myth of JFI success abroad was foreign journalists. These often lacked proper financial or even Japanese background. Courted by foreign financial institutions, chasing fashion, creating excitement—the objectivity of some was suspect.

There were and are, of course, notable professional journalists who have consistently provided interesting insights and accurate reporting on the Japanese business environment. But far too many journalists never escaped the trap of the overseas reporter. Responding to story instructions from editors at home who usually had no understanding of the Japanese situation, they tended to write for their domestic market and its assumptions. Often they had to concoct stories hastily to justify events. Here they would begin with a conclusion, then try to substantiate it, rather than collect and evaluate reliable information objectively.

To cover their story, they would seek out senior officials and executives in the relevant organizations and companies. In Japan, this is a relatively small group, as evidenced by the frequency with which the same group is quoted. Worse, perhaps, these senior officials often had a largely ceremonial role and were not immune from making self-serving comments. The journalists gravitated towards foreign officials who were adept at providing "quotable quotes."

The greatest obstacle facing the journalists, however, was simply involvement. *Talking* to someone about a problem or a transaction is not the same as participating in a business. The journalist's position as temporary spectator, at times, can produce superficial, even misleading impressions—as seen with the September, 1987 cover of *Business Week* which graphically portrayed a Japanese *samurai* grasping the Federal Reserve building in New York, conveying dominance of the American financial system:

The cover story contained a table demonstrating how Japan's brokers dwarfed U.S. investment banks. *Business Week* warned:

> The Big Four (Japanese brokers) are following the same strategy to carve out a piece of the U.S. securities business that Japanese manufacturers have used to sell consumer goods: high volumes and low mark-ups . . . They want to go head-to-head with each other to

sell financial products too. Just as Japanese auto manufacturers flooded the U.S. with plain, inexpensive cars at bargain prices . . . (the Japanese brokers) are launching a long-term campaign to wear down the competition . . .[21]

THE DOUBT BEGINS

Yet, in less than two years *Business Week's* tone and attitude about Japanese brokers in the U.S. changed dramatically. In "Tokyo Brokers Beat a Retreat From the Street,"[22] *Business Week* concluded, "It's so tough to make a buck stateside that the Big Four Firms are curtailing operations."

Apparently, the threat *Business Week* found so real in 1987 was subsiding in 1989—even before the Japanese equity market began its steep decline. At this point, Sony, Toyota, Hitachi, and Matsushita unlike the JFIs were not cutting back on their American activities. Clearly, muscle was not enough and *Business Week's* own 1987 warning was not even mentioned. What was also ignored by *Business Week* and others, however, were the more substantive questions. If capital, hard work, and committed, well-educated employees were not enough, what else could be impacting results? Why weren't the JFIs taking over the world?

The Economist blamed dependence on the government, lack of efficiency, and a copy-cat mentality as the essential failings. But beyond that it gave few insights into the disparity of performance between Japanese manufacturers and the JFIs. The one was described as "super-efficient," the other "primitive."

JAPAN'S UNIQUENESS PLAYS INTO MYTH

One reason why the myth of the JFIs became so pervasive in the 1980s was the belief in the uniqueness of Japan and things Japanese. There is no doubt that the Japanese governmental, educational, corporate, and social sectors effectively promote xenophobia and ultranationalism in Japan. They have been unequivocally successful in making the Japanese think they are separate from the rest of the world. Outsiders, according to Japanese proselytes, cannot understand the Japanese. Many times a *"gaijin"* (foreigner)

---

21 "Japan on Wall Street," *Business Week*, September 7, 1987, p. 34.
22 "Tokyo Broker's Beat a Retreat from the Street," *Business Week*, February 13, 1989, p. 42.

encounters the response, "You will not understand because you are not Japanese."

This attitude has been taken to absurd conclusions. The uniqueness of Japanese snow is said to require special skis. The special length of Japanese intestines is better suited to Japanese beef. Most serious foreign observers have at least one favorite example. Ian Buruma writes of the Japanese brain: "A Japanese neurologist made a name for himself by writing a book about the uniqueness of the Japanese brain, which was uniquely sensitive to the sounds of temple bells, waterfalls, and cicadas, and other natural vibrations."[23]

For Prestowitz, it was baseball bats: "When a U.S. official asked (Japanese) baseball league officials for information (about why two American baseball bat producers were not given seals which would have allowed them to sell their bat in Japan), he was politely told that it would be impossible for a foreign firm to be approved, because (Japanese) rubberized baseball was a 'unique' Japanese variant of baseball requiring Japanese bats."[24] The obsessiveness of the Japanese with their uniqueness has benefitted the publishing industry. There are thousands of Japanese books which seek to define "Japaneseness." Indeed, there is even a name for the genre: *"nihonjin ron."*

This concept of uniqueness helps the Japanese to think of their institutions as being superior because they are Japanese. Manufacturers and financial institutions are viewed as indistinguishable, because their most important characteristic is their Japaneseness. It was an assumption that all Japanese companies, including JFIs, are better than their foreign counterparts and are destined for greatness.

Any short-term problem is dismissed as irrelevant. Senior officials of JFIs have expressed their faith in the ascendancy of JFIs by using a forty- or fifty-year time horizon. This attitude allowed a life insurance company official to express confidence in the value of one of his New York buildings, which had declined by 50 percent within a few years after it was purchased. In 1990, an official at Nippon Life was quoted as citing the purchase of 13 percent of Shearson Lehman in 1987 as a "long-term strategic investment"—although the value had fallen by several hundred million dollars at that point and the strategic value was also questionable. In terms of intelligent deal flow, one does not have to be cynical to think that Shear-

---

[23] Buruma, Ian, *God's Dust*, London: Vintage, 1991, p. 238.
[24] Prestowitz, *Trading Places*, p. 97.

son viewed Nippon Life as a source of capital and that the fee-incentivized Shearson investment bankers were not concerned with Nippon Life's performance or knowledge accumulation.

Nevertheless, the Japanese operate under the premise that they are successful and moving towards goals because they are Japanese. What foreigners think is irrelevant to them. Foreigners succumb to the uniqueness theory, believing that the Japanese have demonstrated their superiority. The foreigner even thinks that the Japanese know something that foreigners are incapable of comprehending. Likewise, Japanese power and long-term approach give their goals a sense of inevitability. Thus, the elements which lead to the extraordinary performance of Japanese manufacturing companies abroad in terms of product acceptance and profitability become the same ones which propelled JFIs to worldwide prominence and potential domination. This simplistic analogy is extended further to include the role of the Tokyo University educated bureaucrats of the MOF. The MOF is compared to its industrial counterpart, the Ministry of Trade and Industry (MITI). In both cases, the bureaucrats are viewed as having provided the leadership and organizational framework that guided their constituencies to their proper goals. Currently, some Japanese politicians are discussing the role of the MOF and its limits, but they do not understand the difficulties in dismantling the structure, nor do they grasp how the MOF orchestrated the development of a deeply flawed financial system.

> **" Foreigners succumb to the uniqueness theory, believing that the Japanese have demonstrated their superiority. The foreigner even thinks that the Japanese know something that foreigners are incapable of comprehending. "**

By the early 1990s, at least, it was clear that the JFIs were not going to overwhelm their U.S. counterparts. Their long-term ambitions on hold, they are retreating, not advancing. Yet, public attitude in Japan, and elsewhere, still holds that the JFIs are part of a Japanese system that is considered superior and, therefore, potentially dominant. The image of success overseas has been tarnished, but the reality is still not fully understood.

CHAPTER 3

THE ILLUSION OF STRENGTH

Examining the origins of the JFIs and the influences which shaped them will enhance our understanding of their overseas activities in the 1980s. For many foreigners, the "enigma" of JFIs contributes to the appearance of strength and the consequent evocation of fear. But, in reality, the JFIs are more impenetrable than mysterious, and if foreigners took the time to study the JFIs within the context of Japanese society, much of the mystery would disappear.

" But, in reality, the JFIs are more impenetrable than mysterious, and if foreigners took the time to study the JFIs within the context of Japanese society, much of the mystery would disappear. "

Historically, the bases of JFI strength are:

■ Regulation and the MOF's role

■ Post-World War II Japanese bull markets in equity and real estate markets

■ Cross-shareholding arrangements

■ Cash generated by the manufacturing sector

■ Savings of Japanese individuals

- ■ Japanese journalistic practices
- ■ Low interest rates in the 1980s

Ironically, what brought strength at home generated weakness abroad in the 1980s.

REGULATION AND THE ROLE OF THE MOF

In the 1980s, the JFIs were—as they are today—granted franchises by the MOF. Every aspect of their business was controlled by the MOF. Deposit rates, commission rates, and a myriad of items were controlled by the MOF's octopus-like tentacles. Historically, regulation and restrictions had insulated the JFIs from foreign competition. Domestic competition did occur, but in a very narrow sphere between members of a specific group, i.e., trust banks competed with other trust banks, securities firms with other securities firms, and city banks with other city banks. There were areas in which different categories of institutions competed with each other, but results were generally compared between similar JFIs.

Because the authority of the MOF was intentionally left vague, its bureaucrats were free to legislate and adjudicate. In addition there was internal competition among the different departments at the MOF. This led, in many cases, to inconsistencies and ambiguities which created an environment in which everyone had to go to the MOF for dispensation because only a particular bureaucrat could "rule" on an issue. This proved to be amateurish as the MOF personnel had very little background in many areas about which they issued decrees, a problem aggravated by periodic staff rotation.

The amorphous nature of regulations is illustrated by the importance of the definition of what constitutes "a security." If the MOF determined that an instrument was not a security, security firms were prevented from trading it. If this definitional issue were handled in a substantive manner, there would be no confusion. However, the discussion of what constituted a security generally degenerated into a superficial examination of form. Thus, for example, even if a preferred stock was a security, it could not be assumed that a convertible preferred stock would be a security. In the mortgage area, a GNMA was deemed to be a security, but it was not safe to assume that a CMO was approved. The MOF personnel spoke to JFIs, and JFI staff frequently visited the MOF to pay homage. On the telephone, the MOF officials would sometimes give permission to do something on a small scale, but would not define what that meant.

When an offshore branch of a Japanese firm purchased an asset overseas, the MOF was extraordinarily curious and would go to great lengths to cajole the institution into providing minute details about the transaction. The drill might start with abusive, threatening language from a middle-level, arrogant bureaucrat. Then, the same bureaucrat would telephone other JFIs to try to uncover information and to inject authority. All this was done in a heavy manner which was designed to intimidate. The offending party was being ostracized, and all other JFIs were being made aware of this failure to genuflect. Often, the transaction in question was quite routine and the MOF bureaucrat generally had no interest in the substance of the matter.

" The MOF encouraged gossip and managed the spreading of rumors. "

In many areas, such as commodity funds, the MOF decided which institutions would be able to market products initially. If a firm was out of favor with the MOF, its chances of being selected were reduced. The MOF generally bequeathed these presents to various firms so as not to exclude anyone. If a firm exhibited independence, the MOF could easily isolate the JFI and this would soon be apparent to everyone in the financial community. There was little need to exert such power, however, because all the JFIs knew their place within the system.

The MOF encouraged gossip and managed the spreading of rumors. In many cases, the content of such rumors was trivial, but important financial leaks occurred as well. The Bank of Japan's decisions were sometimes known via the MOF before they were publicly announced. The JFIs were aware that the proper attitude towards the MOF would be rewarded.

The foreign firms in Tokyo did not fit neatly into this picture. Initially, the technological skills and trading abilities of the sophisticated firms were viewed with skepticism. The MOF, of course, did attempt to control the foreign firms, but without the vigor that characterized its supervision of the JFIs. Indeed, the MOF did not take the foreign firms seriously until they began to do substantial business by the mid-1980s. They paid special attention to the ones with expertise and clout in futures and options, when those markets began in Japan. In the 1980s, the MOF was reluctant to deal with political ramifications, as the U.S. government was pushing Japan to open its financial markets and the JFIs wanted reciprocity in the U.S. (such as primary dealer status in the U.S. Treasury market). The MOF was especially sensitive to European governments, which deal with Japan on an issue-by-issue basis.

As with the JFIs, the MOF tried to create an atmosphere of control with foreign firms. During the 1980s, there were periodic "cooperative" lunches attended by the MOF and representatives of several foreign securities firms. Here, the exchange of ideas was supposed to promote understanding. The discussions usually amounted to a series of intersecting monologues. The MOF had even arranged for one of the lunches to be filmed for Japanese television to show the Japanese people that it was making a great effort to accommodate foreigners. In essence, this was an attempt by the MOF to subtly impress the attendees. Protocol and form were more important than mutual understanding. The MOF hoped to encourage the same type of subservient response that existed among JFIs.

Another less-than-endearing habit of the MOF was its requests that foreigners (in addition to JFIs) hire retiring the MOF staff as advisors. This practice is called "amakudari" or "descent from heaven." It was—and still is—a common practice among the JFIs, and it reinforced the notion that the JFIs had to go to great lengths to appease the MOF. The rationale for the JFIs was obvious: the MOF controlled their destiny, but would rescue them if need arose.

THE MOF BEHAVIOR HARKS BACK TO FEUDAL TIMES

The MOF did not overly concern itself with the proper functioning of markets, JFI performance, reliable information, unfair practices, investor or shareholder protection, or other seemingly relevant matters. Its behavior is reminiscent of feudal notions of loyalty based on power. The revelations of paybacks equivalent to billions of U.S. dollars by securities firms to large clients or politicians were actually commonplace in the 1980s. The MOF ignored them just as it overlooked market manipulations by Nomura and others.

Nor did the MOF pay much attention to or have great understanding of the JFIs' impact on sectors of the market in the 1980s. During this period, when JFIs or other investors purchased various categories of securities (such as zero coupon bonds, mortgage-backed bonds, floating rate notes,

CMOs, U.S. public utility debt, U.S. real estate, high yield bonds, and Euroconvertible issues), the MOF never questioned why these securities became relatively more expensive in terms of normal relationships to other securities. If the JFIs had been diligent about their evaluation process and had identified undervalued assets, there would have been no cause for concern. However, in each case, Japanese investors moved the price of the securities to absurdly high levels and, when Japanese investors stopped purchasing them, the market returned to the normal, pre-Japanese relationships. Japanese investors lost extraordinary amounts of money in this process.

Basically, the JFIs reacted as a group to whatever asset was fashionable at a particular time. The MOF did not seem to understand the process. The Japanese tendency and willingness to overpay caused hordes of financial intermediaries to visit Japan to sell assets. The JFIs began to confuse their inherited purchasing power with sophistication. They had little knowledge about what they were doing. But one vital consequence of the combination of regulation and long bull markets was that credit research and fundamental analysis were not considered relevant in Japan. Regulation, for example, required that corporate bonds be collateralized, so there was no "need" to analyze the underlying credit of these issues. Nor was fundamental analysis applied in the equity or real estate markets, because constantly rising prices tended to cover up any mistakes. That was the JFIs' mindset at home, and it was the mindset they carried overseas in the 1980s.

The MOF should have been aware of this, just as it should have recognized that the ability of Japanese investors to distort markets temporarily was harmful. But the MOF did not care: JFI performance or competence, like investor protection, were not its priority in the 1980s.

Another MOF-condoned practice which came back to haunt the JFIs was the use of deposit schemes by the life insurance companies. In order to circumvent restrictions on the percentage of foreign assets in their portfolios, life insurance companies would make foreign currency deposits with banks that would purchase an asset for a very small spread to offset the deposit costs. Foreign intermediaries scrambled to create assets for JFIs. After the asset was identified, foreign investment bankers would visit life insurance companies to obtain funds for deposits. There was no consideration of appropriate yields or risk-reward analysis. The only relevant consideration was absolute yield. If fixed income asset was trading at a yield of 1-1/2 percent over the yield of a comparable U.S. Treasury bond in the U.S. market, and the asset required only 1 percent more than the U.S.

Treasury issue in order to satisfy the JFIs spread over deposit, then the JFIs used 1 percent as their standard.

Even if foreign intermediaries or money managers were inclined to discuss proper asset evaluation techniques, there would have been little response in the 1980s environment to the promotion of risk-reward analysis or proper portfolio management. The Japanese investors wanted concrete proposals. They did not want to master the process. Neither the JFIs nor other Japanese investors understood the concept of risk-reward, so they would not have even attempted to go through the exercise.

ART OF INTIMIDATION

The MOF granted the JFIs a franchise and protection. In return, the MOF demanded obedience, homage, and the hiring of retired officials. It was a cosy arrangement in which no degree of professionalism was required.

" **The MOF has sent teams of people who appear unexpectedly at the office of a financial firm to 'review the books.'** "

The MOF readily used intimidation, however, to enforce its authority. Kenichi Ohmae, an influential Japanese observer for overseas audiences, commented bluntly in *The Wall Street Journal*: "If financial firms do not comply with its (MOF's) suggestions, the ministry can come in and ransack every page of their books."[1]

Indeed, the MOF has sent teams of people who appear unexpectedly at the office of a financial firm to review the books. This was a show of force calculated to inspire fear. In 1987, an American executive from Equitable Life Insurance Company mentioned to an MOF official that he was visiting the MOF to gain clearance for a proposed asset transaction because of the Japanese financial community's respect for the MOF. The MOF official quickly corrected the American—"They do not respect us; they fear us."

---

1   Ohmae, Kenichi, "The Scandal Behind Japan's Financial Scandals," *The Wall Street Journal*, August 6, 1991, p. A-16.

In 1992, a team of the MOF officials descended on a major American investment bank. They proceeded to spend three months trying to uncover trading violations, especially in derivatives. At the conclusion of the investigation, the MOF officials could find no apparent wrong-doing. Afraid to return to their superiors empty-handed, the MOF officials pleaded with the senior American present to fabricate problems.

In the 1980s the MOF represented that its personnel reviewed all overseas transactions. Financial firms were required to submit volumes of reports, but it was absolutely impossible for the MOF to look at these transactions because the sheer volume was overwhelming. Nevertheless, the possibility of arbitrary inspection of transactions and the vagueness of the supervisory guidelines effectively conveyed the message of the MOF control. There were also periodic telephone calls by the MOF personnel to financial firms over trivial matters. The objective was not supervision but outward subservience to the MOF.

Lawyers could do little in terms of providing guidance or clarity. Each request to check the suitability of a proposal generally received the same reply from a lawyer: "Go to the MOF." Matters in question were often not matters of substance. In addition, there was no recourse. As Karel van Wolferen made it clear in his chapter "Keeping the Law Under Control,"[2] challenging any government decision through the courts was probably futile.

A visit to the MOF was always predictable. The bureaucrats were either self-assured or arrogant, but usually formally polite. Their physical surroundings were contrived understatement. Men shuffled about wearing slippers. Piles of paper spewed forth from old metal filing cabinets. Mountains of seemingly random stacks of reports sat on rows of desks in cavernous, impersonal rooms. The atmosphere reeked of clutter. Yet, there was nothing cluttered about the minds of the MOF bureaucrats. They were smart and articulate polemicists. When policy or routine matters were discussed, they were effective spokesmen for Japan's position, as defined by the MOF. However, when technology or intricate, novel concepts with reference to transactions were raised, the MOF bureaucrats mostly had to listen because of their lack of experience. Discussions with the MOF about the introduction of futures, options and index funds in Japan in the 1980s indicated their substantial lack of knowledge in such areas.

---

2   van Wolferen, Karel, *The Enigma of Japanese Power*, New York: Alfred A. Knopf, 1989, p. 202.

THE MOF AND THE SHOGUN BONDS

In the 1980s, the attempt by the MOF to create the Shogun bond market illustrated the difficulty of trying to transplant Japanese financial practices to international situations. A Shogun bond is a foreign currency-denominated bond issued by a foreign entity in the Japanese market. The market existed between 1972 and 1974 for private placements. It was used briefly again in 1978-79 for four issues.

During the 1980s, the JFIs were significant purchasers of foreign currency-denominated bonds, the bulk of which were denominated in U.S. dollars. The JFIs were such a large factor that they determined or influenced the pricing of various issues. For example, Japanese banks borrowed fixed rate U.S. dollar bonds in the Euromarket. These bonds were swapped into floating rate obligations to give Japanese banks a floating rate obligation. The usual size of an issue was $100 million. In many cases, the entire issue was purchased by Japanese institutional investors. There was little interest by non-Japanese, because the bonds were priced at yields very close to U.S. Treasury bonds. Japanese institutional investors, however, did not distinguish between various Japanese bank issues in terms of credit or liquidity to determine relative value.[3]

In addition, the Japanese corporations were issuing billions of U.S. dollars of units which consisted of long-term (up to five years) detachable warrants and U.S. dollar fixed income bonds with coupons sometimes as low as 1 percent in the Euromarkets. The warrants were detached and purchased by investors who wanted a leveraged way to participate in the Japanese equity market. After the warrants were detached, the bonds had significant yields. Investment bankers attached currency swaps to the bonds, which were sold to Japanese institutional investors. These are only two examples of the enormous purchasing power of the JFIs in the 1980s.

The MOF and the JFIs observed that Japanese institutional investors were a dominant factor in foreign currency-denominated bonds. The MOF and the JFIs wanted to move the market from Europe and the U.S. to Japan. They thought the fees and prestige of underwriting the bonds issued by foreign borrowers could be captured domestically by reinstituting the

---

3 *The New York Times*, July 22, 1992, p. D-6. (Note discussion about how this is changing with respect to domestic debentures.)

Shogun market in 1985.[4] They also wanted to seem to be involved. With much fanfare and publicity, the World Bank reopened the market with a $300 million issue. Within one year, several issues—mainly denominated in U.S. dollars—were offered with proceeds of $1.5 billion.[5] After this brief flurry of activity, there were no more issues, despite the fact that Japanese institutional investors remained large purchasers of foreign securities. The market never developed. One author[6] cited the proposal by Japanese brokers in 1986 to create a clearing system to "remedy the negligible liquidity of the Shogun bond market." He further states that the "growth of the Shogun market had been stunted by the absence of investor interest."[7]

What happened to the Shogun market? After all, the MOF is renowned for its brilliant planning and guidance. The Japanese institutional investors controlled part of the market. The ingredients were present. It should have been simple to bring this overseas market back to Japan. However the market never functioned. JFIs made aggressive publicity-seeking bids to borrowers, who obliged. Brokers marketed bonds by literally begging Japanese institutional investors to purchase them. But there was no secondary market because of the lack of an adequate clearing system, the inability to "short" bonds, and the unwillingness of brokers to maintain a secondary market. Japanese brokers were concerned with selling securities, not making markets. The lack of liquidity and expensive pricing were so obvious that even Japanese institutional investors were reluctant to purchase the issues except under pressure. The deals were placed by asking Japanese investors to accommodate, thus creating yet another obligation between institutions. The Japanese investor knew that he was purchasing a security he might never be able to sell or, if he could sell it, the price would reflect a distressed condition.

Foreigners were duped. Several foreign observers even used the Shogun market as a sign of Japan developing a modern market through deregulation.[8] U.S. investment bankers were telephoning their Tokyo offices, demanding to find out who the buyers were, because they assumed that Japanese intermediaries were more aware of actual conditions and that

---

4   Viner, Aron, *Inside Japan's Financial Markets,* Homewood, IL: Dow Jones-Irwin, 1988, p. 158-159.
5   Viner, *Inside*, p. 159.
6   Viner, *Inside*, p. 159.
7   Viner, *Inside*, p. 159.
8   Burstein, *Yen!* p. 199.

there was real demand for the Shogun bonds. Hence, the U.S. investment bankers believed that the Japanese brokers could make aggressive bids because there was real demand by Japanese institutional investors. The U.S. investment bankers wanted to compete with the JFIs, who were making bids to their clients—the U.S. corporate borrowers. This seemed to validate the concept of mystery and power attributed to the Japanese market, which apparently could only be understood by the Japanese.

The form of the Shogun bond was constructed by the MOF in great detail. The MOF tried to mandate a market rather than create one. In fact, there was no market. The highly stylized, dysfunctional security was an example of the Japanese emphasizing form over substance. They did not understand the dynamics of the market and had done little study except to produce the form of a bond. The Shogun bond resembled a public bond, but it behaved like a private placement. The MOF and the JFIs used their power to create temporary publicity. The scenario was quite common during the 1980s as the JFIs began to participate in the deregulated financial world. Their comfortable environment did not prepare them for the reality of competition. The Shogun market was a study in structural weakness as exhibited by the MOF and the JFIs and in misinterpretation by foreigners.

**" The highly stylized, dysfunctional security
was an example of the Japanese emphasizing
form over substance."**

BENEATH SURFACE OF BULL MARKET

The impact of the ebullient post-war Japanese domestic equity and real estate market on the formation of the JFIs' structure was dramatic. Here again, the influence had very serious long-term implications in addition to the obvious positive contribution to profits and growth. It is common knowledge that Japanese institutions have large shareholdings of other Japanese companies, so that an increase in the value of these holdings directly created growth in the assets and capital of JFIs. Passive investors benefitted as well. The bull markets created prosperity for the investors and reinforced the loyalty which the Japanese people have to their Japanese companies. JFIs enjoyed this halcyon period. The securities firms could sell anything to individuals, because the notion developed that investments could eventually be resold at a profit. Trust banks and life insurance companies could manage pension funds without regard to performance, because market action guaranteed some degree of performance. Commercial banks could expand because their capital was constantly growing as a result of their proprietary portfolio of Japanese equity and real estate.

It also reinforced the Japanese investors' faith in the Japanese system. A loyal investor base never questioned recommendations nor demanded professional advice. Thus, trusting their brokers and the Japanese system, Japanese investors felt secure that they would be cared for and prices would rise. Japanese have been conditioned to respond to authority or power, as represented by JFIs.

Japanese also tend to be more comfortable with what they term "wet" rather than "dry" behavior. Simply put, "dry" is a pure, analytical approach deemed to be Western; whereas, "wet" is a more personal, human relationship-oriented style. Performance measurement was never taken seriously because market prices were improving. Precise calculation of results and comparison of results among JFIs was considered a "dry" western concept. The JFIs and the MOF preferred a vagueness which denied accountability.

The post-war bull markets allowed the JFIs to retain their deposits and sources of funds without regard to proper performance criteria. The JFIs' performance was, for the most part, a function of the direction of the markets and it was fortuitous that the markets were rising for most of the forty-five years after the war. The JFIs were not required to perform in line with the market. They could underperform the market in terms of investment or business results and not worry about adverse client, shareholder, or investor complaints or defections.

The revelations of massive repayments to important clients was only proper fulfillment of the expectations created by a "wet" relationship where mutual obligations demanded compensation. Unfortunately, for most of the loyal individual investors, there was not enough money to reimburse all who had losses. Since the Japanese ultimately respect only power, those deemed most important in terms of political influence or business resources were compensated. This was a longstanding practice which received attention because of the market debacle and the corresponding need to compensate its victims.

The MOF tolerated this practice because it was essentially "wet" and part of the system. If from time to time certain individuals or companies were compensated at the expense of others, the practice was condoned because it allegedly promoted stability. No one would question authority unless the system failed to work. A few casualties on the way did not matter to the bureaucrats. The bureaucrats, even now, are concerned only with the adverse publicity rather than the actual practice of compensation for losses.

Generally, individual Japanese do not like to appear different from other Japanese. This is a trait created and nurtured in the family, educational system and corporate world. There is even a Japanese proverb that cautions that the protruding nail is always hammered. This attitude tends to inhibit any in-depth analysis which may be contrary to conventional wisdom. The Japanese purchased stocks recommended by Japanese securities firms who used superficial reasons as the basis for their enthusiasm. Since the most powerful firms were able to manipulate the price of their favorite stocks, a recommendation would be a self-fulfilling prophesy. This further reinforced the principal that power alone deserved respect. The major firms were able to influence domestic equity prices, and since conventional practices were so dominant, a contrary view—no matter how well researched— would not be accepted.

LOYALTY, CONFORMITY IMPORTANT TO JAPANESE

Outside of Japan, there is certainly a propensity to accede to conventional wisdom, but there are also examples of a healthy tendency towards analysis and a free exchange of ideas that has led to alternative investment and management ideas. In Japan, there are cultural, educational, and historical forces which encourage a blind following of accepted or created wisdom. This can be seen also in the Japanese preference for name brand products or foreign trophy properties, regardless of the cost.

The JFIs, as both investors and intermediaries, thought in terms of absolute returns and security. The problem was that in order to obtain these secure absolute returns, the JFIs had to invest in either domestic equities, or securities with foreign exchange and market exposure, such as foreign equities or bonds. With the low Japanese interest rates during most of the 1980s, foreign fixed income securities appeared to be especially attractive.

JFIs made implicit promises of specific returns in order to attract funds under management through vehicles such as "tokkin funds." These were essentially a form of trust fund that allowed Japanese industrial and financial firms to invest in the market without incurring capital gains taxes on prior holdings. They were predicated on a rising equity and real estate market which JFIs and their clients had been conditioned at home to expect.

The JFIs promoted funds by creating the fiction that the reserve built up by the bull markets would cover any mistake; if the reserves were insufficient, the MOF would always rescue the system or a JFI.

The results of the post-war bull markets were concrete. The low interest rates and high stock valuations gave the JFIs, as well as other Japanese companies, a very competitive cost of capital. The earnings of the JFIs were affected because their businesses were allowed to grow quickly and indiscriminately. Without normal market forces at work, discipline was suspended and analysis neglected. The future seemed assured, so present earnings were fueled by assets which would eventually become problems. Since there were large cross-shareholdings, the strong markets created significant assets which were dubbed "hidden reserves." All of these benefits were significantly reversed when the market plunged.

The positive market environment also created enormous self-confidence which, in turn, reinforced the JFIs' position within the system. Although intangible, this psychological factor, by encouraging participation, facilitated the way business was done.

SPECULATIVE SPIRAL AND CROSS-SHAREHOLDING

The virtually constantly rising equity and real estate markets became intertwined. Money was lent with real estate as collateral. This money was used to buy equities or more real estate. Speculation was rampant. This produced artificially cheap capital, profits, and a sense of invulnerability. There were few complaints as rising prices hid mistakes and postponed the consequences of bad judgment. The JFIs seemed well-managed because their operations appeared to generate good results.

The system of cross-shareholdings provided the JFIs with benefits when conducting business. Since most of the major JFIs were members of *keiretsus*, they received business from affiliates/family/close friends. The keiretsu company feels an obligation to do transactions with a family member. With enough cajoling, one keiretsu company can significantly influence another. Although some keiretsus have stronger internal ties than others, there is undeniably a tendency to cater to a fellow member.

In addition, JFIs had shareholdings in non-bank financial entities, such as leasing companies or finance companies. These institutions became conduits for loans made to further increase their asset size. The leasing companies were regulated by MITI, rather than the MOF, and had fewer restrictions. MITI actually competed with the MOF by allowing the leasing companies to get into areas such as futures in order to expand its sphere of influence.

" Cooperation among the Japanese agencies is fraught with competitive infighting and political turf battles . . . Criticism and strife between ministries can be quite open."

Cooperation among the Japanese agencies is fraught with competitive infighting and political turf battles. Again, harmony among the Japanese needs to be qualified extensively. Criticism and strife between ministries can be quite open. Hideo Nagashima, Director of Corporate at MITI, was hardly diplomatic in his attack on the MOF's inability to develop a domestic bond market:

> We need . . . (a domestic bond market), but it's very limited by the Ministry of Finance. They have a lot of red tape, and they're concerned that the banks will lose their share (of corporate finance).[9]

Hardly the image of Japan's version of mandarins.

Typically, a transaction (such as a loan or fixed income security) was presented to a "family member" such as a leasing company by an investment bank. This asset was priced to yield more than the available cost of funds. In many cases, this spread bore little relationship to market values. If the leasing company approved the asset for investment, it would seek financing from one of its shareholding banks. The personnel at the leasing company were often seconded from its shareholding JFIs. In many cases, they had no background in the credit of the type of transactions which they reviewed, especially if the asset was foreign. The seconded employees were likely to return to their JFI within three years.

One situation which illustrates this situation involved the purchase by a leasing company of a U.S. $75 million subordinated loan of a U.S. bank. The JFIs were prone to ignore categories of credit such as subordinated

---

9   Handy, Quentin, "Japanese Companies Need to Raise Cash, But First a Bond Market Must Be Built," *The New York Times*, October 20, 1992, p. C-1.

versus senior when they tried to obtain ever higher yields. The transaction was introduced by a U.S. investment bank and was funded by the leasing company's shareholding JFI. The JFI lent the money to the leasing company in order to purchase the asset. Within hours after the deal was consummated, the credit rating of the bank was lowered by a U.S. rating agency, and within months the bank's credit had been lowered several more times. There was real concern about the viability of the borrower. The value of the asset was only a worth a fraction of the purchase price.

JFIs SHRINK FROM CONFRONTATION

Interestingly, the JFI and its leasing company did not confront the investment banker because they did not want to jeopardize their relationship. Although the investment bank had inflicted a huge loss on the JFI, either through negligence, incompetence or fraud, the JFI did not blame the investment banker. The JFIs and the Japanese, in general, are averse to confrontation. Even though the offending party was foreign—no Japanese relationship would have been threatened—there was still reluctance to recognize and deal with a problem.

This type of activity with a shareholding company gave the JFI a potential source of cooperative clients and participants. This was a real advantage but, when taken to extremes, led to abuses. The cross-shareholding arrangements constituted a stable system, but there was often a significant price to pay for stability.

MANUFACTURING SECTOR SOURCE FOR CASH

The success of the Japanese manufacturing sector created large sums of money to be invested directly and indirectly by JFIs. In addition, this cash provided cheap sources of capital for JFIs. Investing these sums on behalf of the manufacturing sector endowed the JFIs with enormous power. Since entry of new domestic participants was restricted by regulation, the new wealth flowed through a limited number of JFIs that were not subject to competition or performance criteria. The only new participants were foreign financial institutions, which made their presence felt as investment banks in the 1980s.

Recycling this wealth appeared to be a bonanza for the JFIs in terms of profits, prestige, power, and presence in world markets. The JFIs used this new wealth to gain market share abroad. They were trying to emulate the Japanese manufacturing companies, who emphasized market share en route to market dominance. In the process, the manufacturers humbled their competition in such U.S. industries as automobiles and consumer electronics. After gaining preeminence, they were free to raise prices and control markets. This clearly was the pattern the JFIs were eager to follow—and the pattern so many observers believed they would follow.

Japanese individuals were also the beneficiaries of the success of the Japanese manufacturing triumphs. Limited pension plans, the high cost of housing, and tax laws all encouraged individuals to be prodigious savers. This provided an additional source of business and investment capital for JFIs. The Japanese individuals proved to be a captive source of lucrative business for the JFIs, who were not accountable for performance and were protected by market forces and regulations. The Japanese individuals were also a passive lot, partly from social convention, partly because markets were rising. In any event, their information flow from the JFIs and the financial press was not objective. They endured high commission rates, poor performance relative to the markets, gross favoritism to large clients or politicians, and pervasive market manipulation. They were getting part of the pie, but one suspects conformity and peer pressure fostered in the family, educational system, and corporation prevented them from questioning the status quo.

JAPANESE JOURNALISM SERIOUSLY COMPROMISED

Even today, to say that Japanese journalism lacks objectivity is an understatement. In essence, stories are often planted in the press to gain credibility. There is collusion between JFIs, the government, and the press. The *Nihon Keizai Shimbun (Nikkei)*, the most important Japanese financial paper, is a national paper with a daily circulation of 2,800,000 in a country which has 125,000,000 people. By comparison, *The Wall Street Journal* has a daily circulation of 1,900,000 in the U.S. with a population of 230,000,000. The influence of *The Wall Street Journal* on its readers is just not comparable to the impact of the *Nikkei* on Japanese businessmen. An article in the *Nikkei* conveys instant credibility to its subject matter. Yet there is no concept of investigative reporting, and analytical tools are lacking. There is also the fear of offending an individual or a JFI.

The young portfolio managers at the JFIs candidly mentioned that their only sources of information are newspapers and brokers. Japanese institutional investors have token research departments and are not responsible for producing primary analytical reports. Thus, they do not produce independent research on a given company by visiting it and accumulating information from direct sources. They use secondary material, such as newspapers, magazines and brokers almost exclusively for information, analysis and interpretation. The *Nikkei* is the most important of the written sources.

" Even today, to say that Japanese journalism lacks objectivity is an understatement. "

The influence of the *Nikkei* has been described in *Unequal Equities* by Robert Zielinski and Nigel Holloway,[10] which recounts the Japanese equity market of the 1980's. Writing about "Information Junkies," Zielinski and Holloway explained:

> The Japanese investors are deluged with news, rumors, and on the stock market, and the information is circulated so rapidly that it is very difficult for one group of investors to learn something new before everyone else hears about it . . . The most important source of information is the *Nihon Keizai Shimbun* . . . To describe it as *The Wall Street Journal* or *The Financial Times* of Japan does not do it justice, because economic news is regarded as more indispensable than in the West . . . the *Nikkei* . . . is required reading for every manager in the country . . . the *Nikkei* differs from Western financial newspapers in another respect; it is not expected to be accurate . . . the *Nikkei* is regarded as a business tool to shape reality rather than a strict source of news and comment for businessmen.

---

[10] Zielinski, Robert and Holloway, Nigel, *Unequal Equities* (Tokyo: Kodansha, 1991), pp. 83-87.

Much of the problem, Zielinski and Holloway reasoned, came from the structure of the *Nikkei* itself:

> The newspaper has 1,000 full-time journalists, most of whom compete for space in five morning and four evening editions daily, each averaging 35 pages . . . News-gathering in Japan is a highly competitive business with reporters working frantically to make it into print. Under such circumstances, it is common for mistakes and speculative reportage to creep in, but this is tolerated to a greater degree than in the West.

In this environment, it was easy to manipulate the press. The Japanese reporters were so "cooperative" that they even discussed their articles with interviewees before they were printed. A Western reporter would consider this review as an unacceptable infringement on his or her independence. The government, as well as business, used the press to "shape reality." One can imagine without difficulty the consequences for a reporter if he failed to obey the government. Reporters maintained their networks, especially from university, at the major JFIs.

In Japan, the 1980s was a period of easy money and low interest rates. The strength of the manufacturing sector generated huge surpluses which needed to be invested. These elements, in conjunction with the previously-mentioned factors such as regulatory environment, bull market mentality, psychology, notions of vulnerability, and cross-shareholding arrangements, proved to be a combustible combination.

The 1980s did not create the illusion of strength which led to the problems of JFIs overseas. The conditions of the 1980s accelerated the trends and practices that were imbedded in the development of the JFIs. The resulting abuses in terms of asset problems and poor performance were due to the fact that huge capital flows were being handled by the JFIs, which were ill-prepared to do so. Above all, they did not know how to identify or select assets overseas.

In addition, once abroad, their priorities were muddled. Appropriate goals could have been profit/performance, technology or skill transfer, presence/publicity/market share, or servicing Japanese clients overseas. All of these could be valid within a given strategy. But the JFI operations had no focus. As a result, these goals became interchangeable rationalizations. If an operation lost money, the JFI would say the goal was technology, when no technology was transferred. If transfer of money management skills was the objective of a joint venture and this did not occur, the JFIs would justify their activities by saying that there was a small profit on the investments made through the joint venture. In reality, the costs in terms of management resources, personnel, and expenses were quite large and never considered. JFIs very rarely considered actual costs or opportunity costs.

> **" The 1980s did not create the illusion of strength which led to the problems of JFIs overseas. The conditions of the 1980s accelerated the trends and practices which were imbedded in the development of the JFIs. "**

To be sure, the JFIs could claim with accuracy that they had attained market share and publicity. But market share is a questionable goal in many areas of lending. Any institution can gain market share by aggressive pricing or lending to poor credits. This type of activity does not necessarily lead to market dominance or residual business in the rather fluid financial sector.

CHAPTER 4

THE REALITY OF THE JFIS' OVERSEAS OPERATIONS

*"I can't think of a single important business, a
mainstay of Wall Street, where the Japanese have
made any progress to speak of . . . what is remarkable
is how little penetration they have made in high
value-added businesses."*[1]

—SAMUEL L. HAYES III

The JFIs were simply not successful overseas during the 1980s, in terms of adequately recycling investments or in establishing businesses. They were unable to acquire skills or knowledge effectively, despite having had years of experience abroad. This rendered them unable to compete, either in new areas in Japan or overseas. The coveted technological or analytical knowledge was not absorbed or transferred to Japan, nor integrated within the corporation.

The JFIs overseas were not profitable. Expensive overhead was added. Fully allocated costs were not considered. There was no accountability for profits or performance. Localization of personnel was a failure, except when there was an arrangement by which the employee's main connection was capital.

---

[1] Samuel L. Hayes III, as quoted by Sterngold, James, "Japan's Washout on Wall Street," *The New York Times*, June 11, 1989, p. 3(1).

No strategy, except for publicity, could be discerned in their activities. The Japanese staff abroad could be characterized as overconfident, at times arrogant, and often unprofessional. There were excessive amounts of bureaucracy and internal political maneuvering. All substantive decisions were made in Tokyo. Departments within JFIs operated as independent fiefdoms that did not communicate or cooperate with each other, while presenting a facade of harmony. Coordination between Tokyo and a branch, and among branches, was minimal.

Lack of coordination and overcentralization may appear to be inconsistent. This phenomena can easily be explained because JFI centralization was based on a departmental basis, and often there was duplication among the various departments. This led to wasted resources. Interestingly, prominent historians of Japan use terms such as "centralized feudalism" to describe Japanese political structure. In a way, JFIs are also characterized by centralized feudalism.

PROFIT NOT THEIR MOTIVE

The much-admired Japanese systematic approach was nowhere evident. Japanese employees did not view their assignment overseas as one in which they should build a business. They were unconcerned for the most part with a non-Japanese client base. They attached no immediacy to developing skills. Profit was not their motivation.

> " As for the JFI employee, he could generally assume he would be rotated home or to another department and would no longer have to deal with any problem. He could not be blamed, much less fired, because of the lifetime employment system. "

Rather, their goal was to avoid mistakes and maintain proper political ties with Tokyo personnel. Thus, they generally followed whatever was fashionable—such as real estate and LBOs—with only a superficial knowledge of the credits involved. They were unable to distinguish value or understand risk. Ironically, for all their concern about avoiding errors, they often made huge mistakes.

At the same time, the JFI employee was rarely criticized for making an investment which became a credit problem because the asset was usually introduced by a Japanese or foreign *"Yuumei Na Kaisha"* (famous company), a politically safe source. Since the deal probably also involved other JFIs, and because several internal approvals had been given, no one would want to blame another employee. There could be too many internal political implications.

As for the JFI employee, he could generally assume he would be rotated home or to another department and would no longer have to deal with any problem. He could not be blamed, much less fired, because of the lifetime employment system. The result: JFI employees in the 1980s were risk-averse but, in reality, exposed themselves to enormous risks. Worse, the reaction to any problem was bureaucratic paralysis.

TRADITIONAL MANAGEMENT STRUCTURE PROVES INADEQUATE

Japanese senior management overseas in the 1980s had no control because departments were vertically integrated and decisions were made in Tokyo. Age and political skills determined promotion. Official hierarchy was rigidly followed. The relationship of the general managers, who were in their mid-40s, to the managers, who were in their mid-30s, was not straightforward in a Western sense. The information and transaction flow was generally filtered through the manager. The chain of command was respected so the general manager did not interfere with the manager. The managers were concerned with a narrow transactional area. They never conceptualized about which market area was attractive, only which was fashionable. The general manager often viewed his role as ceremonial, non-transactional, and policy oriented.

Most of the weaknesses described above resulted from structural problems. These, rather than individual incompetence, plagued the JFIs and prevented the proper development of business in terms of profit, performance, skills, client base, personnel management, product capability, investment capability, and market strategy. The JFIs overseas were characterized by a short-term attitude, poor planning, fragmentation, and inability to transfer knowledge and technology. These are definitely *not* traits associated with anything Japanese. Indeed, they were the opposite of all that is thought to be quintessentially Japanese.

JAPANESE MANUFACTURERS VERSUS JFIs

The analogy of the Japanese manufacturers to the JFIs was false. The JFIs did not establish a base from which to grow, whereas Japanese manufacturers are identified with product excellence in terms of quality, service, and aesthetics.

The reasons for such disparate results between the overseas activities of the JFIs and Japanese manufacturing companies were varied. At the most basic level, the manufacturers had been exposed to competition and the JFIs had not. The disparity also relates to circumstance, education, corporate culture, the domestic business environment, government regulation, and the motivation for engaging in overseas business activity. The comparative strengths and weaknesses of JFIs and manufacturers were quite different at the time they attempted to expand abroad.

Obviously, certain sectors of Japanese industry were protected during the post-war period. However, government intervention on behalf of Japanese industry was never as pervasive domestically as the all-encompassing scope of the regulation in the financial sector where every detail of the activities of financial organizations was stipulated by the MOF.

For the manufacturers, competition was a fact of life domestically. In order to survive at home, they had to produce good products. There was severe competition among the market participants, and Japanese consumers demanded quality. By the time Japanese manufacturers exported products overseas, they had excelled in a tough domestic market so they were accustomed to competition. If their products were poorly made, they would not have gained ascendancy domestically. The size of the domestic market allowed economies-of-scale so that pricing was flexible. The government subsidized various sectors and shielded them from foreigners, but generally there was enough competition to ensure that the survivors were strong.

There was no quality control mechanism for JFIs. Performance was no criterion for survival. Japanese securities firms and trust banks did not have to worry about losing a client because of bad relative performance.

In the manufacturing sector, technology could be obtained in many cases from foreigners. The practice of reverse engineering—taking a superior product apart and putting it back together in order to co-opt the technology—was common practice. However, once the Japanese manufacturing company had the technology, it was often able to improve upon it, discover practical applications, or find more efficient ways to build products using it.

> **"** **There was no quality control mechanism for JFIs. Performance was no criterion for survival. Japanese securities firms and trust banks did not have to worry about losing a client because of bad relative performance. "**

In the 1980s, when the JFIs tried to use foreign technology, in many cases they were unable to integrate the knowledge into their operations effectively. The quantitative area, in particular, remained locked in "technology departments," which had no impact on investment or business activities. Only when a technology became so common that it was a commodity, did the JFIs begin to use it. Apparently intent on discovering instant results, the JFIs did not understand that technology could be thought of as a tool in understanding a process, in addition to possibly providing a solution.

The physical nature of an industrial product allows for a certain degree of continuity in that improvements and refinements can often be made in a series. The abstract nature of financial products does not allow for the structural product development similar to that of manufacturers.

Outside of Japan, the JFIs were basically providers of cheap capital, whereas Japanese manufacturers have set standards in many cases in terms of quality and competitiveness. The JFIs were notable for their purchase of over-valued assets.

The Japanese government has assisted its manufacturers unfairly in terms of patent protection, research, establishing barriers to the domestic market, and fostering collusion. The government has protected the JFIs, as well. The difference in results overseas cannot be attributed to protection. The government did more than protect JFIs; it granted strict franchises.

Perhaps there are different skills required in the manufacturing area than in the financial sector. The Japanese educational system's emphasis on nationalism, detail, group loyalty, self-sacrifice, peer pressure, and respect for Japanese institutions and hierarchy may suit the manufacturing sector more than the overseas activities of JFIs. The needs of the financial sector, in terms of direct communication, spontaneity, objective research and evaluation, questioning ability, and conceptualization, are not traits encouraged within either the educational system or apprenticeships with JFIs.

In general, the manufacturers' competitive background, and the educational, cultural, and professional training of the Japanese, are compelling reasons for the failure of JFIs and the success of some of the manufacturers overseas in the 1980s.

JAPANESE MANUFACTURERS' CONDESCEND TO JFIs

In the 1980s, Japanese manufacturers often regarded financial services in a condescending manner. They viewed financial services as a supporting—even parasitic—function which should be considered suspect. They were quite blunt, as evidenced by Akio Morita, the chairman of Sony Corporation, who, in a speech at Yale University in 1991, gave a sweeping indictment of the U.S.:

> Some say I accuse the U. S. of not being competitive and creative, but this is not true . . . What concerns me about the U.S. is that the most dramatic advances I have seen in U.S. competitiveness and creativity have been occurring not in the manufacturing sector but over on Wall Street . . . Over the past 30 years, developments in the financial world have been astounding, and many ways have been invented for making money: the leveraged buy-out, junk bonds, commercial paper, and so many other types of financial instruments I cannot hope to list them all. But this is sapping the attention and strength of the economy . . . It is time for the financial world to return to the supportive role for which it was originally designed. Money should be invested to support needed research and development costs for the future creation of products. Money should not be traded as just another commodity . . . It may be an over-simplification, but the future of a nation will be its ability to produce planes, cars, electronics, and so forth, not by how slick its financial markets can shuffle paper assets around.[2]

---

2 Morita, Akio, *Yale Management*, Spring 1991, p. 11.

Morita has reduced creativity and innovation in the U.S. financial sector to "paper shuffling"—an oversimplification. To dwell on the abuses of the U.S. junk bond market in the 1980s was a convenient way to avoid critically analyzing the weaknesses of the Japanese financial system, which became a burden for the Japanese economy. Its structural weaknesses have led to huge market inefficiencies, bad investment decisions and performance, enormous loan losses, and a misallocation of capital within the Japanese economy. This has hurt Japanese individuals and corporations. Morita fails to recognize the truly valid functions of the financial sector in wishing to relegate it to a supporting role. Unfortunately, his opinion is representative of that of other Japanese business leaders, and the Japanese economy is paying a rather high price for relegating its financial sector to a supporting role.

JFIs IN PERSPECTIVE

Many of the weaknesses of the JFIs are common to all large organizations. Excessive bureaucracy, lack of coordination, home office control, and poor planning are problems non-Japanese companies confront as well.

In the financial area, the U.S. commercial and investment banks were plagued by these problems in their expansion into Europe and Asia in the 1970s and 1980s. Many U.S. commercial banks eventually were forced to retreat from their colonial outposts, which they found to be costly, without profits, and a drain on management and capital resources. Overseas, U.S. employees often adopted extravagant lifestyles, without concentrating on building businesses. The importance of entertaining visiting senior officials from headquarters was emphasized over client contact and product development.

The American banks, in many cases, justified their operations by the need to have a presence in the global markets and economies-of-scale. They assumed that profits would follow. Implicit was the need to have a critical mass overseas. Certainly, in many businesses such as foreign exchange and custodial-related areas, it is necessary to set up a worldwide system. However, in many areas relating to lending and capital markets size can actually be a disadvantage. When operating across borders, the complexity of communication and information flow are limiting factors, and companies need to impose discipline to determine what type of cross-border business is potentially beneficial. The need for proprietary trading or investment capability versus client business raises another set of issues.

The U.S. banks were forced to retrench internationally, their grandiose dreams forgotten. The pace was accelerated for those facing dire domestic situations or mergers. What remains are attempts to establish cost-conscious businesses. Some are successful; others will be forced to change.

CHAPTER 5

DOMESTIC PRACTICES — AT HOME ABROAD

Dear Friend:

After a pleasant two-year stay (in America),
I am returning to Tokyo to assume a position
in our head office.
Mr. . . . will be my successor . . .[1]

—JFI EMPLOYEE

In going overseas, the JFIs attempted to transplant wholesale their domestic practices, corporate culture, and organization. This was, in a sense, only natural. Already prey to the illusion of their own strength and vision of the invincible Japanese system, why should they make changes in what worked so well at home?

ROLE OF PERSONNEL DEPARTMENT

The personnel department of the JFI plays a significant role in the staffing of international and domestic departments. It surprises many foreigners to learn that the personnel department of Japanese companies has the primary

---

[1] Excerpt from a letter written by a JFI employee.

responsibility for staffing departments, including those overseas. Most foreigners consider a personnel department at a financial institution to only be
responsible for clerical matters, benefits, human relations, training, and
some mid-level hiring functions. The Japanese personnel department also
has a major input in career promotions. Therefore, it is a powerful department and most employees want to have a tour of duty there. The ability to
control personnel placements and advancements is critical in these large
JFIs, which operate without traditional profit centers or objective measures
of performance.

**" Japanese recruits are quite immature
relative to western college graduates . . . The
Japanese university, in fact, could be
considered an intellectual wasteland. "**

Japanese companies recruit their domestic staff from Japanese universities. Again, this is the preserve of the personnel department. Japanese recruits are quite immature relative to western college graduates. Although
Japanese college graduates have an excellent background in basic math
from their high school days, they have generally spent the previous four
years in college mainly drinking and socializing.

The Japanese university, in fact, could be considered an intellectual
wasteland. Although the recent recession may alter the process, typically
the students are allowed to play as a reward for their rigorous entrance
exam preparation. Exams are the sole criteria for admittance to the prestigious universities and the preparation process is referred to as "examination
hell." The preparation of the Japanese high school and junior high school
students is mainly focused on passing the university entrance exam and has
little to do with knowledge, communication, or learning. This entails an
enormous effort involving regular courses, supplemented by cram courses
taught at special schools called "*juku.*" A 12 year old who might study
until midnight, seven days a week, with few holidays, is a typical case of a
student wanting to gain admittance to a well-respected university. Foreign
universities would be unthinkable in terms of plans for future employment
at a JFI.

Once a student has been admitted to a prestigious university, his career
is assured. He need not worry about performance in college, or about developing skills and interests. In fact, classrooms may hold only a fraction

of the students taking a course, because it is well-accepted (and antici-pated) that few will show up. A degree from the proper college is the appropriate credential for a graduate to gain admittance to a major com-pany and, hence, job security and status. Until the recent recession, recruit-ment of college graduates was very competitive, and the government tried to regulate the process by prescribing the earliest date on which a company can visit a campus.

As a result, the Japanese junior high and high schools play a more important role in shaping the intellect, character, and personality of the future JFI employees than the university. Japanese children spend an aver-age of 240 days a year in the classroom, as compared to 180 for Ameri-cans. The rigorous school environment has been cited as one of the main reasons for Japanese economic competitiveness. The emphasis is on rote memory. Military discipline, peer pressure, and group loyalty are pounded into the students daily.

The Japanese government has its own recruitment tradition which em-phasizes one university, Tokyo University (or "*Todai*," as the Japanese often call it). This is the most prestigious of all Japanese universities, and its entrance examinations are the most rigorous. In Japanese society, the most elite professional position is that of bureaucrat at one of the powerful government ministries, as opposed to the private sector. Tokyo University supplies 70 percent of the personnel for the MOF and MITI, and 60 per-cent of the major ministry positions.[2] The former Prime Minister, Kiichi Miyazawa, has indicated that he would like to see this below 50 percent within the next few years, as the disproportionate amount of influence of Tokyo University relative to its numbers is becoming a target of resent-ment. The inevitable Tokyo University network of graduates within the ministries has produced an environment that has fostered scandal and pro-moted the status quo, as well as guided the Japanese miracle.

CULTURAL INDOCTRINATION ENSURES CONFORMITY

The cultural indoctrination which takes place within Japanese schools is as important as the academic experience—a point Bruce Feiler, in his book *Learning to Bow* captured extremely well.[3] Feiler taught English in a Japa-

---

2 Lehner, Urban C., "Miyazawa, Making Waves, Seeks to Curb the Clout of Tokyo University's Alumni," *The Wall Street Journal*, March 6, 1992, p. A-10.
3 Feiler, Bruce, *Learning to Bow*, New York: Ticknor and Fields, 1991.

nese junior high school in the mid-1980s. His observations about the way that the government used the schools to instill values, and the interaction among the students and teachers, offer revealing insights into the formation of the JFI employee. The application of peer pressure to ensure harmony, conformity, and hierarchy was pervasive.

In one incident, Feiler reports:

> . . . an eighth-grade student called a ninth-grade student by his name without the use of the honorific "san." (Japanese are allowed to omit 'san' in certain circumstances such as when addressing close friends.) The older student, thinking this impertinent, rounded up some friends and returned to teach the young boy a lesson. The band of six ninth-grade avengers picked up the lone eighth-grade offender, dragged him into a bathroom stall, and began punching him. This continued until a teacher unknowingly walked into the bathroom and discovered the fight in progress.[4]

In a chapter entitled, "The Anatomy of a Junior High School Uniform," Feiler discusses the dress code. Japanese schools prescribe rigid rules for student attire. This code derives from nineteenth century Prussia. It is applied by the school and is supported by the "*sempai*" or upperclassmen:

> The "sempai" code varies from school to school and within each school according to the clubs. For example, while the color and style of each shirt was closely regulated by the school, the way to wear it was untouched. The upperclassmen at Sano Junior High School leapt at the chance to teach their juniors, or "kohai," the value of respect. Seventh-grade girls in the volleyball club were required to wear their top buttons bound, while the ninth-graders kept theirs unbuttoned. Seventh-grade boys in the karate club were ordered to keep their sweatsuits zipped up to their chins, while ninth-grade boys unzipped theirs to the waist . . . The ninth-grade boys also declared that the underclassmen could not make alterations to their uniforms, a common way of defying the code. Any seventh-grader caught with a purple lining in his pockets or a red lining in his jacket would be punished—not by the principal, but

---

4 Feiler, *Learning to Bow*, p. 42.

by a ninth-grade tribunal. Several months before I arrived, an eighth-grade student was caught with an embroidered dragon on the inside of his uniform. He was summarily taken to the bathroom by a band of ninth-graders and beaten up. His jacket was confiscated and secretly passed around the ninth-grade floor . . . For students, the message is clear: Conform. What the teachers do not patrol, the upperclassmen control, until every collar, cuff and curl is covered by convention.[5]

The difficulty the Japanese have in assimilating into foreign society abroad can be seen in the limits which they set for foreigners at home. Feiler was asked by several students and teachers to speak at the school's graduation ceremony to "add an 'international' perspective to the occasion." The principal vetoed the idea. As another teacher explained to Feiler, "The principal said it was not appropriate . . . Graduation is a Japanese ceremony . . . and the format cannot be changed. Since you are a foreigner . . . (the principal) was afraid you might upset our customs. We cannot compromise tradition . . ."[6]

Foreigners have been surprised by Japanese change of character when confronted by tradition, or having to prove their Japaneseness. The foreigner observes that the JFI employee who held a strong opinion at dinner would ignore, suppress, or forget his view at a meeting in front of his colleagues the next day.

Feiler also relates a story of one of the students who committed suicide by jumping off the third-floor balcony of the school. The student, Kenzo Saikawa, was a "*burakumin*," which is a special class of ethnic Japanese who are ostracized. Originally, during the Tokugawa period (1609-1868), the Japanese forced those in certain occupations that were considered demeaning (such as tanners and butchers) to live apart from the rest of society. They constituted the lowest level in the medieval caste system, and their descendants are still regarded as separate, even though they are ethnic Japanese and may have no connection with these past occupations. Today, corporations will examine the background of a person to determine if he is a *burakumin*, ethnic Korean or other "undesirable." Likewise, parents pay private investigators to determine whether an intended spouse for their

---

5 Feiler, *Learning to Bow*, p. 82-83.
6 Feiler, *Learning to Bow*, p. 216.

child is acceptable. JFIs continue this practice by checking the backgrounds of potential employees.

The students at Sano Junior High taunted young Saikawa with jibes, beat him, and tried to coerce him into stealing candy from the local 7-Eleven. The humiliation and stress overwhelmed him and he resorted to suicide.

DIVERSITY NOT WELL-TOLERATED

The well-publicized murder of thirteen-year-old Yuhei Kodama on January 13, 1993 by classmates in Shinjo, Japan, demonstrates another variation on the theme of enforcing conformity. Kodama represented diversity. What did this mean? Kodama was different. His family was slightly more affluent than the community norm. This meant that his house was huge. His father studied art in Tokyo and ran a private kindergarten. Kodama spoke with a standard Japanese accent rather than the local dialect. Kodama's death was attributed to suffocation after he was "stuffed upside down into the center of a rolled-up gym mat."[7] The boy and his brother had been tormented prior to the incident. The slogan *"Death to the Children"* had been painted on his house. Although this is an extreme case, bullying and peer pressure are an integral part of the life of Japanese school children. The community took up silence rather than guilt or remorse. No one wanted to recognize or be associated with a problem. This example illustrated the motivation for violence in Japanese schools, and certainly is not the same phenomenon as the widespread crime in American schools.

When Japanese secondary school students return to Japan after studying abroad because their parents were posted overseas, they are regularly exposed to a hazing process. Their fellow students want to make sure that the returning student is ostracized and aware that he or she has been contaminated.

Japan is hardly a place to be an outsider. Numerous episodes such as this occur in the atmosphere of conformity. As Feiler points out, ". . . most of the victims never speak out."[8] Feiler summarized his views:

---

7 Sanger, David E., "Student's Killing Displays Dark Side of Japan Schools," *The New York Times*, April 3, 1993, pp. A1, A5.
8 Feiler, *Learning to Bow*, p. 247.

Many of the country's (Japan's) strengths, I discovered are passed on to students; discipline is taught through the strict dress code, cooperation . . . and responsibility through the give-and-take student bond. But Japan's shortcomings are born here as well; stress is nurtured through 'examination hell,' pressure through the threat of gang bullying, and intolerance through the lingering myth that Japanese are a breed apart.

Feiler condemned the schools for not encouraging the development of communication skills in their language study. Language instruction was strictly regulated by the Ministry of Education. The goal of studying a language was to pass the government exam, which had little to do with communication. The lack of teaching of communication skills, the failure to teach ". . . children how to get along with those who look, think, and act differently from the majority," and the fostering of the concept of the Japanese as a wholly different sort of people, are all major obstacles for Japanese when relating to the rest of the world.[9]

It is much easier to understand JFI employees after examining the kind of educational background they share. There is a direct correlation between the "shortcomings" related in *Learning to Bow* and the difficulties encountered by the JFIs in the 1980s.

THE SALARYMAN

The personnel departments of the JFIs actively recruit college graduates. It is uncommon for college graduates to do post-graduate work unless a profession requires it. A graduate is inducted into the company for life and, once there, he (it is still almost always a he) has become a *"sarariiman"* (salaryman). Karel van Wolferen aptly caught the salaryman's nature:

He was originally named for the salary he received, as distinct from the wages of factory hands and other workers lower in the occupational hierarchy. But the term "salaryman" connotes much more than "office clerk" or "white-collar worker;" it stands for a behavioral norm to aspire to. The salaryman has such predictable concerns and habits that it has become common in Japan to speak

---

9   Feiler, *Learning to Bow*, pp. 278-283.

of "salaryman culture." The production of books and magazines devoted primarily to acknowledged salaryman taste . . . comprises one of Japan's biggest industries.[10]

Every JFI employee is a salaryman.

SALARYMAN TRAINED AS GENERALIST

The JFI personnel department continues the indoctrination of the graduate, instilling a generalist attitude into each new salaryman. This can be viewed as an extension of group consciousness. The employee is supposed to rotate among departments throughout his career. Thus, the salaryman experiences a broad range of activities; this is deemed to make him a better manager. His varied career is assumed to enable the employee to serve the company better by knowing all parts and feeling totally in contact with the company rather than with a particular department or specialty. By contrast, specialists are defined by their individuality, the antithesis of the revered group loyalty. Furthermore, it is accepted wisdom in Japan that Western specialization leads to disharmony, and that the Japanese generalist approach is a significant contributor to the success of the Japanese system. The rotation system is ingrained in the salaryman's mind and spirit.

Indeed, overspecialization does lead to problems, and the generalist system has many strengths. For example, it is certainly beneficial for the senior management of Japanese manufacturing companies to have experience in production, design, marketing, finance, and overseas business. Being in so many departments fosters connections throughout the company. Similarly, the generalist system has certain advantages for the JFIs. There is no need to condemn the generalist system, only to recognize and provide for its limitations.

These begin with overseas postings. Certainly, in the 1980s, personnel departments assigned staff abroad with almost no regard for suitability. Implicit in the generalist system was the belief that any salaryman was interchangeable with any other. The only concession was for those who had language skills. Even language skills were not always given priority in terms of the type of business undertaken—such as the investment of large

---

10 Van Wolferen, Karel, *The Enigma of Japanese Power*, Alfred A. Knopf, p. 198.

sums of money in complicated areas requiring the ability to read English. In one case, a JFI had assigned a non-English speaking/reading Japanese employee to be the senior manager in a cross-border Merger & Acquisition department. It is difficult to see how he could function; yet, Tokyo management could not see this as a weakness in such a highly technical area necessitating the reading of mounds of material written in English. Consequently, in many cases JFIs fell captive to Japanese intermediaries whose main qualification was to speak Japanese—not that they had any substantive knowledge or interest in any asset category. Likewise, foreigners with no skills other than the ability to speak Japanese were sought after by foreign firms in the '80s. It was not unusual for these people to be less than competent professionals.

> **" In the investment area, it was often the case that novices with only a couple of years' experience were given responsibility for managing assets equivalent to billions of U.S. dollars. "**

The employees who were transferred overseas, or who were engaged in making overseas investments, in the 1980s varied in age from their late-twenties to their forties. They had enough time to exhibit an aptitude for an area, but this was not considered because the salaryman was interchangeable. In the investment area, it was often the case that novices with only a couple of years' experience were given responsibility for managing assets equivalent to billions of U.S. dollars.

In the Japanese system, individual departments are headed by General Managers. The following table shows the levels of management and their typical approximate ages:

Senior Managing Director	50s
Managing Director	50s
Director	late 40s
General Manager	mid-40s
Deputy General Manager	late 30s
Manager	30s
Assistant Manager	30s

The extent of the emphasis on form and hierarchy can be seen in the recent decision by Dai-Ichi Kangyo Bank (DKB), the world's largest bank, to have its employees discontinue the practice of addressing their colleagues by title.[11] Now, DKB employees will use the more democratic form of "*san*" to "promote open and free communication." Formerly, each person was previously addressed as "*bucho*" (general manager), "*kacho*" (manager), and so forth, rather than the name followed by "*san*." Once overseas, JFI personnel operated from much the same almost-military structure as in Japan.

Overseas in the 1980s, as in Japan today, the general manager displayed a concern for broad policy and ceremony. The deputy general manager and the manager controlled the information and transaction flow to the general manager. In dealing with counterparts at other Japanese organizations, people of the same rank interacted with each other. As the salaryman moved up in age and rank, he was less and less involved with transactions and business decisions. If the general manager interfered with the deputy general manager or manager, he quickly gained a reputation as being a difficult person within the organization.

ON-THE-JOB TRAINING

Since performance was not important, the results were generally predictable. For example, in the area of portfolio management, the new manager or assistant manager immediately established relationships with domestic and foreign brokers. It was on-the-job training. The new manager, if he was a portfolio manager, would immediately begin buying and selling securities, relying exclusively on brokers and newspapers.

For most of the 1980s, there was little attention given to research, either fundamental or quantitative. The generalist novice fund manager was supposed to do his own research, make decisions, and trade securities. Indeed, there was a prejudice against research as being Western, dry, and rational. The young fund manager gravitated towards perceived power—the large brokers who would recommend individual stocks, and if the stocks did not perform well, some form of reimbursement could be expected.

---

[11] *The Wall Street Journal*, April 24, 1992, B-1.

The novice fund managers at the JFIs did not have to worry about performance because their client base was captive; performance did not impact on promotion or compensation. Since the novice portfolio manager would be transferred in three or four years, there was no vested interest in developing skills. His position was secure if he did not make a mistake. If he listened to a *yumei na kaisha* (famous company) and purchased equities or bonds issued by a *yumei na kaisha* he could not be challenged, no matter how much money he lost.

ROTATION SYSTEM HAS STRUCTURAL FLAWS

There are strengths and weaknesses in the JFI's personnel rotation system. The staffs of JFIs are smart, loyal, hardworking and dedicated. The salaryman does not generally leave the Japanese company. He is well ensconced in the lifetime employment system of Japanese big corporations. This has enormous implications. It becomes practical to devote a significant effort to training employees who are likely to remain in the same company for their entire career. In the aggregate, the staff of JFIs is diligent and loyal. The salaryman is a potentially valuable resource.

But there was a great structural weakness to the system which more than offset its advantages overseas in the 1980s. Rotation created problems for JFIs trying to accommodate market changes at home when transplanted intact to foreign markets. The rotation system caused problems that could only be compounded many times over by the lack of familiarity with markets, communications, languages, and institutions.

Above all, the rotation system prevented the accumulation of skills and knowledge at the same time it encouraged personnel to be short-term oriented. JFI staff had no vested interest in building a business. It knew that it would be rotated, and anything that happened after the transfer was of no concern to salarymen. Not that performance had anything to do with their careers, or even their salaries. The result was an excessively bureaucratic approach to transactions and concepts, an approach that was not so cautious and conservative as political and passive. The salaryman overseas in the 1980s feared activity because recognition and promotion were derived solely from vague, subjective, political considerations in the mind of the head office.

The system also encouraged discontinuity. It was common practice for the salaryman, when he took a new position, to exert his authority by disassociating himself with his predecessor's activities and mistakes. Since all

Japanese firms rotated personnel, even the counterpart could not be held accountable for poor advice or incompetence. The person who dispensed the poor advice had also been transferred. JFI officials were often concerned about the possibilities of their own staff becoming too close to individual brokers, so they took further comfort in the rotation system. What remained was the juxtaposition of large companies that had a mutual set of obligations and dependencies. Westerners try to superimpose the word "relationship" on this connection, but this word is too narrow. Expectations were based on the power of a given JFI. One salaryman was not important in this process.

Such a short-term perspective obviously contradicts the image of Japanese long-term planning. Nevertheless, the reality is easy to understand if one considers a three-year appointment with no performance objectives. The only requirement was to not commit what was deemed, at the time, to be a mistake.

The rotation system, however, inhibited the accumulation of vital skills in the 1980s. Certain tasks require commitment. Others, such as research, portfolio management, asset selection, credit judgment, and quantitative knowledge, require various degrees of specialization. The generalist system and the three-year rotation period did not encourage the salaryman toward commitment, specialization, or even taking his job seriously. He was actually encouraged to exert minimal substantive effort. The prudent salaryman would adhere to proper domestic form, spending long and often unproductive hours in the office and drinking nightly with colleagues and counterparts. There was little social interaction with foreign colleagues or clients.

This became all the more important when visitors arrived from the head office. Since promotions were won in the political cockpit in Tokyo, overseas employees had to work assiduously to maintain their contact with Tokyo personnel.

The rotation system also severely retarded the ability of the JFIs to generate a client base overseas. The JFIs were able to retain their captive Japanese client base when it appeared overseas in such areas as custodial business or price-sensitive lending. But potential U.S. clients—such as borrowers or money managers—were constantly confused by the bewildering number of inexperienced JFI staff who were always being introduced as a result of the rotation system. Some of the JFI salarymen could have been quite effective in marketing, if they had been truly committed for a significant period of time. In order to monitor the frequent personnel changes, an extensive method of filing name cards had to be used. After years of repeated ritualistic introductions, U.S. clients grew cynical and tended to use JFIs in circumstances where price and capital were the only requirements.

Westerners were accustomed to receiving hundreds of form letters from JFI salarymen such as the one received by this author:

June 3, 1993

Dear Friend:

After a pleasant two year stay (in America),
I am returning to Tokyo to assume a position in our head office.
Mr. . . . will be my successor . . .

The salaryman who wrote this letter had been assigned to a highly technical M&A operation for a major Japanese bank. The bank had embarked on the business without considering the costs, which were $4,000,000 a year. The business was designed to garner publicity, and was staffed with Japanese amateurs who knew that they would be transferred. Commitment was non-existent. Indeed, the JFIs regularly left the impression with the foreign client that he was dealing with the JFI and not an individual. Unfortunately, the foreign client also concluded he was dealing with rotating novices who had capital.

One of the most tedious tasks of the U.S. interest bankers in Tokyo was the ritual visits required when there were personnel rotations. These were time consuming. They were also wasteful in the sense that any effort made to educate a JFI was of little use, as they were transferred so often.

The JFIs, of course, assumed they had credibility overseas because they were well-established in Japan. Hence, they thought they could transplant their domestic practice of personnel rotation without consequence. The establishment of a joint venture illustrated this attitude. In this example, which occurred in 1986, one JFI entered into a joint venture with a large U.S. financial institution. The major purpose was to market the Japanese equity management expertise of the JFI, a major Japanese money manager. The target client base was U.S. pension fund managers.

The JFI, viewing the situation from a Japanese perspective, determined that U.S. pension funds would invest large sums of money in the Japanese equity market as part of a portfolio diversification strategy. The JFI assumed that an introduction by a well-known American institution was all that would be required. The JFI anticipated the U.S. pension funds would hire it to manage its Japanese equity portfolio. The U.S. joint venture partner was given JFI assets to manage in the U.S. markets. The fees from these assets were the incentive for the American institution to enter this joint venture arrangement.

The U.S. institution was also supposed to train several of the JFI employees. This was generally the *quid pro quo* between the Japanese and foreign money managers. It was often detailed specifically that a money manager would accept a Japanese trainee for a specified time if the JFI gave fifty million dollars or another amount for the foreigner to manage. The management fees were deemed compensation.

After several years of attempting to solicit business through the joint venture, the JFI did not have one American client. The venture was an embarrassment, and hours of management time were consumed in discussing how to unknot the tie. Although the joint venture was working badly, the JFI did not want to deal with the issue. The JFIs assumed, from the Japanese perspective, that they would antagonize the U.S. institution. Fortunately, the U.S. company was acquired by another company so that the tie could be severed without the JFI making a decision. Admitting a mistake and dealing with problems are antithetical to Japanese cultural conditioning, because of the implications of confrontation.

> **" Admitting a mistake and dealing with problems are antithetical to Japanese cultural conditioning, because of the implications of confrontation."**

The JFIs' reliance on their position in Japan, where they were *yumei na kaisha*, caused them to transplant their rotation system with poor results in terms of foreign client development. JFI salarymen tend to neglect foreign client development. It is easier for them to rely on capital, i.e., buy business. The rotating JFI salarymen generally entertains Japanese clients—rather than foreign—during his overseas posting.

IMPACT OF ROTATION SYSTEM ON U.S. COUNTERPARTS

The rotation system had predictably negative impact on the development of relationships with U.S. counterparts, except for large U.S. financial institutions and major U.S. borrowers, which were actually positively affected.

By the late 1980s, many American money managers and corporations had made a sufficient number of presentations to JFIs to become frustrated with the lack of continuity of personnel and, more importantly, the need to educate new personnel about their business. The well-known corporate or public borrowers did not have this problem. They were very aware that the JFIs would bid aggressively to lend money, so they were able to treat the JFIs as commodity sources of money. The World Bank, IBM, General Motors, and General Electric were in this category.

Although the American money managers and less conspicuous American companies were often reluctant to make the effort to ingratiate themselves to the JFIs, they normally went through the motions because there was always the hope of cheap Japanese money. After being exposed to the drama of the Japanese meeting, there was a skepticism about developing a relationship. The Americans wanted Japanese money; the Japanese were waiting to throw money at the next trend. If the American firm had properly identified itself, it might be considered when that particular business became fashionable.

Some Americans were impatient and short-sighted, but even successful and disciplined Americans with long-term goals were disillusioned with attempts to establish a dialogue with JFIs. There was never a basis to build upon because of the changing personnel and absence of informational response. Indeed, actual proposals often never received a response. Since the JFI salaryman did not like to give negative replies, he probably let the proposal wander around the maze of departments that might be involved. One highly-paid American advisor to a JFI submitted sixty potential deal proposals to his JFI and never received a single response. The JFI salaryman liked to think that this slow response was due to detailed consideration. In reality, it was due to passiveness, bureaucracy, unfamiliarity, and lack of decision-making ability. The U.S. counterparts were confused by the vagueness inherent in dealing with the JFIs.

SPECIALISTS WITH SPECIALTIES, BUT NO EXPERTISE

The rotation system, as it operated in the 1980s, denied the validity of specialists. The implications of this lack of substantive specialists overseas were staggering. To be sure, the JFIs did call some of their staff "specialists"—a salaryman who had just been transferred to the JFI's New York office real estate department was referred to as a real estate specialist, despite the fact that he had no background in U.S. real estate, or sometimes even Japanese real estate. No matter. The JFI had great confidence in the "fighting spirit" of the recently-rotated salaryman.

" Japanese life insurance company investors would thus dismiss short-term losses of fifty percent by using a fifty-year time horizon. This was a rationalization that could not be challenged for fifty years, hence, no mistake needed to be recognized. "

Real estate is local, but the Japanese attempted to apply formulas, such as cash-on-cash yields, to determine value. Americans obliged, inventing projections which fitted the Japanese formulas. The Japanese made no distinction for regional economies such as New York, Los Angeles, or Atlanta. The packaging was well-understood by Americans. If a "famous" broker represented a "famous" building in a "famous" city, the Japanese prerequisites for consideration, the Japanese and the salarymen were safe. Many of the ultimate purchasers of American real estate were individuals or companies—not JFIs—but behind the purchaser there was usually a JFI to lend the necessary funds. Capital gains were implicitly assumed because, from the Japanese perspective, real estate always went up in the long-term. Japanese life insurance company investors would thus dismiss short-term losses of fifty percent by using a fifty-year time horizon. This was a rationalization that could not be challenged for fifty years, hence, no mistake needed to be recognized.

The poor results of Japanese real estate investment in the U.S. are a testament to unprofessional and arrogant behavior. Americans have also been traumatized by their own real estate investments as well, but it took a special hubris for the Japanese to assume that overseas they would conquer regional, highly specialized markets. It is not surprising they became the dumping ground for overpriced deals.

The losses—both domestic and international—are of monumental proportions. These results are well-known and continue to be reported in the press. A *Forbes* article entitled "Foreign Aid" listed some of the debacles (reproduced from original chart, final column added by author):[12]

---

12 Taylor, John H., "Foreign Aid," *Forbes*, June 21, 1993, p. 96.

TABLE 5-1. LOOMING LOSSES FOR JAPANESE INVESTORS

Property	Buyer	Purchase Price ($mil)	Value Today ($mil)	Loss ($mil)
Pebble Beach	Minoru Isutani	$841	$300	$541
Arco Plaza	Shuwa Investmetns	620	300	320
Grand Hyatt Wailea*	TSA/Kumagai Gumi	600	250	350
Hyatt Regency Waik.	HRW Ltd.	360	100	260
Mauna Kea Hotel/Resort	Seibu Group	315	100	215
Westin Maui	Aba International	290	150	140
LaCosta Resort	Sports Shinko	250	75	175
Hotel Bel-Aire	Sazale Group	110	60	50
Dana Point Resort	Tokyo Masuiwaya	105	40	65
Total				$2,116

* Development cost: hotel built by the Japanese

Since 1985 Japanese investors have poured $43 billion into Hawaii and California. Some of the biggest deals turned out to be the worst.

Reprinted by permission of *FORBES* magazine, June 21, 1993. ©Forbes Inc., 1993.

The Azabu Building company fiasco, with losses of $636.7 million in 1991 is a major headache for Mitsui Trust & Banking Co., its lead bank.[13] Only the vast extent of the JFI's domestic and international losses is still a mystery. The Japanese financial system's dependence on vagueness prevents accurate assessment. The structure which created these losses is not well understood.

EQUITY RESEARCH ANOTHER JFI "SPECIALIZATION"

Equity research was another area of specialization that the Japanese came to recognize in form, but not in substance. Today it is fashionable, at least in Japan itself, to have equity research departments at JFIs' money management operations. Generally though, these are research departments in

---

[13] Chandler, Clay, and Bussey, John, "The Reckoning: Real Estate Collapse in Japan is Hammering Both Buyers and Banks," *The Wall Street Journal*, August 27, 1992, p. A-7.

name only, staffed by a few people who have no real research background. However, not too long ago, research was left to the novice salaryman, a matter of listening to brokers and reading newspapers.

The new research departments may contain women—traditionally a sure indication a position is organizationally irrelevant. Ironically, Japanese women often have better foreign language skills than the men, and have been given opportunities by foreign financial firms in Tokyo. Initially, the foreign firms had difficulty hiring Japanese men, and were somewhat forced to include women. This has benefitted the foreign firms and the Japanese women. Whether Japanese women can progress to senior positions remains to be seen—especially if foreign firms try to become totally Japanese, or Japanese managers at foreign firms revert to form. JFIs have totally ignored women as a resource.

It is doubtful that the JFIs even now are seriously attempting to conduct fundamental research on Japanese or foreign companies. Japanese brokers have had research institutes for years. An examination of these institutes will reveal an emphasis on form. The institutes were separate from the brokers and distinct in terms of business, with superficial interaction with the parent brokerage firm. The research institute churned out volumes of statistical data on individual stocks and economies without providing any penetrating analysis of the subject matter. Japanese brokerage firm employees tended to disregard the "research" produced by the research institute, which operated as an academic think tank. The members of the research institute rarely visited institutional clients. The Japanese brokerage firms conducted their sales activities without regard to research. There were no negative reports for fear of alienating an investment banking client. The recent announcement by Nomura that they would be making negative comments about Japanese companies was considered to be front page news! There is sometimes tension at U.S. investment banks between research analysts and corporate finance personnel, but any comparison with the Japanese brokers on this subject would be so remote as to be misleading.

Traditionally, at Japanese brokerages, salesmen received recognition for customer purchases of stocks, not customer sales. This marketing function has always been the most important training ground—the place where careers could be made—at a Japanese brokerage firm. Generally, senior officials at these firms are men who have excelled at persuading customers to buy whatever stocks the firm was pricing.

The Japanese retail investor was equally vulnerable. In September, 1992, the theme of AIDS-related stocks was popular. Stocks which have small biotechnology research departments, such as Meiji Milk Products Co. and Morinaga Milk Industry Co., were touted as having found cures for the AIDS virus. Even candy company Meiji Seika was included in the rumor. A company spokesman for Meiji Milk was quoted as saying, "We (Meiji Milk) have no idea if we can even come up with a drug (for AIDS)."[14] Despite this denial, securities firms would buy stocks, promote them, and sell after the price had risen. The process is called ramping. The reasons for recommending these stocks were pure fiction and hype. Yet, Japanese retail investors virtually always succumbed to high pressure tactics of the Japanese securities firms' representatives. These investors—because of ignorance, custom, and respect for the system—were pliable. Japanese regulatory authorities, as usual, ignored the practice.

The selection of a recommended stock was determined by the sales managers of the equity departments of Japanese brokers. They arrived at themes—such as a slow economy requires stimulation—so companies that manufacture paper for currency are recommended because the government can easily redenominate the yen to smaller size bills and thus create jobs for the paper manufacturers. The salesmen then enthusiastically begged clients to buy stocks. The technique was pure persistence. The Japanese institutional portfolio manager (American portfolio managers are sometimes not immune themselves) enjoyed the attention and adulation conferred on him by the salesmen. They did not respect the professionalism of the salesmen, only the power of the company he represented. Until the 1990 equity market debacle, the portfolio manager assumed the Japanese brokerage firm could ensure the performance of its recommendations. The research institute had no part in the dynamics of this process. It was plumage, demonstrating internationalization and sophistication. The employees of the research institute, by and large, accepted their passive role.

However, with the advent of foreign firms in the 1980s, several of the research institute analysts moved to foreign firms and blossomed. The structure of several of the foreign firms was conducive to useful research. The removal of the stigma of specialization, the respect for good research, and the integration of research within some of the foreign firms allowed the analysts to perform their tasks effectively.

The inherent contradiction of a specialist within a pure rotation system also inhibited the development of proper overseas credit research and quan-

---

14 Hardy, Quentin, "Japan's Stocks are Surging on Rumors, Cheerleading," *The Wall Street Journal*, September 4, 1992, p. C1, C11.

titative analysis. Japanese participation in the U.S. high yield or junk bond markets of the 1980s illustrated the superficiality of rotation system-inspired analysis at work.

CREDIT RESEARCH NOT A JAPANESE TOOL

The excess of Japanese capital in the 1980s was discovered by U.S. investment bankers. The Japanese were quite unfamiliar with credit analysis of foreign corporations because they had made few investments overseas during the era of restrictive foreign exchange rules. These rules were eased to allow a greater outflow of capital by the early 1980s.

In Japan, there was no precedent for analysis of private sector credits, as Japanese corporate issues were collateralized. Bank lending itself was not characterized by rigorous examination. The post-war economy was growing at such a rate that there were relatively few major credit problems in the private corporate or real estate sectors. When major problems occurred, such as Sumitomo Bank's write-off of loans to Ataka Trading Company in 1977, or Daiwa Bank's loss relative to the Sanko Steamship bankruptcy in 1985, there was little concern because the financial system could absorb the losses easily. Sumitomo Bank never reported a drop in quarterly earnings, despite a loss of three hundred million dollars on its loan. It simply sold part of its hidden reserve of equity holdings in other Japanese companies to mask the loss. Similarly, Daiwa Bank sold part of its proprietary holdings to cover its problem.

Taken in isolation, these examples are not significant. However, they provided yet another illustration to the JFIs and the Japanese people of the invincibility of the financial system and, hence, the Japanese system. This fostered an attitude which engendered bad habits. In January 1992, a senior official of an Industrial Bank of Japan (IBJ) overseas office stated that it was "insane" to blame the JFIs for not understanding credit risk, because they never had to until recently. He was extremely emotional in his defense of the status quo. But he went on to say that, since it was now necessary to evaluate risks and risk-reward relationships, the JFIs will adjust smoothly. All can be seen as a seamless, harmonious process. Never is there any hint the system was flawed and no mistake was ever admitted.

This apologist approach indicated a total reliance on structure. Since the structure did not require credit analysis, then the banker cannot be blamed, for he is only part of the structure. Again, the underlying assumptions are an ever-growing economy, large hidden reserves, and the ultimate safety net—the government.

IBJ is considered to be the most prestigious private sector financial institution. The status of an employee at IBJ is just below that of a government ministry official. IBJ is always cited as being the most sophisticated JFI, and its ties to Japanese industry are legendary. When a foreigner questions the expertise of a JFI, the usual reply by a Japanese—regardless of whether he works for IBJ or not—is that the foreigner must be referring to Nomura or some lesser JFI because IBJ is the standard bearer for excellence of the financial system. As such, if a change is needed, IBJ will initiate the necessary reform and lead the way for all other JFIs. Moreover, it is important to have IBJ participate in a transaction because other JFIs will be inclined to follow.

" Since the structure did not require credit analysis, then the banker cannot be blamed, for he is only part of the structure. "

Without doubt, IBJ employees are more polished than their counterparts at other JFIs. They seem urbane, and generally have better language skills than other Japanese bankers. They exude confidence, which is often indistinguishable from arrogance. Even foreign language skills are looked upon without the usual Japanese skepticism. IBJ employees even speak of the *IBJ* system when other Japanese bankers would speak of the *Japanese* system.

Nevertheless, IBJ evinced the same neglect to credit risk, and has bungled just as badly, as the other JFIs which are thought to be more parochial and less "sophisticated." In a rather bizarre and well-publicized episode, it was revealed that IBJ and its affiliates had lent the equivalent of $2 billion to Ms. Onoue, the owner of a small restaurant in Osaka. Ms. Onoue's restaurant was popular among members of the *Yamaguchi-gumi*, Japan's largest organized crime syndicate. She had pledged fraudulent CDs, among other things, to obtain money in order to speculate on the Tokyo stock market. She now faces bankruptcy, and IBJ could lose as much as $450 million as a result. IBJ's president, Yoh Kurosawa, stated that IBJ had been "fooled" by Ms. Onoue.[15]

---

15 *The Economist*, September 7, 1991, p. 93.

During the 1980s, both overseas and at home, structural problems relating to credit analysis permeated the entire system. No JFI was exempt from folly. All of the banks, securities firms, life insurance companies, and leasing companies were the products of the same system. The system did not reward risk-reward analysis. It did not consider credit analysis a specialty.

With a lot of money, no understanding of credit risks overseas, and the feeling of invincibility, the Japanese began making investments in U.S. high yield loans and securities. U.S. investment bankers gave seminars and conducted meetings with JFIs in order to market high yield, fixed income assets. The meetings were conducted in Japanese, materials were translated, rosy presentations were packaged. The performances were tailored for the Japanese. The marketing effort was effective in its consideration of local preferences.

What U.S. investment bankers discovered in the process was that the Japanese did not consider yield levels in relation to risk levels. Some American institutions were guilty as well. If the JFIs thought a company would not default before the maturity of its obligation, the yield was not significant, as long as there was a spread over the cost of funding. Since junk assets always had a favorable spread over the funding targets, the JFIs were eager to participate. Huge percentages of certain loans or issues were purchased by the Japanese. As much as 50 percent to 60 percent of a single loan or issue might be placed in Japan. The yield levels were distorted, as it was not unusual for the Japanese to significantly affect the pricing of issues. The JFIs played a major role in the booming junk market of the 1980s and it could easily be argued that many deals could not have been done without Japanese participation.

LACK OF QUANTITATIVE ANALYSIS

By the late 1980s, the JFIs all had technical departments, which they advertised as part of their expertise. These were similar in nature and function to the research institutes at Japanese brokers. They existed for publicity's sake. They were not in the mainstream of the organization and existed more as form than as substance. The "inmates" of the technology department of the 1980s did studies. They examined foreign quantitative systems relating to investments or transactions, but they needed fully packaged products. Unlike their manufacturing counterparts, the JFI salaryman was never able to reverse-engineer a quantitative system, improve upon it, and create a system which was better than the original.

The Japanese rotation system hindered the effective integration of quantitative tools within companies. This was ironic because the JFI staff, in general, on a very basic level is more mathematically literate than the staff of U.S. financial institutions. Yet, in many cases the U.S. investment banks successfully assimilated technology, and the JFIs did not. The answer lies in the disdain for the specialist. The JFI system discouraged commitment by limiting an employee's time in the area. Equally important was the lack of understanding of the complexities of adapting quantitative techniques to a particular business environment.

Since everyone in the investment area or capital market area was rotating, there was a constant need to train the new member of the department. The new member wanted to seem productive, so he would begin working on immediate business proposals. For example, the new fund manager at a Japanese institutional investor wanted to seem like one of the crowd, so he would do what they did—talk to brokers and trade securities. He might even be afraid to seem different by beginning to concentrate on quantitative techniques or fundamental research. If he succeeded in outperforming the other salarymen, that could also be a problem.

> " Unlike their manufacturing counterparts,
> the JFI salaryman was never able to
> reverse-engineer a quantitative system,
> improve upon it, and create a system which
> was better than the original."

It might seem blasphemous to assert that the JFIs did not use technology. But there was no apparent system to their investment process. These were huge institutions, with billions under management as agent or principal. The Japanese investors who managed funds of publicly traded securities relied on individual fund managers who made individual decisions about their portfolios without knowing the overall impact of a particular decision. The young portfolio manager was, after all, getting on-the-job training. He could not be seen as a maverick or his superior would look bad.

While much of the Japanese industrial sector willingly accepted innovation in terms of product design or production in the 1980s, the JFIs' structure retarded progress. Again, status quo, rather than performance, was the goal. It was highly unlikely that a JFI would lose a client because of poor results. In the manufacturing sector, however, if Toyota made a defective car, it would lose a customer.

" The Japanese emphasis on education did not extend to practical acceptance for academics with quantitative skills which could be applied to financial services. "

The Japanese emphasis on education did not extend to practical acceptance for academics with quantitative skills which could be applied to financial services. Academics were somewhat suspect. They were not salarymen and were deemed not to have the broad experience necessary to engage in practical business. Since it was necessary to have a postgraduate background in many important areas of technology relating to financial services, the JFI policy of recruiting only college graduates was detrimental.The technology departments of the JFIs could not operate well in isolation. Nonetheless, the various departments at the JFIs operated independently from one another, both in Tokyo and abroad, despite their hazy boundaries. Occasionally, a Japanese with academic credentials would be hired in mid-career to work in a technology department. He was often buried there and was referred to only when the technological credentials of the JFI were questioned. Even today, when pressed, the JFI employees are not quite sure what is actually done by the technology department.

The academic, accustomed to dealing in theory, received no cooperation from the line departments and, consequently, developed little practical experience. The line departments accused the academic and his department of not having any practical experience. He was, therefore, not considered to be useful.

In the 1980s, as now, Japanese institutional investors were intrigued by the concept of a "black box"—a formula which could predict, given proper data. This fit into their world, which needed order and neatness. The search for the "black box" continues in the confines of the technology department. There is little experimentation with real situations, and the dialogue between the fund managers and the technology department is infrequent.

The Japanese brokers also separated the quantitative area from core businesses. The rotation system and the career promotion structure supported the sales management's heavy-handed marketing of Japanese equities and whatever product, foreign or domestic, was deemed important.

It has been suggested that the JFIs did indeed use technology and were integrating quantitative techniques into their business. Nomura's creation of the "heaven and hell" bond for IBM was cited as proof of the JFI's ability to compete with foreigners.[16] The issue was ". . . developed by a young mathematician in Nomura's new product group . . . The 'heaven and hell' issue involved three interest rate swaps and five foreign currency swaps." The net result: IBM saved "forty basis points." The section containing this description was entitled "Innovative Enough" and cited Nomura as praising itself for being "as brainy as it is brawny." The author further stated that Nomura was currently working on swaps technology so secretive that its swaps department in Tokyo had been declared off-limits to visitors.

WHAT IS INNOVATION?

Here, perhaps, there needs to be a clarification of the meaning of innovation. Certainly, Nomura's "heaven and hell" issue was clever, but was it innovative? Without trying to list the entire universe of possible applications of technology within the financial services industry, it would be helpful to look at some of the ways technology is used:

1. *Statistical aid*—Using quantitative analysis to select companies based on certain requirements, such as P/E ratios, cash flow, earnings, and book value is an example of use by portfolio managers. Determining the overall impact on a portfolio of a given decision is another.

2. *Cash flow determinations*—Interest rate swaps and currency swaps are created by arriving at cash flows which match currency and interest rate targets over a prescribed number of years. In many cases, investment bankers start with the needed result, such as a forty basis point improvement on the existing borrowing rate, as in the "heaven and hell" bonds. In the case of a AAA-rated company, as IBM was, the actual borrowing rate is well known as a certain spread "over or off" a U.S. Treasury issue with the same maturity. The spread relationships can be altered by credit changes, supply and demand, and so forth, but there is a working level assumption

---

[16] Burstein, *Yen!*, p. 185.

at any given point about the correct spread—especially that of a AAA- or AA-rated bond. The spread relationship is more difficult to determine for lower rated bonds than for higher rated ones.

In terms of the "heaven and hell" bond, Nomura knew what yield was necessary to interest IBM in issuing debt. There was nothing profoundly innovative about the investment or its creation. It was then possible to manipulate cash flows to arrive at the desired price.

The Japanese institutional investors during the 1980s were always trying to find new ways of making predictions on interest rates and currencies. Investment banking firms were inventing bonds with imbedded interest rates or currency options. These bonds would limit or increase exposure to a particular market. The Japanese institutional investors' speculative habits in the fixed income market were often the driving force behind these transactions. The institutional investor had an income stream from the interest and a maturity, so his commitment was well-defined. In most cases, he paid an exorbitant price for the imbedded option. The investor was buying income, and not really worrying about the cost of the option.

During the 1980s, the Japanese institutional investors had enormous cash flows which they were investing. They did not have to sell one asset in order to purchase another one. They were, in essence, diverting cash flows. In many cases, performance did not mean total rate of return (capital gains plus income); it meant yield. So most of the cash flow was channeled into fixed income assets.

Furthermore, the Japanese institutional investors considered their huge hidden reserves as a safety net. If they lost money, the reserves would mask the problem. Investing was a game, not a serious business.

Taking advantage of these cash flows, however, was a very serious business for investment bankers. The foreign investment bankers created billions of special fixed income bonds for the Japanese institutional investor. The investment banker—in the above-mentioned case, Nomura—quantified the necessary cash flows and issued the bonds. The procedure involved a modification to well-established currency and interest rate techniques. In essence, it was a gimmick. The *sina qua non* of these transactions was the Japanese institutional investor, whose transactions were more brawn than brain.

3. *Custodial and clearance systems*—These obviously rely heavily on quantitative systems.

4. *Investing via index funds*—This is a major example of the use of quantitative methods.

5. *Arbitrage trading*—In the equity area this can mean taking advantage of the difference between the price of futures and cash markets. It can mean discovering market inefficiencies and structuring strategies to profit from this aberration.

6. *Historical trends*—Given a set of assumptions and data, the price levels and trading characteristics of a particular security or a market can be analyzed in isolation or in comparison to another market or security.

7. *Asset/Liability management*—Techniques for quantifying risks, hedging, and managing risks are widely employed.

The main point in providing this list is to show the diversity and scope of quantitative applications. In some cases, such as data processing and securities clearance, the use is very mechanical once the system is constructed. In other examples, the degree of systemization varies enormously. There can be a great deal of subjective input in terms of making assumptions or framing issues. The technology can be a tool, not an answer. There still have to be human decisions about the relative importance of data and evaluations of future trends. Where the use of technology becomes a commonplace, the JFIs have been able to adopt it to some extent in their money management, capital market, or investment banking operations. This assembly line characteristic is important. When the technology is quite new or there is a major subjective component necessary for decision making, the Japanese rotation becomes one of the major hindrances to integration.

Because of the many uses of technology and the JFI's diversity of functions, it is important to examine individual cases of quantitative applications. Still, a pattern emerges as one of mechanical application rather than innovation and complexity.

DRAMA OF THE JFI MEETING

Most of the discussions about transactions, either terms or credit, occur in a meeting, usually at the JFI's office. Very little, other than market input or perfunctory conversation, takes place over the phone. There is an emphasis on personal contact and form. The meeting is ritualized. If the meeting is in Tokyo, the investment banker appears at the JFI's building. He is met in the lobby by a uniformed guard or "O.L." (office lady).[17] The lobby personnel instructs the investment bankers to the appropriate floor, where they are greeted (sometimes at the elevator) by an O.L., who ushers them to a room.

" Foreign managers in Tokyo discovered the strict age regiment when they found that their Japanese colleagues were reluctant to hire anyone who is one day older than themselves, despite qualifications. "

In the 1980s, if the topic was a U.S. credit-related or complicated transaction, the contingent of investment bankers sometimes consisted of a specialist visitor from New York, a foreigner from the Tokyo office, and the Japanese employee or employees responsible for interfacing between the JFI and the foreign investment bank. If the meeting was ceremonial, the foreign investment bank contingent could number five or six people. The Japanese company would want to know whom to expect so that it could plan accordingly. The most appropriate manner was to have an equal number of representatives from both sides with each participant having an equal ranking counterpart. This protocol is extremely important to the JFIs, even with foreign visitors.

This was a little difficult for foreigners because their ranks did not coincide with Japanese titles. Nor did their ages. The Japanese are promoted in age groups. Nomura and others have made minor concessions to this rule and have promoted people a few years younger than at other JFIs. Foreign managers in Tokyo discovered the strict age regiment when they

---

[17] O.L.'s are young women who work in clerical positions in the hopes of marrying a salaryman employed by their company. The general managers are often responsible for trying to promote suitable marriages within their departments. Salarymen who are unmarried and have just been rotated overseas sometimes panic and have been known to investigate the personnel files themselves to find a spouse because it is bad form to go overseas unmarried.

found that their Japanese colleagues were reluctant to hire anyone who is one day older than themselves, despite qualifications.

In a JFI meeting the room size is dependent on the seniority of the officials present. The decoration and furniture configuration are generally similar at each JFI. The guests sit on the couch furthest from the door. They face the JFI representatives. The senior official is positioned in the middle. Those of corresponding rank sit directly across from each other. The younger JFI employees arrive with notebooks for they will record everything. Coffee tables, not a conference table, are used. There is usually a Woolworth-type impressionist painting on the wall. The furniture is spartan. After the guests are ushered into the room, the JFI members will arrive. There is an anonymously polite introduction and formal exchange of business cards. The JFI salarymen study the business cards to determine where the particular person fits organizationally in his company. The JFI salarymen bow reflexively to the foreigners; the foreigners do not know quite what to do. The atmosphere is extremely formal even though the guests and the JFI personnel may have had dinner together the previous night.

The O.L. gracefully serves Japanese tea at the beginning of the meeting. As she exits the room, the O.L. turns and faces the participants. She then bows and excuses herself, while backing out of the room. If the meeting is long, the O.L. reappears and serves coffee, after carefully removing the tea cups. She then backs out of the room. Form, ceremony, politeness, and ritual are paramount in the JFI meeting.

In the 1980s, if the purpose of the meeting was a transaction, the American visitor from New York would be anxious to begin discussing his deal. He would assume the senior person opposite him was the decision maker, but if the senior person were a general manager or managing director, he would likely not be directly involved with the decision-making process.

The senior JFI official always began the conversation with the question, "When did you arrive in Tokyo?" Then, there would be the predictable lamenting about jetlag. At this point the visitor would launch full force into the sales presentation. Since no one would ever interrupt, except the foreigners' translator, the presentation would be a monologue. The Japanese are always reluctant to ask all but the most perfunctory questions, such as, "When the deal is going to be priced?" The foreign visitor would pause repeatedly to encourage a dialogue. As Americans are wont to do, the visitor would allow only a millisecond to elapse, for he was uncomfortable with the silence. If Americans wanted a response, they might have to wait thirty seconds—an eternity for an American—before a Japanese would say something.

If the meeting required translation, inevitably the translator would have to struggle to keep up with the visitor, who would speak much too quickly and for too long a period before pausing. The visitor would also use colloquial expressions which cannot be translated. But idiomatic English was not the worst fate that might befall the diligent translator. It was the dreaded joke. When the foreign visitor tried to amuse the JFI participants, he would want to know why they did not laugh. So he would make the translator explain the joke. A joke is generally a cross-cultural enigma, but at this point, the foreign visitor's ego would be involved, so the explanation might take a long time. Some Japanese translators did not even bother attempting to translate a joke. They would merely inform the Japanese present that the visitor had told a joke and suggest they appear amused.

"... idiomatic English was not the worst fate that might befall the diligent translator. It was the dreaded joke. When the foreign visitor tried to amuse the JFI participants, he would want to know why they did not laugh. So he would make the translator explain the joke."

The foreign visitor would usually indicate that his firm was the best at whatever he was attempting to sell. He would be armed with color graphs and tables to prove this. If the foreign visitor tried to describe more than one transaction, or more than one market circumstance, the JFI employees would probably be confused. They needed a very rigid, outlined discussion. To attempt to move quickly from one topic to another—often an American trait—was to court disaster because the JFI employees often were not aware that the visitor had moved from the first topic. The visitor would desperately want informational feedback. He might ask a question to provoke a response. Again, the silence would last only a short time before the visitor would nervously resume his monologue. The charts, ratios, and spread sheets concerning the transaction would be explained in depth. Everything would be described positively as this was a pure sales presentation.

JFIs WANT PACKAGED TRANSACTIONS

Even today, the JFI employees like fully-packaged transactions. They are accustomed to receiving these packages, which they then review. They crave order and neatness. Questions and dialogue are minimal. They do not like to initiate an idea and develop a transaction. This would require more interaction than they are prepared to allow. In the 1980s, however, it would have also meant coming up with better quality investments.

A one-week seminar on asset allocation in 1990 at the office of a JFI illustrates this propensity. The American lecturer was a fund manager who had employed quantitative methods to assist his organization in determining the asset mix of his portfolio. The portfolio had diverse holdings—U.S. and foreign equities, public and private equities, fixed income securities, and real estate. The American lecturer had an excellent performance record and was able to manage several billions of dollars with a staff of 15 people. For one week, there were almost no questions in an area that was broad and relevant to the audience.

At the end of the seminar, the students suddenly became involved. They wanted to know the specific formulas which constituted the "black box." If they applied the formula, they thought they would understand the secret of asset allocation. Just as they had been taught in school and corporation, the young salarymen wanted to memorize an answer. Rote memorization was all they thought was required. When the fund manager tried to explain that there were no formulas which could be used without subjective input and modification, and that quantitative techniques in this area were only used to assist in making decisions, not in making them, the reply fell on deaf ears. He further tried to explain that portfolios have different objectives depending on their liability requirements. Again, the employees wanted a simple, uniform package which could be approved intact. It was an assembly line mentality.

In a 1980s meeting, the actual discussion about a transaction would be very mechanical. None of the JFI employees would have meaningful knowledge of the company or industry represented by the transaction. The JFI employees were in the involved area only as a stopover during the rotation process. A JFI employee would be assigned the task of preparing, rather than examining, the proposal for the JFI.

Preparation meant putting the proposal in the proper form for consideration. But consideration did not mean critical evaluation. Issues such as understanding the creative nature of rosy favorable projections, the alleged high internal rate of return forecasts, accounting nuances, economic cyclical implications, management quality, competitiveness within the industry, real value of the company, or other substantive matters, were never seriously considered.

" A JFI employee would be assigned the task of preparing, rather than examining, the proposal for the JFI."

Whether the foreign investment banker was aware of the superficiality of the JFI's approach is not important. He would leave the sales documents with the JFI. (By the mid-1980s, the foreign investment bankers had learned that materials had to be translated into Japanese.) The material would be politely accepted by the JFI employees.

At the conclusion of the meeting, the visitors would rise and shake hands with the JFI contingency and then proceed out of the room. At the elevator, there would be another round of handshaking, and the visitors would enter the elevator with the JFI employees facing them and bowing.

NAVIGATING THROUGH JAPANESE ETIQUETTE

Foreigners always would want to know if they should bow and how to bow. It is really not important for foreigners to try to adopt this custom. As long as the foreigner commits no rude act, the Japanese do not care. Foreigners are not expected to engage in Japanese etiquette in these infrequent encounters.

Issues of protocol could be harmless or they could have a serious impact on business. Proper bowing techniques are an example of the former category. Another example of a benign breach of etiquette was one committed by a senior official of Salomon Brothers' New York equity department when he visited Salomon Tokyo in 1986. He invited three senior Salomon Japanese colleagues for dinner—and included their wives. Japanese rarely include wives at business functions, and even then, it is usually an accommodation to foreign colleagues or clients. On the day of the dinner, the three wives called to explain that they could not attend the dinner because they could not find babysitters. The wives had gracefully excluded themselves from an awkward situation. This event was innocuous and did not diminish the status of the New York visitor in the eyes of the Japanese.

A major supplier to Toshiba and Mitsubishi Electric breached Japanese etiquette at a restaurant. The supplier was an American manufacturer living in California. He was highly regarded by Japanese companies because of the quality and price of his product; hence, he was important. The supplier did not like Japanese food and returned the sushi and sashimi that had been ordered for him in a Japanese restaurant in Osaka, requesting they be cooked. The restaurant proceeded to prepare the raw fish in accordance with the desire of the guest. There were no negative business implications for the supplier, because he was foreign and had something which the Japanese wanted.

There are also examples of serious and costly breaches. One occurred at Salomon Brothers in 1985. An employee of Mitsubishi Trust, Mr. Maruyama, had accepted an offer to join Salomon Brother's Tokyo corporate finance department. Protocol would dictate that the prospective employee resign properly. He should have indicated to his superior at Mitsubishi Trust that he was entering another field, working in the family business, or taking some time to reevaluate his career. Under no circumstances should he have indicated that he was resigning to join Salomon (or any domestic competitor or foreign firm in a similar business). This would constitute a serious violation of protocol and embarrass his superior at Mitsubishi Trust, who would thereby lose great face within his company.

Salomon's corporate finance department, with prodding from Salomon's New York-based international investment banking department, disregarded the advice of Salomon's Tokyo management and instructed Maruyama to tell Mitsubishi Trust that he was resigning in order to join Salomon. After Maruyama followed these instructions, the predictable reaction and problem ensued, culminating in Mitsubishi Trust suspending all business with Salomon Brothers for over a year. The resulting loss of revenues was several million dollars, as Mitsubishi Trust was one of Salomon's largest Japanese clients.

The Japanese are only concerned about the power status of the company or the client the foreigner represents. Alienating the JFI salaryman could result from extreme behavior but not from the omission of formal

Japanese etiquette. The multiple handshaking came out of awkwardness on both sides. Since neither side knows when the other wants to shake hands, they both do it often.

As soon as the elevator closes, the U.S. visitor would want to know what the JFI response will be. A Japanese member of the foreign firm, if asked, would present the results of the meeting with the JFI in the most positive of lights, as he would not want to offend. Also, the Japanese have an extreme reluctance to mention a rejection, a failure, or a problem that smacks of confrontation.

Hundreds of deals were discussed in meetings like this in offices of Japanese institutional investors in Tokyo and New York. During the 1980s, the first-class section of flights to Tokyo were filled with eager investment bankers. It seemed as if every part of America was for sale. In a meeting at the Asia Society in New York on December 4, 1991, former Prime Minister Nakasone was asked if he was worried about repercussions from the Japanese purchases of such high profile U.S. assets as Rockefeller Center or Columbia Pictures. He reminded the audience that U.S. investment bankers had been aggressively marketing these assets to the Japanese.

FOLLOWING FINANCIAL FASHIONS

But in the 1980s, the Japanese institutional investor was often predisposed towards the acceptability of a transaction being brought to them by U.S. investment bankers. The yield in the junk bond area, of course, had to be appropriate. There could be no negative press reports about the borrower in Japan or the U.S. The intermediary should be a *yumei na kaisha*. It was also helpful if the borrower had a recognizable name. Themes, as in the equity market, were important too. If American LBOs were fashionable, then there was a good possibility of acceptance. The Japanese institutional investor usually equated activity with strength, which was always interpreted positively. If other Japanese institutional investors were active in the market, then it would be difficult for a JFI to avoid seriously considering a transaction or market. This pressure to conform is a slight variation of the herd instinct.

During any meeting with JFIs, the slightest mention of another JFI will cause JFI salarymen to overcome their reluctance to ask questions and want to know every detail about the reference to another JFI, especially if it is a similar institution—a securities firm, trust bank and so forth. As a matter of fact, the JFI salaryman is often more interested in what another JFI is doing about the transaction than in the transaction itself. Other tidbits of information—especially gossip about new joint ventures, personnel changes, and new policies—are equally welcome.

" Inconsistency of application of a rule is just as effective as vagueness of language in creating dependency on interpretation."

The actual structure of a JFI transaction must seem to conform to the MOF guidelines. For example, during the 1980s, there was the fifty percent (*goju pahsento*) rule—no more than fifty percent of a transaction could be placed with Japanese investors. This rule was circumvented without difficulty. A transaction could be said to be one hundred million dollars with only fifty million being issued at that time. The MOF could easily have discovered huge numbers of bond issues where one hundred percent of the issue was placed in Japan. The rule was a tool which could be used when the MOF wanted to exert power, or when the JFI needed an excuse not to do a transaction. Inconsistency of application of a rule is just as effective as vagueness of language in creating dependency on interpretation.

The Japanese are masterful at devising ways to avoid regulations when they deem appropriate. From the seventeenth, eighteenth, and nineteenth century *ukiyo-e* artists to present day Japanese institutional investors, circumvention is a prized art form. When the Japanese were forbidden to print calendars in the eighteenth century so as not to compete with the government monopoly, the *ukiyo-e* artists cleverly painted designs that represented calendar dates on komonos or otherwise slightly disguised the calendar. Similarly, the JFIs know how to maneuver bureaucratically when it suits them.

NEMAWASHI AND ACCOUNTABILITY

The process of obtaining consensus is called *nemawashi*. In the case of a high yield transaction, the analysis was really a proposal constructed by the young salaryman, according to the guidelines mentioned above. The transaction, having conformed to the generally accepted conditions required at the particular moment, had a good chance of being approved. During the initial phases of the internal approval process, various members of the department would give their tacit acceptance. In most cases, even if the initial presentation was made to the New York office of a Japanese institutional investor, the actual decision relating to the transaction occurred in Tokyo. Many Japanese institutional investors tried to give the appearance that decisions were made in their overseas offices, but this was a charade. Decisions emanated from Tokyo. The foreign staff of Japanese institutional investors had no input.

JFI employees in various related departments such as planning would be aware of credit-related decisions and have some jurisdiction. These departments were even further removed from credit analysis.

If a Japanese institutional investor had spent any time in an international department or overseas office, he was deemed to have experience. Experience, in these situations, had no relationship to knowledge. The formal assignment conferred the illusion of experience. It was assumed that there had been an absorption of knowledge. By the time the transaction was approved, there would have been enough people involved so accountability was obscured. Moreover, enough people had a vested interest so that no one would ever attempt to determine accountability. Actually, no one ever wanted to be accountable. This is a less than constructive view of *nemawashi*.

As the IBJ official said, it would be insane to expect the Japanese to understand credit relationships because their domestic market does not require it. In a tightly regulated market with favorable markets to rectify most mistakes, this attitude was never questioned. To *attempt* to transplant this attitude was, to use the IBJ official's word, *insane*. *Nemawashi* was a perfectly acceptable practice, if properly applied. Within the context of the structural weaknesses of the JFIs overseas in the 1980s, it became a political excuse to avoid making serious decisions.

The JFIs did not consider the substantive value of the LBO market during the 1980s, because internal structural issues did not allow this. They could not understand credits in depth, nor the asset as a category. In a very general sense, the LBO represented an attractive asset category during parts of the early 1980s. The mid-1980s saw highly inflated values, partially as a result of JFI participation. By 1990, LBOs represented an interesting asset category. Clearly the above descriptions are only guidelines, and results could be quite different, depending on the skill of the LBO fund manager. Also, LBO assets could include equity, senior debt, and various categories of subordinated debt—each of which had to be considered a separate class of asset in terms of value. During this period, an individual JFI could have had three or more rotations of personnel involving the credit analysis of LBOs.

Since the JFIs only participated in themes or fashions, it was consistent that they were most involved during the period of greatest activity and vulnerability. They also restricted their participation to major names or firms. There were many medium-sized, highly disciplined American LBO fund managers who were excluded from consideration because they were not famous. Despite past performance, philosophy, or expertise, they could never receive serious attention from the JFIs.

> " Moreover, enough people had a vested interest so that no one would ever attempt to determine accountability. Actually, no one ever wanted to be accountable. This is a less than constructive view of *nemawashi*."

One example will suffice. A small LBO firm which managed a $100 million fund was introduced to a large Japanese investor. The two principals of the firm had been in the field for seventeen years each. Their fund had produced a return of fifty percent compound for the previous nine years. Several of their portfolio companies had strong Japanese ties, either in distributing Japanese products in America or in manufacturing products which could be sold in Japan. The fund had made almost no investments for several years in the mid-1980s because the principals realized values were highly inflated. The firm purchased companies that needed outside capital. They worked closely with their investee companies and assisted them in growing. Their time horizon for assisting in this process was four to five years, after which time, depending on market conditions and valuations, they might sell part or all of a company to realize a profit. All of the fund's original investors still participated because of the performance, philosophy and skill of the managers. The fund was not blind—each investor could approve each deal separately. The fund did not use excessive leverage. The only source of income for the principals was capital gains on the investments, not fees. The fund purchased medium-sized, $50-$250 million in sales, U.S. companies involved in low- to medium-tech industries. There was no financial engineering involved. The principals did not think that imposing a good capital structure on a bad company was effective or proper. In short, it was very conservative and profitable in the long run.

By 1991, the principals had identified several attractively priced companies which needed outside help. They thought the companies had excellent potential for growth. The principals explained their strategy and record to a JFI, that had no way to fit these Americans or their companies into the JFI's structure. They were not *yumei na kaisha*, and their investments, although excellent value, were not recognizable names in Japan. Even though the JFIs made significant investments in LBO-related assets which performed poorly, they could not consider a proposal based on substance rather than form. It would be better not to have made the investment in these complicated areas rather than make them relying on a famous large company.

Once again, the rotation system directly or indirectly influenced this propensity to neglect substance.

RISK/REWARD CONCEPTS AND RELATIVE VALUE

Since the JFI salaryman stayed in a position for only a few years, he could develop only the most rudimentary understanding of the relationships between different categories of assets, the appropriate reward for investing in a particular risk category, the proper sources of information, or basic nuances of various securities. The Japanese institutional investor during the 1980s thought in terms of absolute returns, such as 7 percent in yen. He would be satisfied with that return even if a similar security appreciated 20 percent. He wanted order and was averse to risk. The essence of investing is understanding risk. The Japanese institutional investor wanted a comfortable, predictable return each year. After all, he was going to be in his present job for only a few years, so why make the attempt to understand markets or securities?

Since the Japanese yen bond market was yielding 4 percent to 7 percent during most of this period and money market yields were even lower, the JFI could not hide in their own fixed income market. Worse, many JFIs had promised returns to *tokkin* funds or life insurance policy holders in the range of 7 percent. The portfolio manager was thus forced to look at foreign equity-related securities and bonds and the domestic equity market.

One example of the consequences of naivete based on inexperience, and applying domestic market practices, was the investment in bonds without regard to "call features." Most U.S. bonds (except U.S. Treasuries) have an option whereby the borrower can prepay an issue at a stated price on a stated date. This gives the borrower the flexibility to repay debt before the obligation matures if interest rates fall, and reissue at a lower interest rate. For example, a bond may have an 8 percent coupon and mature in thirty years. The borrower may be able to "call" the bond after ten years at a price of 108, when the bond was originally issued at 100.

The Japanese samurai bond market (foreign yen-denominated bonds) actually have call features. When interest rates were low enough to encourage borrowers to "call" their older issues, the MOF, in a heavy-handed manner, threatened to restrict the borrowers' future access to the Japanese market if the Samurai bond issue was "called." The MOF viewed a "call" as disorderly and knew that Japanese investors who purchased bonds at a price higher than the call price would take a capital loss. Although the Japanese investor knew about the risk when the bonds were purchased, the MOF did not care.

Overseas, U.S. bankers noticed that the Japanese did not consider call features relevant. This is important to the borrower as it gives him tremendous flexibility to adjust his debt costs when interest rates change. Hence, the U.S. investment bankers brought thirty-year fixed rate bonds to the Euromarkets, with one year "call protection" and a small redemption premium. The Kingdom of Sweden and other borrowers took advantage of this. The Japanese investors who purchased these bonds took a thirty-year interest rate risk such that if rates went up, the price of their security would go down, and if rates went down, the bonds were "called." At the time, the usual call protection in the U.S. was ten years.

The Japanese institutional investors were equally unconcerned when they received fixed income returns while taking equity risks. If an investor is taking a credit risk, he should be getting a return commensurate with the risk. The actual pricing of a U.S. dollar bond relates to the U.S. Treasury market, in which there is assumed to be no credit risk. If a U.S. Treasury five- to seven-year bond yields 8 percent, then the price should relate to 8 percent. AAA-rated corporate bonds might yield 8-1/4 percent, and a junk bond might yield 12 percent. The equity market must compete with those returns in order to be attractive. Private equity, such as real estate or LBOs, might require returns of 25 percent to 30 percent to justify the risks.

The JFIs' purchase of assets was often of critical importance in terms of pricing. The JFIs' participation often determined whether a deal could be done. After the Nikkei collapse, *Barron's* estimated that JFI purchases of global equity offerings dropped from 25 percent to 5 percent of a par-ticular issue.[18] Europe's privatization efforts would certainly have been more difficult without the predictable uninformed role of the JFIs.

No matter which market the Japanese entered, they distorted realistic relationships and accepted low returns. In 1987, Japanese institutional inves-tors pounced on the Euroconvertible bond market without doing any re-search on the underlying equity. They moved the conversion premium levels to uneconomical heights. Japanese institutional investors were capable of making such large purchases that only a few investors could influence val-ues dramatically. In several cases, Japanese institutional investors were speculating with their own capital. U.S. investment bankers were ecstatic.

> **" In the 1980s, with enough pressure or persistence, a salesman could cajole a Japanese institutional investor into making a purchase. "**

One curious case illustrates the JFI investing process at work. A me-dium-sized Japanese bank made a $50 million investment in the equity of a U.S. LBO fund in 1986. When a partner of the LBO fund met with the official responsible for the investment, he asked what a normal-sized loan to one of the LBO fund's portfolio companies would be. Although the banker had never made such a loan, he said one to five million dollars. Thus, the bank would have lent only one million dollars to a company, but would invest $50 million in a fund that would purchase equity of compa-nies with which the banker had absolutely no familiarity. Equally impor-tant, he knew nothing about the fund managers. The reason for the purchase was based on the relationship of the banker to the salesman at the investment banking firm which marketed the deal.

In the 1980s, with enough pressure or persistence, a salesman could cajole a Japanese institutional investor into making a purchase. This was certainly the style which was used by the Japanese securities firms. They were given quotas of securities to sell. Even with institutional clients, the brokers were more persistent than informed. The Japanese institutional in-vestors liked the adulation and seemed to view the frequent sales calls as a

---

18 Palmer, Jay, "Europe on the Block," *Barron's*, June 14, 1993, p. 17.

kind of collegial banter. After all, it was not their money, and they would not be criticized for purchasing a security from Nomura or Daiwa.

Some of the successful foreign securities firms in Tokyo in the 1980s did not adopt the typical Nomura approach to client contact. They made a conscious effort to be more professional, even though the constant rotation of fund managers and the obvious inefficiencies, such as the call feature, meant that contact with the Japanese institutional investors was less than sophisticated. The capital flows were so large that the foreigners were constantly identifying new assets which fit the requirements of the Japanese investors. These needs often had little to do with correct asset evaluation, risk/reward considerations, or notions of relative value.

The amount of money to be invested brought additional problems to foreign investment banks in Tokyo. One of the tasks of managers in the Tokyo offices of foreign investment banks was to restrict the influx of visiting investment bankers, as well as monitor the flow of Japanese capital. This was fraught with internal politics. The stakes were high as Japanese capital was funding mispriced deals. In some cases, it may have been all, or a significant part, of the funding available. "Sales" in Japan could easily represent major profits for departments involved in real estate, securitized assets, high yield assets, corporate debt, convertibles, syndication, currency and interest rate swaps, and investment banking. Deals were structured entirely for the Japanese market in some cases.

U.S. investment banks are organized vertically into profit centers. Some are more vertical than others. The consequences can promote divisive internal competition and animosity, in addition to profits. Often, product lines do not fit clearly into one department at an investment bank. For example, high yield asset business in Japan could require coordination of investment/merchant banking, relevant trading, research, sales, capital markets, swaps, and liaison groups. Each time a U.S. investment banker saw the slightest opportunity to access cheap Japanese money, he wanted to fly to Tokyo or he wanted immediate priority for his deal. The inquiry could be an idea, the remote possibility of a transaction, a ridiculously priced transaction, or a real deal. No matter how unprepared the banker, or how ill-conceived or scatterbrained the idea, he demanded immediate attention.

It was very difficult to arrange the formal meetings and prepare the presentations required. The Japanese generalist institutional investors were inundated with proposals. They did not have any particular substantive criteria for selecting assets, so investment bankers were indiscriminately offering assets. The unfortunate Japanese salespeople in the Tokyo offices of

U.S. investment bankers attempted to set up multiple appointments with Japanese institutional investors in this frenzy of activity. Their New York departments gave the orders and vied for the time with Japanese institutional investors competing with their colleagues in other departments.

It should be remembered that JFIs did not dominate the U.S. corporate market, the Eurobond market, or the U.S. Treasury market during the 1980s. When they did participate in these markets, however, they often created temporary and sometimes major price distortions which provided opportunities for investment bankers. When the Japanese were not involved, the market returned to previous levels.

The importance of the profitability of these transactions was not well understood outside the investment banks. The role of Japanese capital was critical. The profits were not visible to the outside world because they were never identified. They did not appear in the profitability statements of the Tokyo branches of U.S. firms because the transactions were "booked" in New York or London, for various internal departments. The successful U.S. banks made huge sums in this area during the 1980s.

THE JAPANESE BROKERS VERSUS JAPANESE INVESTORS

The generalist/rotation system had different implications in the 1980s for the Japanese brokers than it did for the Japanese institutional investors. The Japanese brokerage firms have mutual funds and money management operations. These funds are a captive source of business for their parent companies. The Japanese brokerage firm's money management operations maintain some business with outside intermediaries, especially in the foreign securities area, but the bulk of their activity is internally executed. Their results indicate that their parents' profits are more of a priority than performance.

The rotation system did not hinder the brokers' marketing efforts because their clients—Japanese institutional clients—did not require professional service and quality ideas, especially in the domestic markets. As has been observed, the rotation system was one of the main causes of this lack of emphasis on professionalism. The tendency was for Japanese institutional investors to rely on a personal relationship with the Japanese brokerage community. Therefore, the young, inexperienced salesmen of Nomura and Daiwa could successfully service institutions, in addition to individual investors.

The style of client coverage for individuals and institutions was very similar. This included the "theme of the week" stock selection. The sales manager identified a theme (e.g., construction companies because of the new Osaka airport, or German stocks because of the opening of Eastern Europe, or Japanese manufacturers with large real estate holdings) and then told his sales team to sell it. There was no extensive research support. The typical sales manager of a securities firm prided himself on not using research or originating his own ideas. The salesmen then began calling, visiting, and pressuring clients. If the clients were not responsive, the salesmen became extremely persistent and, if that failed, they begged clients to purchase the "theme of the week stock."

Historically, the Japanese brokers ranked low on the Japanese status ladder. A university graduate usually preferred to join a bank, an insurance company, a trading company, or almost any other Japanese company, before he would join a Japanese brokerage house. This only changed during the 1980s with the increased visibility of the Japanese brokers. There was also a clearly delineated hierarchy within the various categories.

" Although they were viewed condescendingly, the brokers were feared because of their power."

The condescending attitude towards Japanese brokers was witnessed frequently. During a conversation, an IBJ official echoed this when he emphatically indicated that *IBJ*, not the brokers, was representative of the superiority of the Japanese system.

Although they were viewed condescendingly, the brokers were feared because of their power. The brokers knew this. The frenzy, arrogance, and crudeness that one encountered with a Japanese broker in the 1980s was an attempt to project this image of power. They had to maintain their position with muscle; they had to be seen to have brawn.

Overseas, the placing power of Japanese brokers and other Japanese intermediaries compelled borrowers to listen. In many cases, the placing power consisted of the Japanese intermediary buying the security and "placing" that asset in his own inventory. Some of the JFIs based in London were referred to as "warehouses" rather than financial institutions. Also, it was common to subsidize transactions to make them attractive to Japanese institutional investors. For example, a Japanese intermediary would make an aggressive bid to a borrower. The borrower would issue a security through the Japanese intermediary, which would then own an unmarketable security. They would take the overpriced U.S. dollar security and attach a subsidized yen currency swap to it. This would create a marketable yen security. In order to accomplish this, the Japanese intermediary had to lose money on the currency swap because it was overpriced. The Japanese intermediary engaged in this type of activity often for the sake of market share or publicity, especially if it was allowed to share in the glory of being a manager in an underwriting.

LEGACY OF DEPENDENCY

The rotation system was a major factor in defining and restricting the type of business done by Japanese institutional investors and banks in the U.S. during the 1980s. The common denominators for acceptable intermediaries or counterparts were size and presence—in other words, the major U.S. investment and commercial banks. They were the filter for transactions and contact. The rotation system helped create a dependency on large U.S. financial institutions for generation of transactions, whether in conventional areas such as dealing in U.S. Treasuries where it is normal, to more esoteric and complicated areas such as real estate or private equity. The JFIs' international staff waited for presentations to be given to them on a fully packaged basis, i.e., sales promotions. The JFI salaryman did not seem motivated to examine and investigate a variety of sources of information and transactions. Partially, this is the result of his having so much money to invest either directly or indirectly. Secondly, it derived from the desire to have a politically safe source, a foreign *yumei na kaisha*. Large U.S. investment and commercial banks were certainly necessary and useful at times, but they were also opportunistic, and JFIs needed to be cautious when dealing with them. Essentially, they sold assets, and usually did not care about the asset after the sale. These institutions were fee- and trading profit-oriented.

During the 1980s, U.S. financial intermediaries were engaged, among other activities, in merchant banking, such as buying equity participations for investment while collecting huge intermediary fees. Earning fees on transactions which the American investment bank purchased as investments or bridge loans was fraught with issues of conflict of interest. It also led to portfolio problems, as fee generation rather than sound judgement prompted decisions. The JFIs purchased the bridge loans, giving the investment bankers huge profits.

The JFIs transplanted intact their faith in large, well-known companies. Their Japanese background taught them that these were reliable, trustworthy, and stable, and that small companies are risky, unprestigious, and lack resources and skills. In reality, there are both good and bad, competent and incompetent people and departments at large companies, as well as at small ones. Especially at a large U.S. financial firm, the particular individual or department is very relevant. The JFIs focused on large U. S. financial intermediaries rather than critically evaluating a wide variety of sources of information and transactions. They could not do otherwise because the time-consuming process of identifying reliable sources was incompatible with the rotation system. This situation resulted from the inability to institutionalize knowledge-accumulation. Each new manager wanted to have his own contacts as previous ones might not be loyal. With his own contacts, a salaryman was assured of a relationship with personal obligations attached. It would have been better for the JFIs to avoid the complicated credit intensive transactions all together rather than handle them through their existing structure.

> **" They could not do otherwise because the time-consuming process of identifying reliable sources was incompatible with the rotation system. This situation resulted from the inability to institutionalize knowledge-accumulation. "**

The JFIs willingly accepted their dependence on large U.S. financial firms. In 1989, one senior official at a JFI explained the relationship of his institution to the U.S. investment banks as complementary. The U.S. investment banks originated transactions; he purchased them. This JFI had multiple branches in the U.S., various asset managers and loan officers, and had been in the U.S. for many years and, yet, it still could not originate a transaction. He also stated that he had difficulty evaluating his relationship with clients, such as Ford Motor Company. The answer was easy. Ford would accept aggressively-priced bids, but the JFI could not have the multi-layered, dependence based on mutual obligations that existed between his company and Japanese companies. All that could exist was a transactional relationship.

LEGACY FOR BUSINESS

The rotation system encouraged commodity, low margin business rather than sophisticated, high margin activity. Unfortunately, the JFIs in many cases did low margin business, taking risks commensurate with high margin business. Their superficial analytical skills and knowledge were not adequate to screen transactions.

One of the most extraordinary examples occurred in the Euromarket, where the Japanese craving for assets and not profits lead them to dominate the Euro-floating rate note (FRN) market. They had forced the pricing to levels at which only JFIs would participate. After buying FRNs at such narrow level spreads—a few basis points—intermediaries created a variation by bringing ever-longer maturities for borrowers until the perpetual FRN was introduced. It had no maturity, and the JFIs dominated the market. They would be especially pleased to participate if they were allowed to be an underwriting manager because of the publicity factor. Co-managements were actually "sold" to JFIs by specifying the amount of an issue a JFI had to underwrite—in reality, purchase. The borrowers were banks so that, when some of the banks developed problems, certain perpetual FRN issues declined by 30 percent. The JFIs had been making 25 basis points (1/4 percent) per year on these investments in which they proceeded to lose 30 percent of their value.

The tendency to follow fashionable trends, such as real estate and LBOs, created problems. Without proper sources of information and transactions, and lacking requisite skills, the JFIs plunged into dangerous waters and floundered. When interesting opportunities did exist, the JFIs were unable to react because they were accustomed to following whatever is popular and, hence, politically safe. Popularity created activity, publicity, and the participation of other JFIs.

In 1992, there was much talk in Japan about the emphasis on "Asian" business. To reduce costs, the Japanese manufacturers have moved manufacturing facilities to countries such as Taiwan, Thailand, and Malaysia. The Japanese banks have followed, and have had a positive experience lending to subsidiaries of Japanese companies in Asia. The JFIs now speak of their better understanding of Asian business because they assume there is a common culture. If the JFIs operate there the way they have in the U.S., their results will be similarly bad.

Certainly, the rotation system has led to difficulties in training staff in the international area. An employee can move from Bahrain to Switzerland and then to the Tokyo department responsible for cross-border M&A in America, within the space of a few years. He can move from lending responsibilities in Australia, to management in London, to distributing capital markets products to domestic clients in Tokyo. None of these are connected in terms of skill development, except to create generalist managers. Every replacement starts at the beginning of a learning curve. The accumulated knowledge is never institutionalized.

CHAPTER 6

TOKYO CENTER

It is not surprising that the JFIs want their Tokyo departments to retain control of international investing and give directions to their overseas operations. Japan is an authoritarian society. The educational system rigidly imposes a fear of authority, which is interpreted as respect. Schools idealize group harmony and this is enforced by group pressure. Order is emphasized over spontaneity, discipline over questioning. The corporation continues this indoctrination when the university graduate enters the business world. The government and the corporation represent authority. There is by necessity cultural and philosophical opposition to any form of decentralization.

As a result, the JFIs in the 1980s ignored the fact that advances in information technology often make decentralized decision-making an important option. Organizationally, they operated the same way they did for decades when limited technology made it essential to gather and share information via one central location. The world moved more slowly then. There was ample time for this process to occur. By the 1980s, and certainly in the 1990s, as deals grew more complex and the pace of trading-related decisions accelerated, operating internationally in a totally centralized organization was neither necessary nor efficient. The command post needed to be closer to the action and information flow.

The Japanese use of military analogies and terms is an illustration of the depth of their authoritarian attitude. The military is the quintessential authoritarian organization, and Japanese corporations have adopted military nomenclature as ordinary business vocabulary. One JFI described the potential consolidation of U.S. operations as "disarmament." Another mentioned that lack of previous penetration into the Hong Kong market

required a strategy using an "air attack" rather than a "ground attack." A
planning department was a "general staff office." General managers were
"regimental commanders." Overseas offices were "regiments." Trading positions were "weapons and bullets." The tendency towards centralization
was so strong that overseas operations and international business was conducted directly from the "command center."

Centralization and authority are present in every facet of life. The media are located in Tokyo. Television networks are national and based in
Tokyo. The Japanese newspapers are national with large circulations. For
example[1]

Yomiuri Shimbun	9,000,000
Asahi Shimbun	8,000,000
Mainichi Shimbun	4,000,000
Nihon Keizai Shimbun	2,500,000
Sankei Shimbun	2,000,000

The government offices are mainly in Tokyo. The role of the MOF makes it
vital for financial firms to be physically located in Tokyo. Even firms such
as Nippon Life, which has its home office in Osaka, maintains its financial
and investment operations in Tokyo. Some senior executives who live outside the city reside at Nippon Life's apartments in Tokyo and commute
home on the weekend. The educational system is administered by the Ministry of Education, which is located in Tokyo. The curriculum, textbooks,
and every facet of education is standardized and managed from Tokyo.

Centralization is so imbedded in the Japanese system that it was natural for the JFIs to direct operations from Tokyo. The fact that they made
decisions overseas without sufficient knowledge of local markets and cultures was merely an outgrowth of this orientation towards Tokyo where
goals were often framed in terms of political motives. Always concerned
with the impact of a policy or decision in Tokyo, the JFIs treated their
overseas activities as a quest for political gain. Unconcerned with substance, the JFIs looked abroad for publicity.

The centrally-directed expansion of the 1980s was not the result of
careful planning. It came as a series of reactions to external events. If the

---

[1]   Davis, Glenn; Whipple, Charles; and Sakakibara, "The Keepers of the Gate," *Tokyo
Journal,* August 1988, p. 8.

Italian or Spanish market became visible, JFIs would contemplate a Milan or Madrid office. If Luxembourg appeared to be popular, the JFIs would open an office in Luxembourg. If U.S. merger and LBO activity was gaining momentum, the JFIs would look for advertisable names as partners. The JFI's overseas empire thus, in many ways, mirrored Britain's—a number of disconnected responses to outside stimuli.

TOKYO SETS ITS PRIORITIES

Since Tokyo controlled policy, it is important to know what the JFIs in Tokyo stated as their priorities overseas. The same four objectives were repeatedly mentioned:

1. Market share/Publicity
2. Performance/Profit
3. Transfer of technology or knowledge
4. Service Japanese clients located in Japan or abroad

Each was a valid goal separately or as a combination.

The JFIs, however, would have indicated that all four are priorities. By the end of the 1980s, the rhetoric heavily favored performance/profit. Nevertheless, the reality throughout the 1980s was that market share and publicity were the only objectives. The JFI's structure for overseas was established to emphasize form (publicity), and not substantive issues such as profit, technology or knowledge transfer.

> " The JFI's overseas empire thus, in many ways, mirrored Britain's — a number of disconnected responses to outside stimuli. "

The JFIs justified this approach with a simple analogy to the Japanese manufacturers. The manufacturers, they said, expanded overseas successfully by first gaining market share. Market share for the manufacturers meant power, economies-of-scale, recognition, and destruction of the competition. For the JFIs, it meant only a form of recognition. The JFIs never stopped to consider the result of their market share mentality overseas. They blindly followed the Japanese-accepted wisdom. The availability of huge amounts of capital made the objective of formal recognition quite easily attainable.

Concerning the establishment of a U.S. money management operation, a senior IBJ banker told me unhesitatingly that the only one of the four priorities that mattered was market share. When I asked whether this meant domestic or foreign market share, he was suddenly speechless. He had not thought about U.S. or Japanese market share. Nor had he even bothered to identify a particular asset category, e.g., bonds or equities. His answer was a simple conditioned reflex.

YEN SYNDICATED LOANS GARNER PUBLICITY

Transactions need to be identified in order to clarify the motives of the JFIs and to correct the misinterpretations which attribute sophistication and lasting impact to these aberrations. The yen syndicated loan market provides a useful example of the JFIs sacrificing money and energy for the sake of publicity and market share. Major Japanese life insurance companies in the mid-1980s were willing to accept rates of return significantly below market rates in order to receive the glory of being a lead manager of a yen syndicated loan to a prestigious foreign borrower. The yen syndicated loan rate was not an interest rate determined by the market. It was administered, and during the 1980s it was higher than other market rates. No borrower with any credit standing would issue a yen syndicated loan, because the rate was unrealistic. The difficulty was further compounded by the fact that many borrowers did not want to accept the risk of borrowing yen.

The Japanese life insurance companies circumvented these obstacles by allowing investment banks to attach currency and interest rate swaps to the yen loan. This resulted in the borrower's actually having a fixed or floating rate U.S. dollar obligation, instead of an expensive yen loan. The cost of attaching five- to seven-year yen swaps was enormous. The Japanese life insurance companies placed below-market rate deposits with Japanese banks that purchased the loan, which was then converted to dollars at a low interest rate. It did not matter how low the loan rate was because the life company's deposit rate was adjusted to give a positive spread to the Japanese banks. The Japanese banks booked the loan offshore so the MOF would not be able to examine the transaction. This offshore booking also satisfied concern about the *goju pahsento* rule. Countries such as Sweden,

Denmark, Finland, Austria and France borrowed cheap dollars via the yen syndicated loan market.

The Japanese life insurance companies subsidized the transactions and advertised the business with a prestige borrower. They relished the signing ceremonies and attendant dinner which accompanied the transaction. There was a large opportunity cost to the transaction in terms of time and money. It was a typical example of the way energy and money were channeled. Foreign investment bankers were able to make millions on each transaction because they could "bury" fees in the currency and interest rate swaps.

" The transactions were complicated, but not sophisticated or purposeful, and the Japanese financial system encouraged this wasteful behavior."

What had the life insurance companies gained by these yen syndicated loan transactions? The borrowers and the foreign financial community already were well-acquainted with the Japanese life insurance companies, who were among the largest in the world. So there was hardly any need for an introduction. A continuing business relationship was not promoted. The borrowers were responding to an aggressive borrowing rate. They would react similarly to any other below-market rate. This only showed that Japanese life insurance companies could do business if they accepted low returns, even losses. In terms of the domestic market, Nippon Life, Dai-Ichi Life, Sumitomo Life, Meiji Life, Yasuda Life, and Asahi Life did not need to advertise their ability to lend yen to foreigners. The only explanation for their behavior was publicity and market share, but it is doubtful that this publicity served any constructive purpose.

This is an example of what Akio Morita would call "shuffling paper." The transactions were complicated, but not sophisticated or purposeful, and the Japanese financial system encouraged this wasteful behavior.

The efforts in the U.S. market in the 1980s were also based on Tokyo Center's publicity-driven motives. The strategy was implemented by aggressive bids, which resulted in issues being put into Japanese brokers' inventories or stuffed into the portfolios of Japanese investors in the usual, clumsy, power-cum-relationship sales effort associated with the brokers.

Returning to the earlier Prestowitz example, it is easy to see what happened. He stated:

> The (U.S.) service-industry idyll was blasted in November 1986
> when Nomura Securities announced that it had handled, entirely on
> its own, the placement of a major bond issue for the General Electric Credit Corporation. Nomura was the first company to do such
> a thing in the United States.[2]

In retrospect, the language was unnecessarily alarmist and naive. Daniel Burstein described a similar case, writing about Daiwa's "success":

> In 1986, the Daiwa America team raised more than a few investment banking eyebrows by gaining sole underwriter status for an
> important U.S. client—a $125 million GTE issue.[3]

This was yet another example of a JFI transaction which proved to have no relevance outside the one issue. Daiwa was successful in gaining publicity, but not in making money or building a business. The foreign commentators were not describing reality, only contributing to the myth of the JFI threat to the independence of the American financial system.

PLAYING DIVIDEND RECAPTURE GAME

The Japanese "dividend recapture" game provided another opportunity to witness the misinterpretation of Japanese transactions. The transactions were accomplished through Japanese brokers who made negligible money on the transactions but garnered publicity from foreign observers. The brokers were anxious to promote this activity for the sake of appearance.

Until recently, Japanese life insurance companies paid policy holders only from current income—dividends and interest[4] The life insurers could not distribute their capital gains to policy holders. The need for current

---

2 Prestowitz, *Trading Places,* p. 12.
3 Burstein, *Yen!,* p. 213.
4 Forsyth, Randall W., "MOF Beckons Japanese Capital Homeward," *Barron's*, March 2,
   1992, p. 44.

income encouraged the Japanese life insurance companies to participate in the higher-yielding foreign bond markets and the dividend recapture game.

Dividend recapture, or dividend arbitrage, was a simple conversion of the dividend of a U.S. stock to income for the Japanese life insurance companies. In the 1980s, the Japanese life insurance companies had to put realized capital gains into a reserve account. Income, that was defined as interest and dividends, could be paid out to policy holders so the Japanese life insurance companies were eager to convert capital gains to income. High yielding U.S. utility stocks presented an opportunity for this game. The transactions had no investment or trading significance. Aiding the publicity-conscious Japanese securities firms, some foreigners, again, misinterpreted these transactions. Prestowitz observed:

> In 1987, Japan's four largest investment banks accounted for virtually none of the trading volume on the New York Stock Exchange (NYSE). By the end of 1987, they did nearly 10 percent of the trading, and the volume of Nomura Securities alone was approaching that of the giant Merrill Lynch, the largest U.S. trader. (Business Week, September 7, 1987).[5]

Prestowitz misquoted his source, *Business Week*, which actually stated that "the Big Four (Japanese securities firms) now account for an estimated 5 percent to 10 percent of all trading on the New York Stock Exchange." The article further mentions that "Nomura claims" a market share "nearly as big as that held by Merrill Lynch." Furthermore, *Business Week* describes a phenomena, the dividend arbitrage game, that inflated the volume figures used by Japanese brokers. This is contained in a subsection entitled "How to Get on Wall Street's Map; Trade 19 Million Shares a Day" that appeared adjacent to the article estimating the Japanese brokers did 5 percent to 10 percent of the NYSE's volume. The subsection mentioned that, "Some days, this type (dividend arbitrage) accounts for 10 percent of the New York Stock Exchange's activity." It did not say that Japanese securities firms "did nearly 10 percent of the trading on the NYSE by the end of 1987." We shall see how these trades, which were quite large, grossly overstated the activity generated by the Japanese brokers on the NYSE.

---

5 Prestowitz, *Trading Places,* p. 12.

Dividend arbitrage, or roll-over, was simple. *Business Week* described the practice:

> A (Japanese) broker rounds up a block of stock, say one million shares or more, usually borrowing from a Japanese trust bank. The shares are sold to a life insurance company on the eve of the ex-dividend. At the same time, the insurer contracts to sell the stock back to the securities broker a day later for essentially the same price, less the amount of the dividend and a small commission. The broker then returns the shares to the lending institution, paying a modest fee for the rental.[6]

This was a fictitious transaction because the security was repurchased simultaneous to its sale. There was no holding period risk, and the life insurance company received the dividend but at a capital loss equal to the dividend on the sale back to the broker. There was no risk capital involved. The price of the stock—always one with a high dividend, such as an American utility stock—was not affected. The sham took place in one day. American firms were generally prevented from engaging in this type of activity by their internal legal departments, which viewed the transaction as a purely risk-free gimmick which took place solely to circumvent regulations.

The transaction was a non-event except for the volume it generated on the NYSE. Prestowitz interpreted this as the Japanese "process" which "echoed what had already happened in the manufacturing industries."[7] Thus, he had again identified the JFIs with the manufacturers. Burstein wildly exaggerated the consequences of this charade:

> What is known as Japanese dividend arbitrage has become an overwhelming factor in NYSE trading patterns, reaching its current high point on January 25, 1988, when Southern Company set a one-day NYSE volume record: 65.9 million shares, or about a quarter of all stock traded that day. Another thirty-five million shares of Arizona Public Service and Cincinnati Gas & Electric also changed hands.

---

6 "How to Get On Wall Street's Map," *International Business Week*, September 7, 1987, p. 37.
7 Prestowitz, *Trading Places*, p. 12.

The implications are staggering. If a small number of Japanese can move millions of shares in three American companies on a single day simply to gain a modest tax advantage, what would that concentration of power mean if applied to takeover stocks or to a politically motivated move out of the U.S. market altogether?[8]

In reality, this was pure paper shuffling and would not even be a transaction under U.S. tax law. No inferences about power should be drawn from it. These transactions involved no risk capital, no movement in the stock price, and no tax advantage. The Japanese did not "move millions of shares" of stock. High yielding stocks, such as utilities, were the only possible candidates for this game.

The Japanese brokers in the U.S. again succeeded in obtaining publicity and, in this case, the appearance of market share. They were eagerly assisted in publicizing this non-event by the Americans, who were drawing unwarranted conclusions to further their own arguments pertaining to the successful strategy of JFIs in the U.S.

THE RESULTS OF MARKET SHARE MENTALITY

These prestige transactions of the 1980s should be examined in the context of Tokyo's goals of publicity and market share. The substantive issues of profit, continuity, business, relationships, skill development, and real penetration were all absent. Aggressive, often subsidized, bidding was the norm. While manufacturers were able to establish overseas business by engaging in predatory pricing, destroying the competition, building economies-of-

> " These prestige transactions of the 1980s should be examined in the context of Tokyo's goals of publicity and market share. The substantive issues of profit, continuity, business, relationships, skill development, and real penetration were all absent. "

---

8 Burstein, *Yen!*, p. 215.

scale, and developing a reputation for quality, the JFIs were buying deals and distorting markets. The general perception was that these tactics were essentially the same as the manufacturers. They were not.

During the 1980s, Japanese brokers and banks placed high on the Eurobond League tables—a ranking of firms by the volume of transactions which they managed. The reasons, again, were aggressively priced deals as well as a plethora of Japanese borrowers in the Euromarket.

What conclusions can be drawn from this display of strength? Here, the value of market share in the world of global financial services area needs to be explored. Certainly, there are some areas such as data processing, securities custodial business, and securities clearance, that derive benefits from size and economies-of-scale. Trading sectors such as foreign exchange, U.S. Treasuries, as well as any liquid market, benefit from market share, if the share is a result of client base, capital, proper information flow, and/or skill. Market share is not the same as market penetration. If the market share derives only from capital, it will last only as long as the capital is there. Eventually, capital has to yield an acceptable return. This cannot happen without skill, clients, and focus. Price-sensitive borrowers react to transactions, and they will respond to bids—again, only as long as the pricing is aggressive.

Participants in the financial arena in the 1980s had to pay attention to capital flows. If those flows emanated from Japan, the participants wanted to understand the dynamics. If the conduits of those flows were JFIs, they should be sought after for information and business. In many cases, the JFI staff responsible for this flow developed "client syndrome"—a condition that at times affects Americans and anyone who handles large sums of money.

Because JFIs were responsible for investing large sums of money abroad, or represented large sums, the staff received considerable attention, respect, and adulation from borrowers, intermediaries, and money managers. Because of this excessive flattery, the recipients began to think of themselves as powerful. Often, they desired special treatment. This, at times, led to overconfidence and arrogance, and arrogance always leads to mistakes. The JFI salaryman sometimes developed "client syndrome." The real clients were, in fact, other people, other institutions, and the JFI itself.

Market share in deregulated markets could be quite fleeting. There were no cross-sharings to ensure captivity or preferential treatment. Business relationships, whether transactional or advisory, required performance and competence rather than a single aggressive bid. The MOF was not present to grant franchises. Competition was fierce. Size was a positive factor in some cases, but requirements of agility, flexibility, and innovation meant that size could be a detriment in other areas.

The JFIs always defined their competition as larger institutions; however, the competition or partners in areas such as money management, merchant banking, and certain trading areas could be qualified small participants rather than behemoths. All of this was very confusing to the JFI, who tried to play by cosmetic rules and operate centrally from Tokyo.

" Because JFIs were responsible for investing large sums of money abroad, or represented large sums, the staff received considerable attention, respect, and adulation from borrowers, intermediaries, and money managers. "

JFIs TAKE ON U.S. ACQUISITIONS, JOINT VENTURES

During the 1980s, there was a plethora of acquisitions and joint ventures undertaken by JFIs in the U.S. financial market. Publicity and presence were the common themes. Excessive orientation towards Tokyo caused decisions to be made without careful consideration of local markets and cultures. Goals for these entities originated in Tokyo without careful consideration of substantive benefits. There was little understanding of how the JFI and the American firm would interact. For the JFIs, the acquisitions were an attempt to create the appearance of international sophistication and capability. Form predominated over substance.

JFI acquisitions were not intended to impact the JFI's business. They functioned separately, even from the JFI's U.S. operations. They did not exist organizationally within the JFI. There was generally no intention to integrate the "partners" within the JFI's system. They dangled in the U.S. They were painless for the JFIs in that they did not challenge central authority in Tokyo.

Acquisitions were to be displayed on the corporate trophy rack. They indicated to the Japanese market that the JFI had expanded overseas and, therefore, was internationalized. The tie-ups were described as strategic. The pattern of selecting the acquisition partner was usually the same. The targets were "famous" firms or individuals. Again, there was no political risk in being associated with well-recognizable entities. It was the brand name—*yumei na kaisha*—concept revisited.

Once again, the detailed study, thorough planning, and long-term implementation associated with the Japanese manufacturers' strategy was missing entirely. Foreigners were so conditioned to past Japanese success in manufacturing that a focus on proper strategy had become a central part of the stereotype of Japanese companies. The JFI's *modus operandi* with regard to selection of overseas acquisitions could best be described as superficial. The purchases were divided into two categories: general relationship and specific skills.

The JFIs had few stated goals in these tie-ups. One was the requirement that the partners train Japanese staff. The trainees were mostly quite young or middle management personnel. In Japan, there is tremendous faith in osmosis as a learning process. The JFIs thought that by virtue of the fact that their staff was physically near foreigners, they would understand American business or acquire skills. However, they did not want *too* close an association with foreigners because that would lead to individual and institutional contamination.

The Nippon Life trainees sent to Shearson, for instance, probably gained little. Usually, these trainees lacked language ability and rudimentary knowledge about financial matters. The foreign host rotated them quickly through various departments to give the appearance of cooperation. Then, the trainees were relegated to a room where they watched various instructional tapes and slept. The foreign host often considered them a nuisance and joked about their naivete.

> " Even though the Japanese brokers talked about the ability to bring transactions through their foreign partners, the real agenda was image enhancement."

Beyond trainee programs, there was little else required by the JFIs. The sense that no one could be blamed for problems during the first fifty years of the new relationship alleviated the need for specific performance criteria and assured everyone. Thus, the JFIs were free to advertise their new "competence" in overseas markets. The Japanese brokers wanted the Japanese market to know that they could introduce "sophisticated new products." Even though the Japanese brokers talked about the ability to bring transactions through their foreign partners, the real agenda was image enhancement. Domestic publicity value was paramount. They wanted to be seen as something other than purveyors of Japanese equities to Japanese individuals. Nomura's Tabuchi even spoke grandly of the international component of Nomura's earnings rising to over fifty percent.

As a media exercise, the mission was clear. But there was little discussion of how acquisitions would give the JFIs a U.S. base of business, or generate profits. There was no substantive strategy at all. By contrast, the U.S. counterparts in these arrangements had a very clear motivation—cheap money. The U.S. firm would sell a percentage of its equity from as little as 1 percent to 20 percent. The Japanese would pay dearly for the equity and promise access to the Japanese market. The promise was mainly an illusion, but the JFI spoke of a global alliance. The U.S. firms' only apparent obligation was to provide training for the JFI's personnel.

TOKEN PURCHASES DEMONSTRATE OVERSEAS PRESENCE

The most general types of partnership investment that JFIs made during the 1980s were token purchases of the equity or foreign firms. Outside of the U.S., some of the Japanese life insurance companies owned a few percent of the equity of large European life insurance companies. Dai-Ichi Life and Meiji Life purchased 1 percent each of the shares of the Hong Kong and Shanghai Bank (HKSB). This was another practice which the JFIs attempted to transplant. In Japan, it is customary to purchase shares of a company with which one has a business relationship. The JFIs were demonstrating to their domestic market that they now had a presence in Hong Kong and their global network was expanding. The shareholdings were supposed to give the JFIs a privileged position with HKSB in terms of training and, presumably, business. The choice of HKSB was natural. It was the largest financial institution in Hong Kong, and it also played a quasi-governmental role in terms of regulating the currency and monetary policy.

It is doubtful that any alliance-related goals resulted from these token purchases other than an increase in assets under management, or a few transactions flowing from the JFI to the foreign institution. Nevertheless, the formal and publicity goals were accomplished.

Another example was Nippon Life's purchase of 13 percent of Shearson Lehman in March 1987 for $508 million. Nippon Life's only discernible tangible expectation from Shearson was the training of over a hundred Nippon Life employees. In other words, Nippon Life paid over $500 million to establish a training program. At one point, the value of the investment in Shearson declined by over $300 million.[9]

This was an egregious example of the JFI's acquisition strategy. Nippon Life then owned 3 percent of the shares of the Tokyo Stock Exchange, was one of the largest holders of real estate in Japan, and was among the world's top three life insurance companies in terms of premium income. It was simply not concerned with the investment value of its holding of Shearson stock; the amount was negligible in such a large portfolio. Quite apart from publicity goals and the theory of osmosis, the size of such assets as their holdings in Shearson created the illusion of competence, and fostered a lack of concern for details and substantive issues. This was not a serious investment for Nippon Life; it really did not matter to the employees at Nippon Life whether they made or lost money. After all, "This is a long-term, strategic investment," a Nippon Life representative stated in 1990.[10]

The Nippon Life/Shearson example is noteworthy because it was so conspicuous, and it also proved to be typical. After Yasuda Mutual Life paid $300 million for 20 percent of Paine Webber, it was reported to be able to send 150 trainees per year there.[11] Yasuda Mutual Life sold part of its shares in February, 1992. Sumitomo Life had a minor holding in the ill-fated E.F. Hutton. A group of Japanese investors, including Mitsui Trust, invested in Credit Swiss First Boston.

Sumitomo Bank lent $500 million to Goldman Sachs and received an equity participation in Goldman's profits. This was sometimes interpreted as purchasing an equity participation in Goldman Sachs. However, it really was only the right to participate in Goldman's profits for five years, with a renewal clause. The deal, as originally conceived by Sumitomo Bank, provided for training in the investment banking area and cooperation in a London venture. The Federal Reserve, citing the Glass-Steagall Act, allowed only the passive investment and prohibited Sumitomo Bank from sending

---

9 *Business Week*, February 19, 1990, p. 118.
10 *Business Week*, February 19, 1990, p. 118.
11 Viner, Aron, "The Emerging Power of Japanese Money," Tokyo: *The Japan Times*, 1988, p. 199.

trainees to Goldman. Although the return on investment was not a significant consideration for Sumitomo Bank, Goldman's superior earnings performance justified a renewal of the participating loan.

Again, Goldman wanted cheap capital and was able to retain a controlling interest while avoiding the need to make a public offering. Sumitomo Bank wanted training and access to clients. One source indicated that:

> Goldman appeared willing to give Sumitomo (Bank) exactly what it wanted—training, expertise, network access—just as America's great innovators in high technology were always willing to license their breakthroughs to the Japanese for small fees.[12]

Sumitomo Bank may have had grandiose visions of taking over Goldman in the future. If so, it showed a lack of understanding of how financial markets work to assume that the type of originally anticipated interchange between Goldman and Sumitomo Bank would have produced training, expertise, and network access, even if the Federal Reserve had permitted the trainees to visit Goldman. The sojourn at Goldman would have produced the same static encounter witnessed throughout the 1980s between Japanese trainees and U.S. firms. The rotation system would have further diluted any gains. The Japanese would have again been dependent on their capital to acquire a fleeting American client base which would rapidly disappear as soon as Japanese money vanished.

" If an American institution had made this investment, it would have been considered foolish and ego-driven. When a JFI made the purchase, it was regarded as long-term oriented and strategically motivated."

Tokyo's ego and ambition were present. There was no well-conceived, well-orchestrated effort. The only nuance was Sumitomo Bank's aggressiveness, which was its trademark before overzealous lending finally surfaced in the 1990s. In one such problem, Sumitomo Bank was the lead lender to Itoman, a Japanese trading company, which was humbled by ill-

---

12 Burstein, *Yen!,* p. 225.

fated speculation in the Japanese real estate market. Sumitomo Bank had not focussed on a U.S. strategy—that would have required patience and commitment. They wanted a quick solution which looked good at home, and at the time $500 million was not a large amount of money for Sumitomo Bank.

In 1984, Fuji Bank paid $425 million for two finance subsidiaries of Walter E. Heller International. Poor due diligence caused Fuji Bank to underestimate the amount of problem loans in Walter E. Heller's portfolio. Fuji had to put an additional $300 million into Heller, thus raising their total investment in Heller to $725 million.[13] Fuji Bank was constantly surprised by the problems at Heller. Again, the JFI had not examined it purchase with diligence and had overpaid for its "strategic" thrust. If an American institution had made this investment, it would have been considered foolish and ego-driven. When a JFI made the purchase, it was regarded as long-term oriented and strategically motivated.

JFIs BUY FOREIGN NAMES AS SPECIALISTS

When a specific overseas activity became sufficiently visible in the 1980s, the JFIs wanted to have a presence. Officials in Tokyo felt they should demonstrate to the Japanese market that, as international institutions, they were not only abreast of the latest trends, but could also purchase the best foreign names or individuals as specialists. The publicity value of these investments was deemed sufficient to justify the expense and effort.

The scenario was straightforward. The JFI would purchase equity in a U.S. firm, give the U.S. firm money to manage, and hire a famous person or set up a subsidiary managed by a famous person. All were more evidence of the Japanese penchant for brand names at work. There was always a formal structure which was advertised to the Japanese market. In most cases, there was not extensive history of the parties working together. Often the parties did not even know each other before the discussions began. JFIs sometimes had no prior experience in the businesses that were started. Money was no object. U.S. investment banks assisted in identifying these famous individuals or firms. The JFIs had been in the U.S. for decades, but they seldom had many contacts. Once again, the personnel rota-

---

13 Viner, *Inside Japan's Financial Markets*, Homewood, IL: Dow Jones-Irwin, 1988, p. 204.

tion system prevented the establishment of substantive relationships and networks.

> " The scenario was straightforward. The JFI would purchase equity in a U.S. firm, give the U.S. firm money to manage, and hire a famous person or set up a subsidiary managed by a famous person. All were more evidence of the Japanese penchant for brand names at work. "

The JFI, as usual, would require training for its staff, a privileged deal flow, the right to market the U.S. firm's product or skill in Japan, introductions to U.S. clients, or some other variation. The JFI assumed that within a few years it would have the skills and network that would make the foreign partner redundant or unnecessary. The initial investment was regarded as a token initiation fee.

The JFIs commonly felt that the willingness of the Americans to "sell their franchise" was another demeaning example of the short-sightedness and money orientation of American society. One Japanese banker, upon returning from a year at the Harvard Business School's (HBS) Advanced Management Program, echoed this attitude. He declared that the HBS experience had taught him an extremely valuable lesson—that American businessmen are personally motivated, mainly, by the desire to make money quickly—that they could be bought, and showed no loyalty to anything except for money.[14] His impression has a great deal of validity and many Americans fit this description. But the JFIs never truly figured out how to exploit this weakness.

---

14 The Japanese businessman was only echoing what another foreign observer, Alexis de Toqueville, had stated after his visit in 1830. Ironically, both Toqueville and the Japanese businessman stayed in the U.S. for nine months. Among the least admirable of American traits, Toqueville noted, was the singular fixation on money: "I know of no country, indeed, where the love of money has taken stronger hold on the affections of men (than in the United States) . . . The love of wealth is, therefore, to be traced, either as a principal or an accessory motive, at the bottom of all that Americans do." (Alexis de Toqueville, *Democracy in America*, Richard D. Heffner, ed., New York: Mentor Books, 1956, pp. 52, 255.)

JFIs GROW INTERESTED IN QUANTITATIVE INVESTMENT

During the 1980s, the JFIs made many types of specific purpose acquisitions and joint venture arrangements. The fields included quantitative investment, M&A/merchant banking, U.S. Treasury trading, futures and options trading, money management, real estate, leasing, and commodities.

Despite having set up research institutes, the JFIs had no real knowledge or capability in the area of investment technology. True, they paid homage to technology. But their activities amounted to little more than ostentation. When Americans began to emphasize quantitative analysis, then marketed this to Japanese institutional investors, the JFIs had no choice but to look outside their own organizations for help. The use of quantitative systems for investing has always appealed to the Japanese institutional investors' need for order and assembly-line consistency. They think technology will provide the magic answer. As usual, after the Americans popularized certain techniques, the JFIs grew interested.

A *Wall Street Journal* article mentioned that Nomura was attempting to develop "in-house . . . (capability in) computerized investment methods" without success since the late 1970s.[15] Actually, Nomura had been making an effort since the late 1960s when Nomura representatives visited Salomon Brother's pioneering bond portfolio analysis team. Nomura's representatives took notes and photographs, and proceeded back to Tokyo to try to replicate Salomon's work. Certainly in the 1980s, they were never able to threaten American supremacy in quantitative fixed-income analysis. JFIs preferred to have this new idea, as any, introduced from outside, both because they were unwilling to risk failure, and they were loathe to alienate other salarymen by successfully introducing a new idea. The same habit of mind could be found then at U.S. investment banks: Japanese employees often liked to be accompanied by a foreigner when making out-of-the-ordinary presentations, even when the Japanese knew more about the subject than the foreigner. Sometimes presentations like this just sounded better coming from a foreigner—or so the Japanese felt.

Some of the major acquisitions and joint ventures undertaken by JFIs during this period were Nikko's purchase of 50 percent of Wells Fargo Investment Advisors, one of the pioneers in index fund management.

---

15 Sesit, Michael R., and White, James A., "Japanese Firms Have Yen for U.S. High-Tech Investment Skills," *The Wall Street Journal*, June 11, 1989, p. C-1.

Nikko's joint venture with Barra, Nomura's joint venture with Rosenberg Institutional Equity Management[16] and Daiwa's association with Harry Markowitz, a Nobel Prize-winning economist.[17]

Nikko paid $125 million, or almost 20 times earnings for its Wells Fargo Investment Advisors' stake. Nikko was to market Wells Fargo's product in Japan and, it hoped, learn vital "black box" techniques. There was talk of jointly working on projects which would fit the Japanese market. The Japanese would master the formula and use it in the domestic market. Size, order, famous name, and assembly-line mentality provided a neat package. But it was inherently flawed.

> **" It was doubtful that brokers would make a sophisticated sales pitch based on quantitative research. Such effort could only draw resources away from the activities that were generating profits. "**

Although the JFIs had ample exposure to quantitative techniques in the 1980s, the profitability of Japanese brokerage houses, for example, relied heavily on commissions on sales of Japanese equities to domestic clients. What made the massive sales volume possible was the strong equity market and the brokers' aggressive sales approach. Even in Europe, the profitability of the business of underwriting Japanese equity-related issues depended on demand based on the assumption of a strong equity market.

It was doubtful that brokers would make a sophisticated sales pitch based on quantitative research. Such effort could only draw resources away from the activities that were generating profits. It is not surprising, then, that neither Japanese brokers nor other JFIs were ever terribly serious about assimilating technology fully into their investment business operations—whatever rhetoric they might broadcast.

Even if the JFIs were serious about technology, organizationally, assimilation was impossible. One requirement for integrating technology and communication is a high degree of coordination and communication be-

---

16 Sesit and White, *Japanese Firms.*
17 Siconolfi, Michael, "Nobel Economist Objects to Daiwa Exploiting Prize," *The Wall Street Journal*, December 13, 1990, p. C-1.

tween technology specialists and other departments. Dialogue and experimentation are essential. U.S. firms, such as Salomon Brothers, have a long history of interdepartmental cooperation between quantitative departments, sales, trading, back-office, and corporate finance. This tradition was carefully fostered by Salomon's research department under the leadership of Sidney Homer, Henry Kaufman, and Marty Liebowitz. As will become evident in the next chapter, the JFIs fragmented structure, Tokyo's pre-occupation with publicity, the JFIs disdain for specialists, and the rotation system all inhibited such interaction, making assimilation virtually impossible.

Thus, the JFI in the 1980s was left with a partner—whether acquisition or joint venture—that might offer some PR value, but whose skills could never be assimilated. Here, perhaps, an analogy to Japanese baseball might be appropriate.

U.S. baseball players are recruited by Japanese teams mainly for their ability to hit home runs. There are a few pitchers, but the most sought-after specialists are hitters who can produce crowd-pleasing home runs. The players, basically, have one-year contracts and are not expected to integrate into the team. They are viewed with suspicion, as a possible contaminating influence. The U.S. players generally are there to make money and leave. The number of foreign players is restricted to two per team. The ownership of Japanese baseball is not by individuals but rather by corporations, which justify their participation by virtue of the publicity gained from their sports franchises.

So it was when Daiwa Securities established a joint venture with Harry Markowitz, a Nobel-prize winning economist. The Daiwa-Markowitz example illustrates the actual interface between JFIs and their partners. *The Wall Street Journal* quoted Markowitz[18] as indicating that he would not renew his contract with Daiwa. The article continued, "Mr. Markowitz cringed when he saw a Nikkei news service report that ran . . . under the headline: 'Daiwa to Sell Nobel Prize Fund.' In addition, the *Journal* said, "Daiwa ran a U.S. newspaper ad . . . that referred to 'Nobel brains' managing . . . (Daiwa's) fund." Daiwa tried to bury the incident by stating that newspapers incorrectly quoted Daiwa's spokesman. Anyone with the most cursory contact with a Japanese broker knows that Daiwa was exploiting Markowitz's name in a manner that was misleading to investors who might assume there was now no risk in the investment.

---

18 Siconolfi, *Nobel Economist*, p. C-1, C-9.

The most important element of this episode was the clarity with which it revealed a typical JFI's motives for entering into a joint venture with a foreigner. Publicity was the goal, crude advertising the means. The objectives of technology and knowledge transfer were lost in the process.

U.S. SCOUTS PROSPECTS FOR MERGERS AND ACQUISITIONS, MERCHANT BANKING

The enormous flows of capital from Japan in the 1980s led the U.S. banks to recognize the potential for acquisitions and merchant banking activity in Japan. It took only a few deals, such as Bridgestone's purchase of Firestone Tire & Rubber, Sony/CBS, Dai-Nippon Ink/SunChemical, Sumitomo Bank/Goldman, and Shuwa Reality/ARCO L.A. Plaza to encourage these investment bankers to pursue the JFIs with vigor in terms of corporate, financial, and real estate offerings. As well, they sent Mergers & Acquisitions (M&A) specialists to Tokyo to interface with the JFIs and to develop contacts with Japanese corporations directly.

The JFIs also observed how much corporate activity was being handled by foreign financial firms representing Japanese companies. The highly visible M&A activity in the U.S. provoked the typical JFI reaction. Eager to appear internationally competent, the JFIs rushed to establish an M&A presence. They pursued the same plan as in other areas. Although the JFIs had development departments in Tokyo and sometimes these had extensions in New York, they lacked expertise, background, and a track record which could be advertised.

Japanese domestic M&A had been dormant since the World War II period, except for the occasional speculative fling. The steady growth of Japanese industry and the cartel-like operation of the companies in concert with the Japanese government meant that change was orchestrated from within the company. The role of the investment banker was non-existent in this process. If a large Japanese company encountered severe difficulty, it was not unusual for Japanese banks to play a role in terms of providing financial or organizational support, as *IBJ* and the Bank of Japan did for Yamaichi Securities in 1965.[19] It was, however, highly unusual for companies to sell divisions to other companies.

---

[19] Viner, *Inside*, pp. 227, 259.

Further, estate tax problems had not yet forced private families to think about selling large blocks of stock that, in effect, would transfer control of a company in order to settle estate tax requirements. Since the wealth in Japan has largely been created during the present generation, the problems associated with passing wealth from one generation to another have not been encountered.

There was a psychological inhibition to M&A. Selling divisions or restructurings might be construed as a sign of weakness in a company. In the financial sector, troubled banks were simply absorbed by larger banks, as in the case of Sumitomo Bank's purchase of Heiwa Sogo Bank, in 1986.[20] The MOF and BOJ were actively involved in planning absorptions, and nothing transpires without their blessing.

Moreover, conventional M&A in the Japanese domestic market had pejorative connotations. It was associated with speculators who bought large blocks of stock and tried to force the company or a friendly company to purchase the stock, at an inflated price—a form of "greenmail." Sometimes, these Japanese speculators had underworld connections. The activities of the American Charles Knapp in his struggle with Minebea and Boone Pickens with Toyota reinforced the Japanese stereotype of the unsavoriness of corporate raiders. These activities, and the individuals who have engaged in them, were viewed as peripheral, not worthy of consideration.

JAPANESE HOP ON M&A BANDWAGON

Once M&A activities came to be seen as a potential part of the mainstream of Japanese corporate activity abroad, the JFIs quickly followed the trend. The visibility of the U.S. merger boom of the 1980s was immediately associated with power. Japanese banks participated in the loans which propelled the deals. The desire for publicity and the fear of not being associated with this new force, drove the JFIs to seek tie-ups.

The Sumitomo Bank/Goldman and Nippon Life/Shearson deals were examples of how the JFIs sought to achieve their merchant banking goals within a general relationship. Other JFIs tried to attain such a presence by taking equity positions in firms started by well-known individuals or estab-

---

[20] Viner, *Inside*, p. 211.

lishing joint ventures with such individuals or firms. The U.S. counterparties often received investments in LBO funds they managed or equity in their own firms.

Nomura invested $100 million in a fund managed by Wasserstein, Perella & Co. in return for 20 percent of the equity of the firm. Bruce Wasserstein and Joe Perella were formerly with First Boston Corporation. They were linked to many of the major mergers of the 1980s. Similarly, Nikko Securities invested $100 million in an LBO fund run by the Blackstone group for a 20 percent equity stake in the firm. Blackstone was headed by Peter Petersen, who had been co-head of Lehman Brothers before becoming Secretary of Commerce. Yamaichi Securities participated through Lodestar, a firm run by an ex-Merrill Lynch investment banker. Daiwa scurried about to find "global alliances" with entities such as the large French bank Credit Agricole. Daiwa announced the partnership with great fanfare in Tokyo.

The Americans gained capital and a certain credibility because of their connection with a major JFI. Their only apparent obligation was to "train" JFI personnel and provide a deal flow. The JFIs would receive instant recognition by their association with high-profile Americans. They could announce that they were acquiring expertise, a network of clients, deal flow, and information. Performance on their investment was hardly a priority. Again, the initiation fee would be small—another case of short-sighted Americans who were partners with long-term oriented Japanese, or so it seemed to many observers.

" The Americans gained capital and a certain credibility because of their connection with a major JFI. Their only apparent obligation was to 'train' JFI personnel and provide a deal flow. "

The Japanese banks' approach was comparatively subtle. They established joint ventures with Americans or set up companies run by Americans. IBJ and the Long Term Credit Bank (LTCB) formed companies headed by people who had been senior officials at U.S. investment banks. Fuji Bank established a joint venture with James Wolfensohn's company. Wolfensohn had been head of Salomon Brothers' investment banking department before he set up his own firm to advise corporations. He was well-known because of his role in the Chrysler bail-out, his extensive U.S. and international contacts, and his charitable activities on behalf of Carnegie Hall and the JFK Center.

Again, the pattern ran true. The JFIs dealt with form, not substance. Money was not an object, nor was there an objective measure of performance in terms of profit or skill transfer. In general, the only thing the Americans took seriously about the JFIs was their money. Americans who benefitted from Japanese largesse were often quite candid. One ebullient American investment banker who was selected to manage a Japanese joint venture in the merchant banking area boasted that he did not have to make a profit for ten years. The American had been a senior official at an American investment bank. The prestigious JFI was looking for credibility. The match was perfect. As the American escorted this author around his palatial office, he remarked casually, "They're paying for it; I'm not." In February, 1993, the American sent out his usual form letter indicating his alleged "remarkable progress." At the end of the letter, he had written, by hand, "The Japanese are asleep!"

M&A ENTHUSIASM NOT BACKED BY HOMEWORK

Accountability was not an issue, as fifty-year time horizons obviated the need to show results. Tokyo's authority was not challenged as the new entities were created outside of the JFIs' structure and would not infringe on anyone's political territory in Japan. The association with "famous" firms or individuals was not only politically safe, it fulfilled one of the main tenets of the Japanese domestic business ethic—size and fame equal credibility and acceptability. The transplant of this principle regarding size and fame to the U.S. market was consistent with their established practice.

There was little attempt to study, investigate, or examine possible partnerships which did not fit this Japanese concept. The JFIs did not put much substantive effort into making these entities work properly. Unlike the Japanese manufacturers who made an enormous effort to understand the U.S. market, the JFIs relied on headlines. The process was superficial; the results were predictable.

The JFIs set up their vehicles to pursue cross-border M&A without understanding the nature of the business. The excesses of the U.S. domestic M&A during the 1980s usually blinded them from the routine bread-

and-butter business of restructurings, divestiture of divisions, liquification of assets, tax-related equity acquisitions, implementation of new strategies, and technological impact.

Even if that were not the case, the JFIs' own experience or lack thereof worked against them. In Japan, the bank's or investor's role routinely was that of rescuer, not transaction initiator. They were not expected to create deals, nor was there any pressure to do so. Employees were not rewarded for transactional activity. If they had any role, it was merely as a conduit for information about deals.

Japanese companies do not react with alacrity to proposals. Unless a Japanese company has a strategy in place to consider a possible acquisition, it would be extremely difficult for a JFI to influence a decision. Japanese companies—and this includes JFIs—like to think of themselves as being independent. They prefer to have an idea originate, or appear to originate, from within the organization, although investments relating to publicly traded equity securities or fixed income purchases can be influenced by financial intermediaries. The combination of the passive attitude of the JFI and the lack of response by the Japanese companies produced very little M&A business.

The idea of responding to and servicing Japanese clients was, a theme permeating the JFIs' attitude in the 1980s. In a sense, the JFIs had defined their role as "responsive" and could justify their involvement in areas accordingly. Moreover, when the JFIs themselves became clients—for example, when they were acquiring entities—they expected the financial intermediary to present a fully packaged presentation, which might or might not be reliable or objective. The process was extremely brittle in that there was little dialogue. The information or the presentation was given at a "Japanese meeting" and seemed to disappear.

The JFIs entered into formal arrangements with foreigners and sent staff to be trained, but they never understood M&A as a business, the communication issues which surely arose between the Americans and the Japanese staff, or how M&A fit structurally within their own operations. As in most matters with JFIs, the business was supposed to somehow evolve organically.

The JFIs invested in LBO funds managed by investment bankers who were motivated by fees, not long-term strategic investments. The difficulties encountered by most U.S. investment bankers who made loans to facilitate take-overs in anticipation of refinancing the loans, i.e., "bridge loans," indicate the recklessness with which these investment bankers then evaluated risks when a large fee was involved. In most cases, the opportunity to collect a large fee—at times, in excess of $100 million per transaction—immediately enticed the U.S. investment banker to purchase an illiquid investment in a hasty manner. The JFIs never distinguished between the activity of their partners as investors or as intermediaries. The Americans who were entrusted with money were experienced, often, only as intermediaries.

LONG-TERM INVESTMENTS VERSUS SHORT-TERM TRANSACTIONS

The discipline required for long-term investment in private equity is very different from the short-term transactional skills of the investment bankers. The former has a vested interest in the performance of their investments. The latter do not have any commitment to the transactions after the fee has been collected. Also, there can be long periods of time when inactivity is warranted because no proper values are available for investment. In order to be successful as a principal, it is necessary to have the discipline to wait until opportunities present themselves. Fee-oriented investment bankers are not known for their patience.

The JFIs plunged into the M&A arena during an active period in the 1980s. They did not stop to consider the cyclical factors inherent in the activity. They were unaware of the inefficiencies of cross-border M&A, unaware that theirs was not a simple task of finding deals and perfunctorily presenting them to Japanese clients, that currency rates, interest rates, corporate liquidity, and business outlook are only a few of the variables which helped to determine activity. Certainly, the JFIs had access to corporations, but they had little influence and could only wait to receive an inquiry. The slow decision-making process, or lack of decision-making ability, compounded matters. Absence of dialogue yielded poor information flow, so the deal origination process could not be refined. The personnel rotation at the JFIs and the Japanese corporation precluded continuity.

As the BOJ raised interest rates, and as shares on the TSE began to plummet in 1990, many Japanese corporations needed to look at restructuring. Cross-border interest waned except for a few conspicuous deals. The JFIs had not anticipated this, nor had they planned for the domestic situation which presented itself. They had largely engaged in a publicity campaign in the U.S. that did not produce the knowledge required at home.

Had they actually learned investment banking and merchant banking skills, JFIs would have been better prepared for the changes in the Japanese market.

The inevitable communication problems between the JFIs and their American partners appeared. The Japanese were accustomed to working in a highly structured environment without accountability. The Americans wanted to complete deals hastily and had no concern about the advisability of a particular transaction. Articles appeared which mentioned the "cultural conflict" at Nomura Wasserstein Perella Co.[21] The Americans were described as "aggressive Western deal makers" as contrasted to the "more conservative Nomura men."

In those days Nomura men were not often described as conservative. They were conservative only in that they wore grey or blue suits. They were better known for their persistent sales efforts, which were ax-handle aggressive. They did not care about product quality. If the Nomura sales manager ordered his men to sell something, Nomura (or any other Japanese broker's) salesmen did not question the appropriateness of the investment. They tried to reach their assigned sales quota.

Nomura operated successfully while purveying Japanese equities to Japanese individuals or Japanese institutional investors. There was a great deal of difference, however, between peddling Japanese equities to Japanese investors and selling American companies to Japanese corporations. The difference had nothing to do with the character of Nomura's staff. The article's use of the word "conservative" is an example of the problems encountered when English words are superimposed on a Japanese context. Nomura's staff did not have the influence to sell transactions or generate inquiries. They simply knew how to present a transaction, and could gain admittance to most corporations. There were no sales quotas, nor could they force Japanese corporations to buy American companies the way they forced investors to buy stocks. So, they did not bother; the bulk of overseas Japanese investment in the 1980s consisted of fixed income securities with maturities, liquidity, and coupons. Nomura's brokers did not focus on the actual operation of their M&A business or their U.S. tie-up.

One JFI's M&A unit in America provides an example of the confusion surrounding the inception of such vehicles. The senior American in the unit was so skeptical of the performance that he refused to take any equity in his operation. The most important Japanese senior manager in the entity

---

[21] *Institutional Investor*, June 1991, p. 36.

was transferred within a year after his assignment started. Within a few months after establishment of the operation, the Japanese staff identified the main purpose of the M&A group as information-gathering, not transactions—because they could not complete any transactions.

The need to accommodate form required that the JFI establish a separate vehicle to conduct the M&A business when none was necessary. The unit could be advertised in Japan and displayed in the JFI's annual report. The goal was setting up the entity, not in establishing a successful business. Since the aim had been achieved, the general manager could claim success immediately. All the personnel would be rotated so no one had any vested interest in the operation. Since the Japanese departments operate independently, no one at the JFI was concerned about the increased fragmentation fostered by another appendage. Costs did not enter into the decision, when the amount was only several million dollars a year. The opportunity cost in terms of resource allocation of personnel was never a consideration when the project was evaluated, as internal political considerations predominated. The limited supply of staff with English reading and writing ability should have provided some degree of discipline in establishing new operations, but it usually did not deter this JFI any more than the others.

The inefficiency of the M&A process in Japan can be further highlighted by one example of a large Japanese trading company's handling of a proposal. The trading company was approached in 1989 to discuss the merits of purchasing an equity participation in an American firm which distributed Japanese products. Since the American firm was a public corporation, significant information was available. It had a focused and highly effective marketing philosophy. The earnings were growing steadily, the company's management was very conservative, and the company had little debt.

There appeared to be synergy between the Japanese and the American company. The trading company expressed initial enthusiasm and wanted to proceed in its examination, going so far as to sign a confidentiality agreement and indicate an interest in visiting the American firm.

Then, the Japanese individual who was acting as intermediary announced that the trading firm no longer had any interest. However, he took me to visit the trading company, as he did not want to probe or risk confrontation. I was told by the young salarymen at the trading company that a new policy had prevented them from exploring this opportunity further. The new policy could not be defined, and the salarymen were rude and condescending throughout the conversation. They were unaccustomed to providing any information about their actions. This totally whimsical method of operation was usually never questioned by other Japanese. The Japanese intermediary never said a word during the proceeding because he genuinely feared the trading company.

> **" When operating in the world of cross-border mergers in the 1980s, the ambiguities, inefficiencies, erratic decision making process, lack of continuity, and lack of accountability made the business very difficult to quantify."**

There could have been valid reasons for terminating the discussions, but one suspects that this case reflects the haphazard, careless nature of the decision-making process. This kind of vagueness and lack of dialogue created an inefficient process which, in turn, generated a lot of wasted time.

Patience is always cited as a prerequisite for doing business in Japan. The patience involved in setting up distribution outlets for physical products, such as Coca-Cola and McDonald's is obvious. But these involved a series of acts that can be measured in terms of market penetration, profit and personnel considerations. When operating in the world of cross-border mergers in the 1980s, the ambiguities, inefficiencies, erratic decision making process, lack of continuity, and lack of accountability made the business very difficult to quantify. Too often, success seemed to depend completely on being in the right place at the right time. Nevertheless, the JFIs set up operations without fully realizing the nature and scope of the business.

JAPANESE INVESTORS LINK WITH U.S. MONEY MANAGERS

Many Japanese institutional investors developed informal arrangements with U.S. money managers in the 1980s. Starting a decade earlier, the JFIs solicited U.S. financial firms to accept trainees, sometimes for as long as two years. The results of these educational efforts have been described earlier.

U.S. money managers were eager to participate in the Japanese market and sorely tempted by the possibility of competing to manage Japanese pension funds. Regulations that provided that only Japanese life insurance companies and trust banks could manage Japanese pension funds were relaxed in the late 1980s. American money managers were aware of the relatively poor performance of the Japanese life insurance companies and trust banks in managing this money, although this was difficult to ascertain because there were few benchmarks and little reliable information.

At this point, it is virtually impossible to find reliable data to accurately compare performance among Japanese money managers. This was painfully obvious to Lawrence Repeta, president of the Japanese operation of Frank Russell company which specializes in comparing performance among money managers. Repeta's frustration was apparent when he described the unwillingness of JFIs to release data about their performance. He bluntly stated that "The fact is, there is no useful data base for comparing funds or their returns . . . There is a screaming need for unbiased information."[22] This is a phenomenon which I have witnessed consistently over the years.

The JFIs have lived in a world of vagueness and obfuscation. Clarity, disclosure, and useful information are antithetical to the present system. Rhetoric about reform sounds good and is especially sought after by journalists, but actual reform is hardly a realistic short-term possibility in a structure where information flows are so limited. Public disclosure would be very unpleasant for JFIs. It would also hamper the MOF control over the system.

The difficulties of gathering assets in Japan without a Japanese partner in the 1980s was illustrated by the experiment of an American money manager. In 1987, the money management arm of a major U.S. financial institution was ready to perform its proselytizing role and teach the Japanese institutional investors about performance. The firm had $28 billion under management and a meaningful presence in Tokyo. The financial institution had a well-recognizable name and was quite prestigious. At a meeting in New York in January 1987, the senior American official explained that his strategy was to market his past performance record in order to attract funds from Japanese institutional investors.

---

22 James Sterngold, "A New Leaf for Japan's Mutual Funds?" *The New York Times*, January 2, 1994, Sec. 3, p. 13.

It was mentioned to him that American notions of past performance had little relevance to Japanese investors at that time. It was suggested that an initial approach might include marketing specific expertise in managing fixed income funds relating to mortgages or high yield securities. The Japanese institutional investors were interested in becoming more involved in both areas. In addition, products relating to options and futures, if structured properly, would provoke attention as well.

The senior American money manager replied that specialized fund management was of no interest. He wished to market general money management expertise and emphasize performance. He proceeded to hire six Japanese money managers, who began to solicit funds. After two years without acquiring a base of assets to manage, the six Japanese money managers were no longer in the money management department. They were either at other firms or other departments of the same firm. The firm was able to raise a fund for investment in high-yield securities, and their mortgage-related activity was profitable.

Most American money managers were aware of these difficulties, as well as the costs of establishing an operation in Japan. If a firm managed Japanese equities for non-Japanese institutions, it could justify having personnel in Tokyo to do research and manage existing portfolios and, secondarily, to solicit new funds. The Japanese cross-shareholdings, longstanding domestic ties, preference for "wet" relationships which can bail them out of difficulties, bull market mentality, suspicion of foreigners, lack of available information, inability to objectively evaluate different money managers, and lack of concern for performance were imbedded in the Japanese system of money management.

These formidable obstacles remain, and structural change is necessary to alter the status quo significantly. The impact of evolutionary deregulation will be slow. Only a protracted crisis which would challenge the system can hasten the process.

Also, the employees in charge of pension funds are generally part of the rotation system and therefore, unskilled. The cross-shareholdings and business ties make it difficult to isolate performance as a sole criteria for retaining a manager. How could a Mitsubishi company fire Mitsubishi Trust & Banking Co. as its pension fund manager, even if the results are dreadful or the fund wanted to invest in areas where Mitsubishi Trust had no expertise?

As a result of deregulation in the 1980s, the Japanese institutional investors such as insurance companies, trust banks, and securities firms, were joined by the long-term banks and city banks. They established small money management operations. The long-term banks and city banks generally funded their money management operations internally, but they still felt the need to indicate that they were competitive with other JFIs.

In the 1980s, the JFIs took less interest in forming partnerships with U.S. money managers who had general investment skills than with specialists. The JFIs assumed their staff could master the U.S. equity and bond markets. Japanese investors did not seem to grasp the significance of the different categories of U.S. equity investing, which included asset allocation, value, growth, small capitalization stocks, and indexation. There were relatively few equity participants such as LTCB/Miller Anderson & Sherrerd, Yasuda Fire & Marine/Brinson, and Tokyo Marine & Fire/Delaware. There were joint ventures such as Sumitomo Bank/Bankers Trust, which had been established for the usual reasons—investment credibility and publicity for the JFI and market access for the Americans.

There were also a number of equity participations in commodity firms for their options and futures skills. In general, however, the Americans were quickly disillusioned about the possibility of obtaining significant assets to manage in Japan, as their Japanese partners were either reluctant or unable to market effectively.

In one case, a prominent New England money manager sold a small percentage of his company to a JFI in 1989. A few months after the sale, this senior American official scheduled a trip to Tokyo for a week to see his new partner and visit institutional clients. After arriving in Tokyo, he discovered that the salaryman who had negotiated the purchase of equity in his company had been rotated to a subsidiary. The JFI had advertised the "strategic alliance" with this well-known American, and had then virtually forgotten about him. The American was not well-acquainted with anyone else at the JFI, and few appointments had been arranged. He left disillusioned after a couple of days.

A FEW OBSERVATIONS

In the 1980s, JFIs were forced to look outside their organizations for people or organizations because skills and contacts were needed. Centralization in Tokyo caused these attempts to be relegated to exercises in form rather than substance. Similar patterns of concern for market share and publicity prevailed. JFIs tended to mimic each other by following the same course. Tokyo was directing activity without regard to local people or conditions. In summary, trends in the JFIs overseas operations in the 1980s were the following:

- Tokyo control meant that U.S. offices of JFIs waited to receive orders. The local offices tended to react rather than initiate. Theoretically, local offices should be better acquainted with matters pertaining to the U.S. than Tokyo is and should have a major influence on business, but Tokyo staff dominated decisions in departments conducting business abroad.

- There was no focus in Tokyo on how the various internal departments and foreign partnerships could fit into a comprehensive business strategy. Each department or business area was allowed to pursue whatever it considered to be proper. When a general manager was rotated, the entire philosophy of a department could shift. A Tokyo-based general manager could terminate a plan initiated by his predecessor and begin a different policy. These moves were never questioned. In many cases, the general managers stationed overseas had mainly administrative functions. The actual business was directed from Tokyo.

The lack of consistent policy was revealed in one example of a Japanese institutional investor's use of four major mutual fund groups. Each choice was based on a different individual at the JFI having an acquaintance at one of the American firms. In many cases, a department was unaware of the activity of the multiple relationships. The choices did not derive from careful considerations or long-term partnership arrangements. Fragmentation and Tokyo departmental control were again in evidence.

- The internal departments involved with overseas business and the foreign partners were not organizationally integrated. There were overlapping responsibilities and duplications. A particular transaction might be introduced to more than one department; each department might have to do separate analysis. Overseas offices had their own portfolios so that London, New York, Singapore, Tokyo, Hong Kong, and Brussels offices might have had an interest in similar securities. In the 1980s, U.S. equity portfolios might be managed in New York and more than one department in Tokyo. Each was supposed to have discretion, and each wanted separate attention. U.S. brokers showed the same idea to multiple sources at the same Japanese institutional investor. The lack of trained personnel made this duplication of effort even more difficult to fathom. The ultimate reason had nothing to do with performance; it related to the fragmentation of departments and the "on-the-job" training mentality.

In the U.S. equity area, for example, Japanese institutional investors occasionally indicated that they wanted their inexperienced portfolio mangers to be contacted by Americans working for U.S. brokers in New York. They thought this would be a better training ground than Tokyo because the American firms had Japanese or Americans who spoke Japanese contacting them. It was assumed that brokers were the only source of information rather than primary research or dialogue with other fund managers. The Japanese institutional investors also felt some resentment about having to speak to a unit whose expertise was contacting JFIs rather than whose specialty was the U.S. market. In response, the U.S. brokers set up Japanese units in New York to speak to the Japanese institutional investors in New York. The Japanese required special units because of their inexperience, lack of language skills, and restricted activity. Virtually any report had to be translated into Japanese before it could be read by the Japanese institutional investors.

During the 1980s, the Japanese investors kept encouraging U.S. brokers to increase their contact with their New York units because New York would increasingly become the center of their equity business. This never happened; Tokyo retained control, and the New York operations generated very little activity. They were used as a conduit for information, but the information was exactly the same as what was being given in Tokyo by the American brokers.

■ One of the reasons the JFIs never made any serious plans or contemplated any commitment when considering their foreign partners was their refusal to acknowledge that they might be dependent on outside—especially foreign—sources. They willingly established an infrastructure of many offices in the U.S., committed scarce English-speaking staff, made countless trips, and spent enormous amounts of management time to build their own physical presence. The results of these efforts to build from within were superficial in terms of actual business contacts and skill development.

■ The JFIs were able to build an asset base and accomplish their goal of market share. They never asked what market share meant in different sectors of the financial markets. Market share can provide economies-of-scale in certain areas and diseconomies in other sectors. The emphasis on size of the asset base was always the priority, to the exclusion of profits and quality.

- The JFIs never examined the failures and successes of U.S. financial firms in order to better devise strategies.

- The JFIs casually entered into partnerships that satisfied their thirst for publicity.

- Technology transfer was supposed to occur by osmosis. A JFI employee was sent to the U.S. to study. It was hoped that somehow he would be able to impart his knowledge to the JFI, despite the fact that he had been rotated. The JFI hoped to accumulate expertise in this way.

- The JFIs did not distinguish between domestic, foreign, and cross-border business. They were lumped together.

- Substantive communication problems between Japanese firms and individuals and American firms and individuals were never considered or dealt with properly. The Japanese employee viewed his stay as short-term. He approached his job ceremonially, and his biggest fear was making a mistake, not failing to perform. The JFIs, in most cases, were not prepared to engage in a dialogue. The seconded employee or trainee was not accountable for performance in terms of profits or skill development. During his sojourn with the partner, the JFIs major goal was the maintenance of political ties with Tokyo.

- The JFIs looked at their partnerships' businesses as appendages that were never attached to their mainstream business. When questioned in detail about the lack of profits and penetration from his American activities, a senior official of a JFI stated that the whole operation was not significant within the firm's business. This was a rationalization, but it shows how cavalierly the JFIs treated their overseas business. They could spend huge sums of money without any expectations.

The JFIs were concerned with creating in Tokyo the illusion of achievement. Despite the frequent trips made by JFI personnel to their overseas offices, they were isolated from reality. The trips tended to be ceremonial and visits mainly internal office affairs, whereby the JFI's local staff was able to glean information from Tokyo personnel. Overseas travel was somewhat of a perquisite for Japanese businessmen, as it is for many foreign businessmen. The Tokyo personnel did not objectively evaluate the activities in the U.S. because their status depended on everything appearing to be running smoothly. Uncovering a problem would have created a difficult situation for a colleague. The rotation system covered up mistakes by allowing each salaryman to enter his position blameless, so faults had to be disguised until the rotation occurred.

It is important to consider whether the overseas activities and subsequent results in the 1980s were a learning experience for the JFIs. Tokyo's goals of publicity, market share, and asset growth were accomplished. The dark side of Tokyo's priorities, however, yielded poor asset quality without regard for proper returns and stagnant partnership arrangements with foreign firms.

Tokyo centralization may imply tight control, order, direction, and planning. Superficially, this is plausible. With respect to JFIs, the reality was different. As we have observed, centralization occurred on a departmental basis. This led to overlapping responsibilities, unconnected responses to issues, uncoordinated planning, political infighting, conflicting goals, no accountability, and an obsession with publicity. Tokyo control yielded a fragmented approach to overseas business that emphasized form over substance. The overly centralized approach of the JFIs overseas business in the 1980s inhibited the establishment of profitable businesses.

CHAPTER 7

BUREAUCRACY

MEET MR. X, THE ARCHETYPE BUREAUCRAT

Mr. X had successfully adjusted to bureaucratic conditions. He had been promoted consistently, even ahead of his peers, to a senior position. He was bright, extremely articulate and smooth, and had mastered the art of dealing with foreigners. His sojourn in the U.S. had made him a self-anointed expert on American business. He equated the number of years of residence in the U.S. with knowledge of the American market.

A conversation with Mr. X occasionally started with his disparaging remarks about Tokyo colleagues' lack of understanding of the American business environment. He was most interested in gossip about either Japanese or foreign firms. He liked to discuss the seating arrangements at particular events which he attended in order to determine political significance.

He viewed large U.S. financial firms with great favor, enamored of their names. He did not relate to strengths and weaknesses of different individuals or departments at those firms, only to the company itself. In 1988, he described the relationship between JFIs and U.S. investment bankers as perfectly complimentary—the JFIs purchased assets created by U.S. investment bankers. By 1992, even he had grown skeptical about the reliability of U.S. investment banks and did not remember his 1988 opinion. Now he respected the power of the U.S. investment banks and recognized a certain dependency on them.

Mr. X was careful to indicate the profitability of his operation when the most cursory examination revealed major problems. He distanced himself from the obvious mistakes that had been made. He could always find another individual or department to blame. He cited the progress made in terms of localization of his U.S. operation when there were no Americans with any responsibility.

JAPANESE SYSTEM—FANTASY VERSUS REALITY

Mention the term "Japanese system" and most observers, foreign and Japanese, will immediately think of careful, methodical, painstaking planning. The logical assumption was, and still is, that the JFIs' rapid expansion overseas in the 1980s was the result of such systematic thinking.

The reality was quite different. There was little planning and less analysis of the fundamental issues facing any business start-up. The organizational structure was excessively bureaucratic, both in terms of control from Tokyo and from the organizational structure transplanted abroad. As shown in the last chapter, the deal evaluation process was totally politicized. This was not a case of rational "dry" Western methods being overtaken by looser, more intuitive and personal "wet" Japanese style. The JFIs bureaucratic mentality was so extreme that operations were often paralyzed, leaving only in-house politics functioning in the conduct of overseas business.

> " Mention the term 'Japanese system' and most observers, foreign and Japanese, will immediately think of careful, methodical, painstaking planning. The logical assumption was, and still is, that the JFIs' rapid expansion overseas in the 1980s was the result of such systematic thinking. The reality was quite different. "

It is important to remember that the JFIs were not alone in being bureaucratic. Every large financial institution, like every large enterprise, is to some extent bureaucratic. The JFIs, however, because they were part of the Japanese system, were thought to be different. Their bureaucratic features were considered organizational strengths when they were actually weaknesses. The JFIs suffered from the same problems that Western firms encountered. In many cases, they were actually less equipped to handle these issues than Western firms.

Institutions frequently encounter tension in finding the proper balance between entrepreneurial activity and structure, form and substance, profit and presence, and short-term considerations and long-term planning. Decisions relating to internal strengths and weaknesses are vital in planning businesses. Limitations in terms of management and personnel resources, communication, capital, expertise, technology, and organizational structure need to be considered in deciding the appropriateness of a business. It should be recognized that "overstretching"—trying to accomplish too much with the available resources—will diminish results and cause failures. It must be determined whether the growth of a business will likely create economies- or diseconomies-of-scale.

In the case of the JFIs going abroad in the 1980s, goals such as profit, technology and knowledge, presence, and servicing Japanese clients needed to be prioritized beforehand in order to evaluate overseas business potential. This was not, could not be done because the nature of the JFIs' bureaucratic structure prevented it.

> " Individual departments were not conventional profit centers; they were organizational centers."

WHEN PERFORMANCE MEANS POLITICAL ACCEPTABILITY

During the JFIs' march overseas in the 1980s, performance generally meant internal political acceptability. Recognition and promotion were derived from subjective considerations which were intentionally left vague. Compensation was determined mainly by length of employment, and salarymen were predominantly motivated by security and recognition rather than money. The bureaucratic hierarchy required that the JFIs promote staff within specified age limits. It was difficult for an employee to have as a boss a younger employee. A potential employee's exact birth date was always checked. (This obsession with protocol and form has been taken to absurdity. Witness the recent concern voiced by some Japanese about the new Princess, Masako Owada, because she spoke for 28 seconds longer than the Crown Prince at a news conference.)[1]

Individual departments were not conventional profit centers; they were organizational centers. If a department did not produce a profit, the JFI explained it away as a result of cyclicality, a poor business environment, or the fifty-year time horizon.

It was virtually inconceivable that a salaryman would be fired for bad business judgment. Under normal circumstances, an individual or a department was never officially "blamed" for a problem. There would have to be a supplementary factor, such as a scandal or negative publicity, to accompany the error in order for an individual to be terminated from his firm. Even then, there would possibly be an intermediate step, such as the famous *madogiwa-zoku* position given to an employee who is out of favor; the employee is relegated to an office where his only task is to gaze out of the window. At one point, when the foreign brokers and money managers descended on Tokyo in vast numbers, some of the *madogiwa-zoku* were used to meet with foreigners in a polite and meaningless exercise.

> **" The JFIs were addicted to comparing their activities with those of other JFIs. As long as the other JFIs were having difficulty in an area, a particular JFI felt secure. "**

The JFIs were addicted to comparing their activities with those of other JFIs. As long as the other JFIs were having difficulty in an area, a particular JFI felt secure. Since all the JFIs' activity, competence, and approaches tended to move in lockstep, each could almost always find at least one other JFI to cite in a problem situation. This reinforced the disposition of JFI salarymen, if not to follow the lead of other JFIs, at least to move together with them in transactions or businesses.

If it had no earnings, the JFI could always re-interpret the goals of a department. The new responsibilities of the department could easily become gathering information or serving clients rather than making profits. In some

---

1   Sterngold, James, "A Ceremony Both Regal and Restful," *The New York Times,* June 6, 1993, p. A-12.

cases, changing a department name accomplished the same purpose, e.g., the U.S. real estate department could become the restructuring department.

Since individual performance was equated with political success, there was a corresponding lack of concern with making money during the 1980s. To be sure, the earnings and capital adequacy problems which appeared in the 1990s caused the JFIs to add such terms as "return on assets" and "return on capital" to their vocabulary. Until then, though, these were never mentioned. After all, publicity, presence, market share, and size were the criteria for political success. But, however fashionable, the use of such terms made little difference because JFI personnel did not know how to cope with the concepts they represented.

JFIs' ORGANIZATIONAL STRUCTURE BAFFLES

Even today, the organizational complexity of a typical JFI's international operation is often baffling. Departments do not necessarily correspond to specific products or geographical territories. They are sometimes quasi-autonomous units with overlapping responsibilities. During the 1980s, in the international area, these departments were vertically integrated, with their personnel abroad reporting directly to Tokyo. Overseas offices had little autonomy, with Tokyo's approval required for most matters. Yet these departments were not required to coordinate in terms of communication or activity. Scheduling meetings which included two different departments was often difficult, even when the presentation was relevant for both. The JFIs considered this a violation of protocol—another example of form winning over substance.

Decision making was not a function of rank. A managing director at a large JFI generally had mainly ceremonial responsibilities. He was dependent on information from subordinates. Indeed, subordinates sometimes used the analogy of a farmer feeding a chicken whose head was sticking through a wire fence. The managing director was the chicken, isolated behind the fence. The subordinates were the farmer, doling out the amount and type of information represented by the feed.

Even a general manager usually was not often involved directly with specific transactions. Information was supposed to percolate up through the organization. As a result, approval of transactions and joint ventures was managed, not decided, at the manager and assistant manager level. Routine money management decisions were decided by individual portfolio managers.

Most JFIs had more than one planning department, each bearing inter-departmental and inter-office responsibilities. These departments were politically important waystations on any salaryman's career path. Planning departments had a general mandate which might include originating transactions, devising business strategies, giving input on personnel resources or training. They were supposed to work closely with the departments in their designated areas, albeit in an ill-defined manner. They did not have any supervisory control. Foreigners were often perplexed by the planning departments because they were ubiquitous and their responsibilities were amorphous.

> **" During the mid-1980s, Morgan Stanley's
> New York officials, for example, had
> to prohibit the Japanese managers at
> Morgan Stanley Tokyo from holding
> meetings from which foreign managers
> were purposely excluded. "**

As for the JFIs' offshore offices, they had no autonomy within this organizational structure. Each Tokyo department was responsible for its overseas personnel and business strategy. Deals that might originate overseas were passed to Tokyo where they would drift along the bottom of a department's hierarchy. Ultimately, they would either conveniently disappear or emerge once responsibility for approval had been sufficiently diffused through the organization.

Foreign employees were not considered part of this organizational structure. They were usually hired as specialists with no management responsibility. Like it or not, they could be terminated at will. Indeed, the exclusion of foreigners is a characteristic which is deeply ingrained in the Japanese salaryman. Sometimes, the Japanese even retained this trait when he worked for a foreign firm. During the mid-1980s, Morgan Stanley's New York officials, for example, had to prohibit the Japanese managers at Morgan Stanley Tokyo from holding meetings from which foreign managers were purposely excluded.

JFIs' LACK OF CONCERN FOR PROFITS

Since recognition was not determined by profits, the JFIs' overseas businesses in the 1980s were characterized by growth of infrastructure and business without regard to the bottom line—in other words, empire building. Costs, both in terms of cash outlays or management and resource time, were ignored when acquisitions and joint ventures were undertaken. Business plans and transaction analysis alike generally did not consider cost of capital. The staff was only accustomed to looking at gross revenues as significant. Building up the number of staff—body count—and assets were regularly cited as measures of success. The overall revenues were not compared to the size of a particular commitment in terms of people, offices, or effort, let alone risk. The bureaucracy in Tokyo wanted the appearance of growth. At the departmental level, both in Tokyo and overseas, salarymen were conditioned to deliver this "growth" without question. Their career prospects depended on meeting the organization's collective will.

Opportunity costs, therefore, was an unthinkable concept. Each department reacted to its own self-interest by staffing its projects, developing its own partnerships, and evaluating its own transactions. There was little consideration given to prioritizing business or recognizing that there were capital, management, or personnel limits. It was better to initiate many activities, in other words, to appear to be growing, than to concentrate on profits or coordination.

Each major Japanese bank had several offices in the U.S., with large aggregate costs in terms of expense, communication, and manpower. These offices often had departments with conflicting or overlapping responsibilities. This generated confusion among American bankers who were unclear about which office should receive a presentation of a transaction. It might have been shown in New York, Los Angeles, or Tokyo. There was even a question of which department was responsible if the transaction required distribution in Tokyo. U.S. investment bankers ultimately showed the same transaction in various offices of the same Japanese bank. The question was never to find the resident expert, for there was none.

Many of the joint ventures and acquisitions created further cost problems for the JFIs. If a JFI took a minority position, as Nippon Life did in Shearson Lehman, the JFI could not attempt to exert influence when an expensive problem developed. If a joint venture was a failure, the JFI had to endure the cost because dissolving the "vehicle" was an admission of defeat, which the bureaucracy was unwilling to do. Once created, if it did not function properly, such an entity would die a very slow death. To close an office involved an enormous struggle. Recently, the JFIs have been forced to close international offices in the 1990s. One JFI, which had boasted about its international presence, has quietly abandoned four offices in Europe, North America, and South America. These can be viewed as peripheral actions which in no way reflect the JFIs' understanding of their problems.

Inevitably, given the nature of the approval process, market ignorance, and the lack of due diligence, the JFIs encountered non-performing loans and bankruptcies. Here, the cost could be another serious drain because domestic Japanese practice, which was vague and subject to administrative change, could not be transplanted. In Tokyo, regulations or situations such as treatment of non-performing loans could be interpreted differently by JFIs and even by individuals within the same JFI. The JFIs were ill-prepared for problems they encountered in the U.S.

Where was the MOF? In difficult situations in Japan, the MOF had found a way to ameliorate matters by altering rules. In the deregulated U.S. environment, harsh realities and American lawyers could not be ignored by U.S. banks or JFIs.

SALARYMEN SEEK OUT POLITICAL SAFETY

The JFIs' highly politicized bureaucratic structure made it all the more imperative for the organization and the individual salaryman to seek out politically safe sources for transactions. Remember that the JFIs' large infrastructures notwithstanding, they never developed a deal-generating network. Nor could their cumbersome approval process handle any transaction that did not come pre-digested.

They had to rely on U.S. investment and commercial banks to package transactions—something the U.S institutions became adept at doing, producing so many deals that even if the JFIs accepted only one, the effort was well-rewarded. But the nature of the bureaucracy, with its many layers of inexperienced salarymen and non-specialist departments meant that no one wanted to take the political risk of relying on foreign intermediaries whose names did not resonate with safety through the organization. This usually excluded small or medium-sized firms who lacked name recognition in Japan.

There was nothing inherently wrong with the JFIs using large U.S. financial intermediaries. However, the JFIs were unable to critically evaluate the people within these organizations, or the transactions which emanated from them. The U.S. personnel at large intermediaries are compensated mainly by bonuses, which are calculated on a yearly basis. Both bonuses and promotion are largely determined by production, which can be either fee income or trading profits. The American intermediaries, their departments and individuals had a strong vested interest in completing as many transactions as possible, not in creating quality transactions for the Japanese. The JFIs did not understand, or care, about the incentives that propelled their American intermediaries.

" A Japanese institutional investor required merely an understanding of its operational protocol."

American institutional investors, aware of the deal orientation of American financial intermediaries, usually know they have to be careful. As indicated previously, the skill and integrity of American financial intermediaries covers a broad spectrum from positive to negative. Japan is different. It is both easy and valid to generalize about Japanese financial intermediaries. The good American intermediaries know that professionalism leads to continuity and business with their clients. In the 1980s, though, the JFIs did not demand professionalism. A Japanese institutional investor required merely an understanding of its operational protocol.

Ultimately, this put the JFIs at a serious disadvantage. The U.S. financial system, in some aspects, is relatively mature. There are many sub-categories of assets and a large number of people with expertise, experience, and integrity who understand the variety of opportunities available. The process of finding the assets and the people is not easy and is a business in itself. Unlike Japan, many of the top people do not work for large companies and, therefore, in the 1980s were excluded from consideration by JFIs. Thus, the JFIs shut themselves off both from good intermediaries and good business opportunities.

Within the JFI bureaucracy, it was important to determine which transactions were politically acceptable. Sponsorship by a large American intermediary or, even better, a large JFI, enhanced the credibility of a transaction. Trends and fashion were also vital. Publicity and activity were signs of positive momentum, which enticed the JFIs. This momentum was advanced by planting articles in the *Nikkei*. For example, if a U.S. foreign specialist traveled to Japan to market a transaction, an interview would be arranged with the Nikkei to allow the foreigner to discuss his area generally. In the 1980s, these articles would appear during the foreigner's visit and would add stature to the visitor's product.

JFIs FALL INTO REAL ESTATE TRAP

In the real estate area, the JFIs frequently looked at the U.S. market with preconceptions borne of the long, post-war Japanese real estate boom. While superficially applying valuation concepts to U.S. transactions, the JFIs could become mesmerized by the apparent cheapness of U.S. real estate compared to Japanese, where cash-on-cash returns were extremely low during the 1980s. The JFIs' involvement could either be by owning the real estate or by lending to individuals or institutions that purchased the real estate and used it as collateral.

The JFIs too often fell into the trap. The Tokyo bureaucracy relied on the outward form of the transaction to determine political safety. "Famous" name intermediaries soon learned how to package properties at trophy locations to fit the formula.

Unfortunately, a high proportion of these investments proved to be disasters.

During the 1980s, the U.S. press interpreted this differently. Stories about the Japanese owning 30 percent of downtown Los Angeles and the loss of Rockefeller Center were common. The articles viewed the real estate transactions as a threat in that the Japanese were taking over America. The Americans viewed this activity as part of the plan of the Japanese to subjugate another aspect of the American economy. The transactions, in reality, resulted from no plan or detailed analysis. Once again, JFI bureaucracy was responsible for ill-timed, poor investments which derived from evaluation and the desire for politically safe deals.

Mitsubishi Real Estate's purchase of an equity participation in Rockefeller Center in 1989 is especially instructive. The American press and "experts" viewed this as yet another example of Japanese power and empire creation. Rockefeller Center is an American symbol. There was an emotional response as Americans felt violated. By mid-1993, though, the press began reporting that the Rockefeller Center deal had clay feet and had declined in value by 50 percent in the previous year.[2] These newspaper accounts are important because of their factual content as well as the context in which the facts are presented. When JFIs were viewed as threats, the articles conveyed the image of power. Then, when it was apparent that the Japanese real estate purchases were in trouble, the articles often reported this without reflecting on their past interpretations.

This is not to say that the JFIs were the only institutions speculating and making bad decisions. American financial institutions were at the forefront in making disastrous real estate loans. It does, however, take special hubris to throw money at these highly regional situations as a foreigner. Also, it provides insights into the way the JFIs operated. It would take a separate discussion to examine the American financial institutions' problems. The JFIs were not exempt from blundering because they were part of the Japanese system.

DEPARTMENT FRAGMENTATION CREATES PROBLEM

The JFI bureaucracy was a quasi-feudal entity. It did not promote coordination among departments. It did not encourage information flow. Usually, there was no communication between departments about transactions or policy issues. Each concentrated on pursuing its own objectives, which often had less to do with building a profitable business than departmental aggrandizement and fostering internal patron-client relationships.

> " The JFI bureaucracy was a quasi-feudal
> entity. It did not promote coordination
> among departments. It did not encourage
> information flow. Usually, there was no
> communication between departments about
> transactions or policy issues. "

---

2 Pinder, Jeanne B., "Rockefeller Center With Clay Feet," *The New York Times*, June 12, 1993, p. D-1.

A good illustration could be found in the equity operations of Japanese securities firms. Japanese equities, convertibles, and equity warrants were often not handled by the same people, trading desks or, in some instances, even departments. The emphasis was on selling individual products, and new issues were, accordingly, given priority. The secondary price movement, like the relationship between a company's equity, convertible, and warrant securities, was never carefully monitored.

This gave rise to enormous market inefficiencies, which were exploited by foreign firms such as Morgan Stanley and Baring Brothers. In many cases, the convertibles or warrants traded at a discount to parity; purchasing the derivatives amounted to buying the equity at below its quoted price. Arbitragers could purchase the convertible securities, simultaneously sell the equity on the market, and convert the bonds to equity. The entire transaction was riskless and profitable. There were also inefficiencies existing in the relationship between Japanese government bonds and the futures, a discrepancy Salomon Brothers fully exploited. The relationship between the Japanese equity market and its futures index was yet another large source of arbitrage profit for foreigners.

JFIs FAIL TO RECOGNIZE RISK

The bureaucratic approval process was cumbersome and undiscerning. Transactions were considered in a perfunctory manner, once the political safety had been assured. Little attention was given to determining the appropriate return for a given risk. Equity-related risks were often taken without demand for equity returns. This happened in such areas as high-yield bonds and real estate loans. Transactions were subject to an assembly-line process which failed to grasp fundamental spread relationships and risk-reward concepts. Bureaucratic decisions created pricing which did not account for major risks. Because of their size, JFIs distorted prices, raising them to unrealistic levels in virtually every market into which they lumbered.

If the credit of a transaction was approved, the JFIs participated almost without regard to yield, as long as there was a positive spread over the cost of funding. Considerations such as cost of capital, return on assets, or appropriate returns were not considered relevant. The bureaucracy wanted gross revenues to indicate size and growth. All used the same criteria, so they began to compete with each other for over-priced assets. Sovereign borrowers, or "acceptable" banks, received numerous proposals from intermediaries based solely on Japanese interest or perceived Japanese interest.

During the 1980s, the JFIs often distributed investment products to their clients without any real knowledge of the product. The example of the U.S. regional bank, whose credit was downgraded within hours after the JFI purchase, provided a glimpse of this activity. The JFI had placed the issue with its clients. The JFI had done only superficial analysis, having trusted the "famous" U.S. intermediary to provide a creditworthy product. A lack of skills as well as a lack of familiarity with the borrower did not deter the JFI from entering the transaction and subjecting clients to unnecessary risk.

In many cases, JFI employees were given presentations by U.S. investment bankers in new, highly specialized areas, and the JFI chose a product based on a brief presentation, then distributed it to his clients.

The implicit guarantees on investments given by JFIs during the 1980s showed their disregard for the difficulties of performance. The bureaucracy sanctioned the arrogance that allowed the practice to take place. The inexperienced salaryman was then expected to find politically safe transactions, in some cases overseas, to fulfill the expectations created.

The JFIs were, however, conscious of one area—management fees paid to intermediaries. Whenever possible, the JFIs would negotiate for a lower rate. A deal might be significantly overpriced, and the risk underestimated, but the JFI salaryman would focus on the fee—at times, an infinitesimally small part of the overall transaction. This was his way of exerting control and power, as well as demonstrating his diligence and effective negotiating skills. The foreign intermediary was well aware of this, so that fees were embedded in interest rate swaps, currency swaps, or other means—as trading profits rather than as fees. The salaryman did not care about the total return or embedded costs. He was only interested in the visible fee, which satisfied the requirement of form.

The lack of coordination between the quantitative units and other areas meant little substantive use of derivatives in the 1980s. There was much discussion about the use of futures, but the actual use seems to be confined to speculative activity rather than pure hedging.

ACCOUNTABILITY IS CONSPICUOUSLY ABSENT

The theme of specific accountability within the Japanese system is one of the themes permeating Karel van Wolferen's *The Enigma of Japanese Power*. At one point, when describing how difficult it is for countries to work with Japan, he stated "there is no one to deal with (in the Japanese government),"[3] hence there is no one who is really accountable. When describing the Japanese government, he stated:

> No one is ultimately in charge . . . There is, to be sure, a hierarchy or, rather a complex of overlapping hierarchies. But it has no peak; it is a truncated pyramid . . . Hence, there is no place where, as Harry Truman would have said, the buck stops. In Japan, the buck keeps circulating.[4]

The trait is, to some extent, present in all bureaucracies but is evident in its purest form in the Japanese government and in the JFIs, which resemble government agencies more than private corporations.

" The trait is, to some extent, present in all bureaucracies but is evident in its purest form in the Japanese government and in the JFIs, which resemble government agencies more than private corporations. "

This lack of accountability should not be confused with ritualized responsibility. For example, Yoshihisa Tabuchi was forced to resign as President of Nomura Securities in July 1991 in order to officially "take responsibility" for Nomura's participation in the scandal by which Japanese brokers were compensating favored clients for losses, manipulating markets, and maintaining close business contacts with the Japanese criminal underworld. These were all quite common practices and well-documented previously, but negative publicity surrounding the disclosure caused much embarrassment to the government so someone had to atone, and Tabuchi was the candidate. It is generally assumed that he still wields power at Nomura. It is difficult to imagine that the MOF was not aware of the dubious practices, with their constant communication with JFIs and massive reporting requirements. The actual discovery of the compensation

---

3 van Wolferen, Karel, *The Enigma of Japanese Power*, New York: Alfred A. Knopf, 1989, p. 413.
4 van Wolferen, *Engima*, p. 5.

kickbacks was made by one of the MOF's departments, the Bureau of Taxation.

Kiichi Miyazawa's political resurrection provides a parallel in the government. Miyazawa had to resign in 1988 as Finance Minister because of his connection with the Recruit scandal. In 1991, he resurfaced as the Prime Minister. His resignation, which constituted ritualized accountability, did not damage his career.

By contrast, when John Gutfreund had to resign in September 1991 as Chairman of Salomon Brothers, it was hardly ceremonial. He had failed to immediately report the illegal activities of Salomon's government bond operation to the Securities and Exchange Commission (SEC) after he became aware of the improprieties. Unlike Tabuchi, it is highly doubtful that Gutfreund will have any contact with Salomon until he is absolved. Indeed, Gutfreund has sued Salomon for $16 million dollars, which he alleges Salomon owes him as his 1991 compensation. The thought of Tabuchi similarly suing Nomura is preposterous.

In the 1980s, JFIs did not hold anyone accountable for their various failures in conducting overseas business. Promotions and recognition were not correlated to success nor blame correlated with failure. A partial list of the non-achievement, non-accomplishment, and non-performance of the overseas activities would include:

- Losses related to U.S. real estate and LBO loans made with inadequate knowledge and poor analysis.

- Poor acquisition and joint venture strategy and execution.

- Low or negative return on equity in overseas operations.

- Inability to transfer technology effectively.

- Neglect of proper securities research.

- Failure to employ hedging techniques in investment or trading areas.

- Absence of localization in development of client base, information network or foreign staff.

- Lack of focus and planning in establishing overseas business.

- Failure to develop a system which produced a skilled and knowledgeable personnel base to handle overseas business.

- Inability to learn how to communicate with foreigners.

- Low profitability and emphasis on mindless asset growth.

The JFIs' bureaucracy exhibited traits common to any governmental bureaucracy but especially similar to those of the Japanese government. Political savvy was rewarded. The self-correcting aspects of accountability and market forces were buried in the bureaucracy. The bureaucracy encouraged overlapping responsibilities, vague mandates, and multi-level approval requirements. This was not planned; it evolved. The results were not a conservative system of checks and balances but a predictable reliance on politically safe choices of transactions, partners, or businesses. The structural faults of this system became apparent when the JFIs began operation overseas in a deregulated, unprotected market. The reaction to problems engendered by the bureaucracy was paralysis and shelter within the fifty-year time horizon.

MISTAKES OBSCURED BY HARMONIOUS APPEARANCES

The JFIs' attitude toward individual or institutional mistakes was akin to the issue of lack of accountability. The bureaucracy exacerbated a tendency to avoid accountability and acknowledgment of mistakes. It is well known that the Japanese emphasize harmonious appearances and dislike any form of confrontation.

> **" . . . in Japanese society . . . reality is seen as negotiable. It is important to remember that relationships and truth are contextual. The Japanese are extremely pragmatic. Everything is relative."**

Mistakes can also be embarrassing. Van Wolferen stated what foreigners often observed, "In their daily lives, the Japanese are very helpful to one another in minimizing embarrassment."[5] This is made easier in Japa-

---

5   van Wolferen, *Engima*, p. 235.

nese society because reality is seen as negotiable. It is important to remember that relationships and truth are contextual. The Japanese are extremely pragmatic. Everything is relative. There is no need to be consistent, and contradictions are accepted as "complementary facets of the same truth."[6] In short, Japanese are not bound by what Westerners would call the truth.

Appearances and public impression are bound by rules of outward harmony. The Japanese, however, are prone to attack other Japanese even viciously in private or behind their back.

The JFI employees are even fond of the saying that holds "he who makes the fewest mistakes wins." This could be rephrased as "he who recognizes and deals with the fewest mistakes wins the bureaucratic game."

The implications of this attitude in overseas business were straightforward. The JFIs did not have to admit or correct mistakes. They were not penalized, nor did they apparently learn from the mistakes in the deregulated markets. One encountered numerous rationalizations when discussing problems. A favorite phrase was "due to poor market conditions." There was not a trace of an admission of a mistake by an individual, department, or firm. Therefore, there was no need to look for the underlying causes of a problem or consider past mistakes when engaging in future activities. Other popular rationalizations were:

1. The situation has long-term strategic value.
2. There is a forty- to fifty-year time horizon.
3. The problems existed before the present staff rotated into the area.
4. Other JFIs are in a similar position.
5. The MOF will intervene if there is further deterioration.

JFI personnel did not have any regard for consistency. The salaryman could change his public stance concerning an issue without acknowledging his previous policy, even one which was diametrically opposed to his present one. JFI personnel regularly contradicted themselves when explaining decisions. Vagueness and contradictions were effectively used by the salaryman to obfuscate issues. The rotation system intervened to remove any obligation to continuity or consistency.

The only kind of mistakes which were not tolerated were bureaucratic breaches of etiquette. The salaryman was fearful of making even trivial

---

6 van Wolferen, *Engima*, p. 235.

mistakes, which could often affect his career. An interesting fictionalized account of the impact of such a mistake is found in a short story written by Keita Genji, the pseudonym of Tomio Tanaka, who wrote 240 short stories and 90 novels about the life of a salaryman. Tanaka himself was a salary-man who retired from the Sumitomo Real Estate Company in 1956. He captures the spirit of the salaryman's dread of mistakes in his story, "The Lucky One." Genji described the disaster that befell the salaryman, Mr. Machida, shortly after he joined his company. Mr. Machida and another new employee were stationed outside the room in a restaurant where the senior officials of their company were entertaining an important client:

> Their job was to wait in the anteroom and be ready to answer the telephone, arrange cars, etc. It was a pretty lowly task, but occa-sionally a Geisha, taking a breather from the party and appearing like a flower out of season, would look in and reward the virtue of the two bored men.[7]

Unfortunately for Machida, an unidentified message was phoned in for the client to come to another party. Machida didn't know the call was from a rival company and passed the message directly to the client, Yamanoue, who immediately left, much to the consternation of Machida's president—before a deal had been concluded.

" There was not a trace of an admission of a mistake by an individual, department, or firm. Therefore, there was no need to look for the underlying causes of a problem or consider past mistakes when engaging in future activities."

For the next twenty years, Machida received no promotions because of his naive blunder. He was never allowed an opportunity and was given only menial jobs or meaningless tasks, such as representing the company at funerals. Machida consoled himself with alcohol, and by creating a mock office environment at home, he pretended that he was a director, and his

---

7 Genji, Kieta, (translated by Hugh Cortazzi), *The Lucky One and Other Humorous Stories*, Tokyo: The Japan Times, Ltd., 1980, p. 112.

wife cooperated by assuming the role of his secretary. One room in his house was furnished as a director's office. Occasionally, he would become drunk and maudlin. He bore his plight stoically and was rewarded when Yamanoue, reappearing to take over the company, stumbled upon Machida and his twenty-year curse.

In another story, "The English Interpreter," Genji describes another salaryman, Soichi Mogi, who, while drowning his sorrows in saki "glared at his colleagues and the hatred which had piled up within him without thinking about the consequences" and a physical altercation ensued. Lifetime employment means that people who may dislike each other are trapped together. Mogi had only been permitted to be a "temporary" within his company because he had never gone to university. His frustration is evident when he chastises his son for becoming an artist rather than attending university:

> Do you realize that your father has been humiliated every day of his working life and forced to remain a temporary because he did not go to university and only had a primary school education? I wanted you to go to university so that you would not have to suffer the same humiliations as your father. I would have done anything to get you to university and then into a firm where you would have the status accorded to graduates.[8]

Mogi, as well as Machida and Genji's other characters, were always taking refuge in alcohol. Status, politics, and risk avoidance permeate these simple stories. Stoicism and acceptance of one's place, without creating confrontation, are also found in these stories.

The tendency to avoid the recognition of mistakes takes many forms in Japanese society. Although not a JFI salaryman, the builder of one of the financially-troubled resort hotels in Hawaii rationalized, rather than recognized, his mistake:

> The Japanese are still in elementary school in terms of their U.S. investments . . . When they come back, they will be in middle school.[9]

---

[8] Genji, *Lucky One,* p. 60.
[9] Carlton, Jim, and Barsky, Neil, "Underwater: Japanese Purchases of U.S. Real Estate Fall on Hard Times," *The Wall Street Journal,* February 21, 1992, p. A-1, A-4.

He did not acknowledge that the Japanese's initial forays into U.S. real estate were a disaster. He just moved along to the second phase of investment, assuming that the Japanese had "graduated" to a higher level of competence. His use of the school analogy made it seem as if all was on schedule and planned.

> " The tightly controlled Japanese financial system did not penalize this tolerance for mistakes. The ability to critique a transaction, business, or trend were unappreciated skills in a bureaucratic system which valued appearance above all else. "

One searches in vain for an institutional memory in the 1980s. Yet, without understanding the problems of the first phase, it is difficult to anticipate success in a subsequent phase, especially if the personnel are new and lack awareness. The tightly controlled Japanese financial system did not penalize this tolerance for mistakes. The ability to critique a transaction, business, or trend were unappreciated skills in a bureaucratic system that valued appearance above all else.

The absence of adequate performance criteria, combined with the JFIs' tolerance for mistakes, meant that problems were not solved. They were simply ignored. The post-war bull markets, the strong economy, and the lack of competition masked the JFIs' mistakes and created a halcyon days mentality whereby the salaryman expected to be bailed out of difficulties.

HARMONY WITHIN BUREAUCRACY

One of the characteristics of Japanese society often praised by Japanese and foreigners alike is its harmony. The homogeneous Japanese society, as depicted, is a smoothly functioning organism without the strains of other societies. This harmony is said to allow government and business to work together in a way which is unthinkable in the U.S., where the two have an adversarial relationship which often requires monitoring by laws and courts. Decisions within organizations are supposed to result from *nemawashi*, the legendary consensus-building technique. This method allegedly allows the people involved to gain support for an undertaking

informally, before a proposal is officially presented. This support is tantamount to approval, for the group has arrived at a consensus. The process
appears smooth and resembles a political compromise rather than a substantive evaluation.

Again, it is useful to look at van Wolferen's observations and apply
them to JFIs. He indicated that, "Japanese society has no less conflict than
other societies . . . The effort to keep up a surface decorum is supported by
numerous subtle methods of avoiding and suppressing open conflict."[10]
Peer pressure, rather than harmony, is the operative word; van Wolferen
called this "informal coercion."[11] Feiler adeptly described the indoctrination
methods employed in the education system to create fear of hierarchy, of
being different and of being ostracized.[12] Every aspect of Japanese life re-
inforces the tendency towards submission to hierarchy and to the group.

Van Wolferen's analysis is accurate when applied to the JFIs' overseas
activities in the 1980s. The JFI salaryman, like Westerners, had strong
negative and positive opinions about his colleagues. In some ways, the
salaryman had even more pronounced feelings because of the likelihood of
working for the same company for an entire career. A great deal of hostil-
ity can develop between individuals who have an antipathy for one another
when they are forced to work in the same environment for thirty to forty
years. In Japan, this lack of harmony is never publicly acknowledged, but
bubbles below the surface.

The deference to hierarchy within the JFI bureaucracy should not be
mistaken for harmony. In order to be promoted and recognized, there had
to be the appearance of cooperation. Political infighting, tension, and inefficiency were present in the JFIs, just as in Western organizations.

Relationships between individuals, as well as between firms, are more
accurately portrayed as contextual, rather than harmonious. The salaryman's relationship with a colleague or a foreigner can be described as contextual. For example, there is a well-defined relationship between the
general manager of a department and the deputy general manager. There is
rigid protocol that describes how the general manager treats the deputy
general manager and the degree of loyalty expected from the deputy general manager. The general manager will usually not interfere with the functions delegated to the deputy general manager. The same will be true for

---

[10] van Wolferen, *Enigma,* pp. 315-316.
[11] van Wolferen, *Enigma,* p. 343.
[12] Feiler, *Learning to Bow,* p. 2.

the deputy general manager's relationship with the manager. The only occasion when the protocol is allowed to be violated is when a salaryman is under the influence of alcohol—which is often, as they are required to socialize virtually every night with clients or their colleagues. Conversations which occurred during a state of inebriation are usually not referred to or deemed inoffensive after the event.

" The situation between JFIs and foreign firms was based on a coincidence of interests and perceived specific usefulness or power of the foreign firm. This interaction should not be confused with what Westerners call a relationship, either personal or institutional. "

Foreigners were often misled by the apparent friendliness and personal feelings that JFI salarymen express in a social gathering, such as dinner or a reception. The JFI salarymen engaged in social protocol appropriate to the position or power of the foreigner. The esteem and power of the firm represented by the foreigner was also a factor. If the Japanese perceived a need for the foreigner or his firm, he would pay deference over many years. If the foreigner was removed from the context—if he left his firm or served no useful purpose—he would find, in most cases, that the salaryman's deference and friendliness disappeared and was replaced by formal politeness or indifference.

Relationships between firms were contextual as well. Japanese firms could be tied by cross-shareholdings or other forms of mutual dependencies. The scandals involving compensation for losses paid by Japanese brokers were a fulfillment of the expectations of this contextual and "wet" relationship. The rotation system lessened the importance of personal ties between employees at different firms because the individuals were constantly changing jobs. The situation between JFIs and foreign firms was based on a coincidence of interests and perceived specific usefulness or power of the foreign firm. This interaction should not be confused with what Westerners call a relationship, either personal or institutional.

A corollary of "harmony" within the bureaucracy was the rule that prevented territorial infringement by departments or individuals. The overlapping product and administrative departmental jurisdictions would seem to encourage infringements, and it did. But, rather than labelling the event infringement, it was called "duplication" and deemed positive. The JFIs managed to avoid open conflict because each department operated autonomously without any obligation to communicate or coordinate with another department. If the departments attempted to coordinate activities, the areas of infringement would be exposed. Therefore, the departments of Japanese banks and brokers liked to be represented by their own personnel, even when this led to duplication and wasted personnel resources.

During the 1980s, the JFIs were distributing billions of dollars of fixed-income assets to Japanese clients, as well as purchasing assets for their own accounts. The JFIs had personnel in the U.S. and Tokyo examining potential assets. The departments responsible for distribution had difficulty coordinating their activities with their colleagues who were creating assets. The distribution departments were almost always dependent on foreign intermediaries to provide complicated products, rather than on their own internal sources, until the product became a low-margin commodity.

OUTSIDE INFLUENCE REJECTED

The JFI bureaucracy thought of itself as a self-contained entity. The JFI invested in various overseas markets in a perfunctory manner. It received information and proposals from outside sources. The information and proposals then moved through the bureaucracy in an assembly-line process. The JFI guarded its "independence." It wanted its own infrastructure, despite costs or profits. It viewed foreign employees and advisors as outsiders and treated them as such. The JFIs arrogantly tried to enter new markets and locations without dependence on foreigners.

The JFI selected outside advisors as ornaments. They were generally "famous" people or had advertisable resumes. Their functions were not clear. The advisors typically might give a monologue about local or international subjects. JFI staff did not engage in an interchange of ideas with the advisor. JFI personnel liked to receive their information in the same form as their transactions, i.e., fully packaged. There was no critique. The JFI personnel, at most, offered an opinion but rarely asked a penetrating question. Their questions generally pertained to superficial mechanics, statistics or gossip. Without an interchange, the contact became largely a formality. The JFI assumed that knowledge and skill would be transferred by memorization of techniques and data. The Japanese educational system instilled this method into the salarymen and the firms.

" **The JFI selected outside advisors as ornaments. They were generally 'famous' people, or had advertisable resumes. Their functions were not clear.**"

This could be observed in the interface between the JFIs and their acquisitions and joint ventures, as well. The JFI was not penalized for this superficiality because, unlike the Japanese manufacturers, it had no profit or market-related constraints in the 1980s. In the manufacturing sector, the physical product was the focal point for analysis in terms of design, market, and quality. Success was ultimately determined by market acceptance, cost, and profit.

Effective communication might occur in different ways in the financial services area. If the JFI had made a passive investment in an entity which traded U.S. Treasuries or commodity futures and options, the requirements for communication were minimal. If the JFI hired foreign employees to perform a specialized function and installed a profit-sharing arrangement, little interchange was required. But the JFI expected to learn skills, an exchange of ideas was vital. As many new trading techniques and practices became common, the JFIs were more apt to learn them because of evolving standardization. Financial services products were easily copied by competitors. Widespread usage reduced market inefficiencies. The JFIs were willing to enter these markets without regard to costs or expected returns. They set up cost structures with no earnings constraints. Also, profit margins were lowered so that the successful high profit product became a price-sensitive commodity by the time the JFIs got involved. Unfortunately, there was still a requirement for judgment of risk, which cannot be standardized. In many cases in the 1980s, the JFIs tried to superimpose standardization on areas requiring judgment, such as the U.S. real estate market.

Asset growth and market share mentality reinforced this tendency towards restricting communication and emphasizing capital. Capital was critical. The JFIs were able to achieve asset growth wherever they had sufficient capital. If their capital was unlimited, they would be able to choose areas to dominate—those characterized by size, low margins, and standardizations but not necessarily those with low risk. Risk could relate, for instance, to change in interest rates as well as to credit.

The inability of the JFIs' bureaucracy to admit outside influences, either directly or indirectly, hampered the evaluation process. Accustomed to a closed, tightly controlled market in Japan, the JFIs were impervious to proper outside sources.

The JFIs frequently treated communication with foreign investee companies in a passive manner. This led to less and less contact and, hence, to an unproductive association which was characterized by brittleness.

JFI personnel tended to select foreign advisors and special outside relationships on a personal level. If there was no formal structure created, a relationship ended when a personnel rotation occurred. The salaryman wanted to establish loyalty with his own selections and did not want to be encumbered by his predecessor's appointments. Thus, it was very difficult to institutionalize a relationship. Stated differently, institutional memory was a problem for the JFIs.

MANAGEMENT RESPONSIBILITIES OFTEN CEREMONIAL

Business was conducted according to specified rules within the hierarchy. The general managers and managing directors were mainly concerned with personnel and policy issues, but a managing director's role could become largely ceremonial within a JFI. The general manager was responsible for a department, which could be either line or staff. Promotion to general manager meant that a salaryman was allowed to manage a department. One suspects that, at times, the creation of new departments might have been a function of an excess supply of general managers, rather than of organizational or economic necessity.

General managers managed, but did not run, departments. The responsibility for handling projects or transactions was often dealt with by deputy general managers and managers. JFI salarymen were very ambitious. The deputy general managers and managers wanted to be promoted. Personal compensation was not an issue; recognition and promotion were. In order to be promoted, the individual had to have the support of his immediate superior in the hierarchy. The most important factor in obtaining a superior's recommendation was loyalty. In addition, avoidance of mistakes was important, although mistakes were not necessarily defined to include bad investments, poor decisions, or lack of performance. As long as the salaryman followed the prescribed, politically safe path, he satisfied the requirement of avoiding mistakes. The salaryman could be described as averse to risk, yet he took substantial risks overseas. These risks were politically acceptable.

> **" Promotion to general manager meant that a salaryman was allowed to manage a department. One suspects that, at times, the creation of new departments might have been a function of an excess supply of general managers, rather than of organizational or economic necessity. "**

Performance and profit were not part of the criteria. JFI salarymen who had dismal records managing international securities were, nevertheless, promoted. Vaguely defined "management skills" were appreciated. These could be seen as the ability to cultivate appropriate relationships within the bureaucracy. The process was highly subjective, even in areas such as money management, where performance was easy to quantify and should have been the determinant for evaluation.

Foreign institutions were politicized as well; however, the extent and consequences of politicization were more severe at JFIs. Moreover, JFIs were supposed to be different. Again, it is possible to cite the forty-five-year halcyon market environment, lack of competition, and lack of concern for performance as forces that removed normal discipline and proper perspective from the JFI world. The promotion criteria of JFIs is only one illustration of the bureaucratic ossification that developed during this period. American banks may have been subject to political forces as well, but mistakes ultimately forced change.

The hierarchical management structure of the JFIs resembled that of a government bureaucracy or army. Both were certainly respected role models in terms of power, organizational structure, and long-term objectives, however the attempt to impose that structure on overseas business activity inevitably resulted in failure.

JAPANESE POSTAL SAVINGS SYSTEM GIVES INSIGHTS

The Japanese Postal Savings System (JPSS) provides a useful insight into the way the Japanese financial system functioned in the 1980s.[13] The JPSS was a huge institutional investor with deposits of 104.5 trillion yen, or the equivalent of $685 billion in 1985. The deposits were acquired because the 23,000 post offices were given permission to set up tax-exempt, interest-bearing accounts for up to 3 million yen ($19,000 US equivalent) per individual. Japanese individuals, however, opened up multiple accounts, such that there were more than twice as many accounts as there were residents in Japan. The Japanese government could not prevent this proliferation because the widespread nature of the practice made intervention extremely politically unpopular. The JPSS was administered by the Ministry of Posts and Telecommunication, which often had territorial battles with the MOF. The JPSS underwent revision in the late 1980s, which, among other things, removed the tax-exempt privilege. By 1992, the foreign press had discovered the JPSS and was writing about its size and influence.[14] It is important to examine how they operated in the 1980s.

Salomon Brothers was the first foreign firm allowed to sell securities directly to the JPSS, beginning in 1985. The JPSS, like other Japanese institutional investors, was forced to look at the foreign bond market because yields on Japanese bonds were low. In 1983, Salomon began to contact the JPSS. This mainly consisted of hand-delivering a list of bond offerings daily to JPSS. The JPSS would only accept hand deliveries, as opposed to offerings made via telephone, which is customary. This arm of the Ministry of Posts and Telecommunications relied on the most basic form of communication, totally devoid of technology. (Fortunately, the Salomon Brothers' Tokyo office was only two blocks away from the JPSS building.)

---

13 Viner, *Inside*, pp. 7, 236-238.
14 Chandler, Clay, "Japan's Banks Find Tough Rival in an Aggressive Postal System," *The Wall Street Journal*, October 29, 1992, p. A-10; "Safe as Post Offices," *The Economist*, December 26, 1992, p. 104.

The JPSS started doing business with Salomon indirectly in 1984. Salomon would offer bonds to the JPSS directly. If the JPSS accepted the offer, Salomon would have to sell the bonds to a Japanese broker as intermediary. The Japanese broker would officially sell the bonds to the JPSS. The Japanese broker was simply a booking agent, because the JPSS technically could not deal directly with a foreign firm, even though it had a registered branch in Japan. In 1985, the JPSS altered its rule to allow official contact with a foreigner. This event was unusual enough to be accompanied by a ceremony and announcement in the Japanese press. Any concession to a foreigner was significant.

The JPSS is an extreme example of the bureaucratic approach to investing, but it does illustrate the state of development of the large Japanese investors as late as the 1980s. The JPSS had no concept of money management. It was simply purchasing high-yielding assets on an almost whimsical basis without regard to currency risk, relative value, liquidity, or its own liability structure.

LEADERSHIP LACKING WITHIN BUREAUCRACY

Leadership, as opposed to management, was not evident among the senior people at the JFIs. The senior people did not have a reliable objective flow of information. Their role was primarily ceremonial. Direction did not emanate from them. There was extreme reluctance to take responsibility for an action. JFIs' senior officials did not establish priorities. Individual departments followed the latest business or investment fashion, rather than attempting to focus. The senior officials could not infringe or interfere with the bureaucratic hierarchy. This yielded overlapping jurisdictions that slowed the pace of activity but was a poor substitute for proper checks and balances.

Many observers assumed that the Japanese system operated effectively in any environment. Peter Tasker, in his otherwise perceptive book, *Inside Japan*,[15] saw the JFIs as comparable to the Japanese manufacturers:

> Can the Japanese do the same to financial services as they have done to the car and camera industries? Skeptics cite the need for

---

[15] Tasker, Peter, *Inside Japan*, London: Sedgwick & Jackson, 1987, p. 73.

high-level political contacts (overseas), sophisticated risk-management, and fast, imaginative decision making, none of them obvious Japanese strengths . . . There is nothing especially complex about the banking and securities business. New financial products, unlike new electronic gadgets, cannot be patented; once developed, they are available to be copied by everyone. The essential ingredients of success are power, organization, and ambition, qualities the Japanese have in abundance. Political influence and experience can both be bought. Japanese financial institutions number amongst their consultants former high officials of the Bank of England and the Federal Reserve, and an ex-chancellor of the Federal Republic of Germany.

> **" Leadership, as opposed to management, was not evident among the senior people at the JFIs. The senior people did not have a reliable objective flow of information. Their role was primarily ceremonial. "**

Tasker was wrong. He thought that the world was again underestimating the Japanese. He accurately portrayed certain mechanical aspects of the securities and financial markets as being easily duplicated. These are also likely to become price-sensitive commodities with little or no profit margins, and risks which need to be understood, as these techniques are more likely to result in trading activity rather than fee business. He does not mention the areas of judgment and risk evaluation that created problems for the JFIs. He does outline how the JFIs will correct these flaws. He mentioned the Japanese strengths—power, organization, and ambition—which were assumed to be present in the JFIs' structure. It is here that bureaucracy was confused with organization. The JFIs' organization evolved into a bureaucracy which was protected by rules, a bull market, a strong economy, and no competition. When the JFIs operated in overseas markets, they still retained the power and ambition, which, without the proper organization, led them astray.

In a recent op-ed article, Tasker barely mentions the JFIs. He seems to blame the "bubble economy" for the difficulties. He observes that "The financial system is gravely impaired," but nowhere does he refer to his misplaced optimism of 1987, as expressed in *Inside Japan*.[16] As we shall see, several writers in recent publications fail to correct the false impression they created in the 1980s about JFIs.

[16] Tasker, Peter, "The End of Japan, Inc.," *The Wall Street Journal*, June 30, 1993, p. A-14.

CHAPTER 8

THE PITFALLS OF PROVINCIALISM

Harmony, homogeneity, and group consciousness are characteristics generally associated with Japan and the Japanese system. Carefully nurtured by
government, family, school, and corporation, these traits are usually credited with much of corporate Japan's spectacular success. At home and
abroad, Japan's growth is always attributed to collective effort, its awesome competitiveness to monolithic strength.

But the reality is that Japan's emphasis on cohesiveness is excessive,
and this excessiveness had serious negative implications for the JFIs' forays into overseas business in the 1980s. Japan's homogeneous culture is a
nearly closed society. Security, order and control are everywhere present—
and so, too, that pervasive spirit of Japanese uniqueness and aloneness in
the world which government, school, media, and corporation also work
diligently to build.

The Japanese system carefully screens what ideas and influences can
be admitted. It rejects the Western emphasis on individualism, dialogue,
and criticism while taking as prized imports Western science, fashion, and
usable concepts, such as Edward Demming's theories on quality control.

The Japanese system does not allow objective criticism about its past
to be introduced to its citizens. It prefers to erase history, rather than encourage meaningful discussion about its past. The Japanese government
does not understand the implications of promoting uniqueness, conformity,
and exclusion. On March 16, 1993, the Japanese Supreme Court upheld a
decision to "whitewash . . . (its) wartime history."[1] The Court ruled in

---

[1] "Erasing History," *The Nation*, April 19, 1993, p. 508.

favor of the Japanese Ministry of Education that had "demanded that (Professor Saburo) Ienaga delete all sections on wartime atrocities (from his textbook)." Professor Ienaga had been commissioned by the Ministry of Education to write a textbook, *The History of Japan*. When the Ministry censored the textbook, Professor Ienaga filed a lawsuit challenging the Ministry. The suit was filed *twenty-eight* years ago! The Japanese system prefers to manufacture truth. Reality is not a factor. It overlooks mistakes.

The same Japanese system that did not analyze its past had difficulty understanding how it could not assimilate foreigners, or why its methods could not be transferred abroad. Those who suggested that JFIs could easily adjust did not realize that their flaws were fundamental and structural. These weaknesses were societal and cannot be corrected by reading a how-to-do-it book or hiring a few foreigners.

Such an environment does not encourage or even tolerate assimilation. The core of Japanese culture must be pure in order to be unique. This made the JFIs' task difficult, if not impossible. How could a JFI retain its purity when it established a significant physical presence in overseas business? How could a JFI salaryman live abroad and not be contaminated? How could a JFI salaryman relate to his foreign colleagues? How should a JFI treat its foreign employees? Could a JFI incorporate practical Western business methods and technology into its operation without modifying its Japanese structure? Was the Japanese manufacturers' experience a precedent? Was a foreigner expected to matriculate through the bureaucracy, or was he distinct? Could the foreigner become a specialist, generalist, or manager within a JFI? Could the foreigner assimilate? If not, was the foreign employee, therefore, a temporary fixture to be replaced by a JFI salaryman after skills, market dominance, and clients were developed? Did the foreign employee ultimately occupy a subservient role?

MYTH OF LOCALIZATION

As the JFIs rapidly expanded their U.S. operations in the 1980s, they encountered the issue of assimilation head-on because they had to hire larger and larger numbers of Americans to meet rising manpower requirements. As has been described, the JFIs had to enter into multiple joint ventures and make numerous acquisitions to rectify their lack of skills. Foreign observers identified this as *the* critical need for JFIs and assumed that successful coopting of foreign talent would be easy—it could be bought. JFI officials were speaking loudly about the goal of "localization." Their aim, they said, was to hire local staff so that business could become local in nature.

Many reporters and some prospective employees believed them. But pronouncements about localization had more to do with the rhetoric of corporate policy—formed to make the JFIs look like international institutions to its Tokyo audience—than with the realities of business practice. Implementing localization was never seriously considered by the salarymen and departments establishing overseas beachheads. Instead, the JFIs struggled to impose a Japanese system on their U.S. offices.

Foreign employees were certainly necessary. Language ability, skills, and U.S. clients were in limited supply. The JFIs' ambition and overconfidence of the 1980s demanded that they establish major operations in overseas businesses, either abroad or in Tokyo, to recycle assets and expand their organizations. In the 1970s, JFIs were content to allow some of their European and Asian offices to operate passively as a booking venue for syndicated loans or floating rate notes. Neither operation requires major commitments in terms of staff. By the 1980s, though, the JFIs wanted a higher profile.

The JFI salarymen's feeling of separateness and superiority was surely reinforced by their physical contact with the U.S. in the 1980s. They were the target of so much attention and so many requests for money from foreigners that they naturally felt as if they belonged to an elite system. As with most people who travel or live abroad, there is a natural inclination to want to be with fellow countrymen, to eat familiar food, and to compare the host country with one's native country. When the JFI salaryman arrived at JFK airport in New York, he did not find order, security, and homogeneity. He found apparent chaos, filth, poverty, diversity, and rudeness. The customs officials at JFK airport were not the neatly attired, serious people whom he encountered at Narita. The American customs officials were often chatting socially with their colleagues. When the salaryman entered the lobby to find transportation, he was accosted by a mob of drivers, all offering trips to Manhattan at various prices, most of which were exorbitantly high.

If he survived this turmoil, he entered the taxi line. The New York taxi ride from JFK to Manhattan would reinforce his view of the superiority of the Japanese system. The JFI salaryman may have been exposed to Third World cities such as Lagos, Bombay, or Beijing, but this rite of passage was shocking. The taxi was likely to be filthy, and the JFI salaryman must have been perplexed by the plexiglass barrier—translucent because of the grime—between the driver and the passenger. He would sit in this hazy capsule, which often reeked of stale food or worse. He could not smoke because it was prohibited. The driver, whose comprehension of English was often poor, seemed unsure about the destination. The taxi's defective shock absorbers ensured a rough ride. The decaying infrastructure, pot-holes, drab houses, and dilapidated surroundings en route underscored the decline of America. The scene at the New York hotel was also unfamiliar, with brusque people seeming to emerge from everywhere wanting a tip. The salaryman was accustomed to clean taxis driven by men who some-times wear white gloves, where tipping is not practiced but service is.

The prevalence of homeless people and panhandlers was a stark con-trast to Tokyo in the 1980s, where the only derelicts visible were a handful of alcoholics wandering around a few train stations. If the salaryman was stationed in New York and commuted, he invariably compared the disre-pair and foul odor of Grand Central Station to the efficiency and cleanli-ness of Tokyo Station. The two-hour, crowded commute to a small, tidy house outside Tokyo seemed less onerous than before. He sensed that peo-ple were not connected to New York; everyone seemed to be hustling. At its worst, it was a form of chaos.

The JFI salaryman's tendency to generalize created false impressions in a nation as diverse as America. The salaryman's Japanese frame of ref-erence was very different from that of the American, and his foray into American business was not an attempt to understand, but to conquer. The hostile physical environment could only encourage his feeling of separateness.

The need to gain access to American skills, however, remained. The rotation system added pressure to hire foreign specialists. Fortunately, spe-cialists could be viewed as separate entities who would not pollute the organization, just as American baseball players could hit their home runs for the Yomiuri Giants or Hanshin Tigers without becoming part of the team. The techniques could be learned by observation and then incorpo-rated into the system. There was never any consideration of interchange of ideas, only debriefing. The JFIs expected their foreign advisors and foreign intermediaries to present fully-packaged information or transactions. Im-plicit in this process was the assumption that the foreign specialist would be made redundant. In a worst case scenario, the JFI could "buy" any American expert or provide capital to a targeted group, thus co-opting the desired skill. In the latter case, the JFI would have the benefit of the spe-cialist and manage him outside of the organization.

The JFI salaryman generally spent most of his time abroad with his Japanese colleagues and Japanese clients. The contact with foreigners—either associates or clients—was generally perfunctory.

AMERICAN MBAs BECOME STATUS SYMBOLS

In addition to specialists, the JFIs experimented with younger American employees. They hired recent graduates of America's most prestigious business schools. The M.B.A. was a much sought-after symbol. The JFIs assumed that the business schools were significantly responsible for the American sophistication in financial services. Furthermore, glamour and popularity of these schools in the 1980s contained elements of trend and fashion that the JFIs found enticing to follow. They wanted to buy this expertise.

" **The symbolic value of the M.B.A. degree was significant to the JFI salaryman.** "

In order to do this, they recruited graduates and also sent their Japanese staff to American business schools for two years in order to learn practical American skills. Symbolically, this effort followed the JFIs' rhetoric about localization, in that U.S. business would be better understood, and local practices would be co-opted. In many cases, the JFIs paid for the employees' expenses and tuition. Since very few employees leave Japanese corporations to work for competitors, the JFIs felt secure in making long-term investments in training people. This does not mean that the training had any substantive merit. As has been shown, it was often superficial, with no impact. In theory at least, the JFIs have an advantage in the time, effort, and money expended in preparing their employees. Ironically, in 1992, some of the JFIs spoke of curtailing the practice of sending their Japanese employees to U.S. business schools, because many of these employees left JFIs to join foreign firms.

The symbolic value of the M.B.A. degree was significant to the JFI salaryman. The Japanese degree-holder was often introduced as being knowledgeable about American business because he held an M.B.A. from Harvard, Stanford, or Wharton. Sometimes the English side of a Japanese business card (which are often printed with each of the two languages on opposing sides) would indicate the M.B.A. also.

The JFI employees at American business schools, however, usually pursued the same pattern of separation as their colleagues in business. An American graduate student who was fluent in Japanese described his salaryman classmates at Wharton as totally group-oriented. The group was confined to Japanese. They sat next to each other in class and spent all their time together. It never occurred to them, either in terms of curiosity, interest or future contacts, to extend themselves outside of their group.

The impact of the business school was minimal on the salaryman. He was there to obtain a degree for its prestige content. He was supposed to absorb practical techniques by memorizing formulas and listening to lectures. No interchange or participation was expected. When he returned to his position at the JFI, the newly-acquired information could be imparted to his firm by osmosis. Since he had learned little and even had less opportunity to share it without being seen as politically or culturally unreliable, the benefit to the JFI was at best suspect.

NOMURA TRIES TO SNAG AMERICAN GRADS

Most observers in the 1980s viewed the Japanese hiring of American and British graduates as part of their long-term strategy to dominate the U.S. and world financial markets. One wrote as follows, "Nomura reportedly hires more new graduates from Oxford and Cambridge than the Foreign Office, traditionally the leading employer of Britain's best and brightest."[2] These graduates were hired to better "fulfill (Nomura's) . . . ambitious goals."

It is easy to trace the results of Nomura's efforts in Al Alletzhauser's *The House of Nomura*,[3] a book that Nomura tried vigorously to suppress both abroad and in Japan. (Incidentally, the interpretation of libel laws in Japan is quite loose in that an accurate, fully verified fact about a person might nonetheless be libelous because it embarrassed him.) Why was Nomura, a hugely powerful company, so fearful of this book? Why did it

---

2 Burstein, *Yen!*, p. 243.
3 Alletzhauser, Albert, *The House of Nomura: The Rise to Supremacy of the World's Most Powerful Company--The Inside Story of a Legendary Dynasty*, London: Bloomsbury, 1990.

even think it could stop publication abroad? Michael Lewis' book, *Liar's Poker*, which painted an amusing but highly unflattering portrait of Salomon Brothers, was not the target of a comparable campaign by Salomon Brothers.

In the chapter on "Ivy League and Oxbridge," Alletzhauser describes Nomura's experience with the "best and brightest" American and English graduates. The policy as he describes it was direct: "Nomura would hire students straight out of America's and England's finest universities to shape their minds and control their lives."[4] Nomura used an agent to interview the students and hired twenty-eight graduates in 1982 and thirty-five in 1983. By 1985, none of the class of 1982 remained at Nomura, and most of the others had "left of their own accord."[5] Some were enticed away by non-Japanese firms; almost all were repelled by the Nomura environment.

During this period, Nomura received considerable recognition because of its power and visibility. It would seem to be a likely employer for young Americans and Britons to select. The JFIs' reputation for professionalism, long-term planning, excellent training, and overseas ambitions had to be alluring. To be sure, the graduates took very little risk in their adventure with Nomura. Their exposure to the Japanese language, culture, and business was useful experience. In many cases, the Nomura program led them to responsible jobs and high salaries at foreign firms who needed people with some understanding of Japan to staff their Japanese equity departments.[6]

Japanese training, with its—in a Western sense—stultifying emphasis on conformity and company loyalty, however, was not suitable for foreigners. Nomura, as well as others, ignored the Westerners' need for interaction, stimulus, competitive wages, and feedback. The JFIs' staff in the U.S. went to prestigious schools and hired Americans without considering their career paths or needs. Indeed, the JFIs never really could reflect upon the career paths of the young graduates because the individual departments were managed from Tokyo. How could important personnel departments in Tokyo manage the graduates' careers, when even a cursory investigation would have revealed incompatibility with the JFI bureaucracy? They could never become prototypical Japanese salarymen. But then, deep down, the JFIs never had any intention of integrating the graduates. The "localiza-

---

4 Alletzhauser, *The House of Nomura*, p. 227.
5 Alletzhauser, *The House of Nomura*, p. 235.
6 Alletzhauser, *The House of Nomura*, p. 235.

tion" policy initiated in Tokyo was designed to advertise presence. Body count, not personnel development, was what mattered.

The scenario of one American employee who managed to stay with a JFI for several years after graduation, is revealing. She requested that the company transfer her to Tokyo for one year so that she could improve her Japanese language ability, which was already adequate. The JFI allowed her to do this. She moved into the company dormitory with young married couples. The housing provided by this huge company was in disrepair. The apartment walls were shedding plaster, and there was little hot water. The American woman was ostracized by the Japanese women who lived in the dormitory. Upon returning to the U.S., she spent several more years with the company but finally resigned, realizing that despite her skills, loyalty and ability, she had no future. The constant rotation of people, the lack of planning, the absence of performance criteria, and the overwhelming weight of bureaucracy was too frustrating.

In 1992, a bright JFI official confided that he did not know how to evaluate an American's resume. In Japan, it is relatively simple for a JFI official to look at a Japanese student's resume and determine acceptability. Graduates of prestigious Japanese universities are generally always acceptable, the only problems in the 1980s being the scarcity of available students and the keen competition for them. In fact, the Japanese government has regulated when the recruitment process can begin—a date regularly violated by Japanese companies, which need to start as early as possible. Even when there is a shortage of students, the JFIs are likely to run secret checks to determine whether a candidate is proper; for example, he cannot be ethnic Korean or burakumin.

The JFI official's quandary regarding American resumes was the result of a diversity of backgrounds, personalities, capabilities, and ethics of Americans. The mechanical, superficial methods of selection used by JFIs would not be effective in screening Americans. The fact that a recruit attended an Ivy League school might be a positive indication but might also be irrelevant when viewed in the broad context of qualification and job description.

Overall, the official concluded that foreigners could not really be integrated within the JFI structure. When asked if his firm should distinguish between specialist and management roles for foreigners, he recognized the dilemma. Without hesitation, he stated that the Japanese were excellent managers. Implicitly, the foreigners were outside his system, and the Japanese were inside his structure. Unfortunately, he still was left with the task of selecting the foreigner.

FOREIGN SPECIALISTS NEEDED, IF NOT WANTED

The JFIs' need to hire foreign specialists became increasingly critical during the 1980s. The Japanese salaryman did not have the skills required for the JFIs' new business activities. The system precluded developing qualified people internally. Outsiders had to be found.

The list of possible specialist skills is endless. For example:

1. MONEY MANAGEMENT

    - Public overseas cash markets
        - equities and fixed income
        - U.S., Europe, Asia

    - Derivatives
        - equities and fixed income
        - domestic and foreign
        - options and futures

    - Private equity

    - Foreign real estate
        - U.S., Europe, Asia

    - Venture capital
        - U.S., Europe, Asia

    - LBO equity and debt
        - U.S., Europe, Asia

2. ASSET-LIABILITY MANAGEMENT

3. FOREIGN LOAN PORTFOLIO

    - Private credit analysis

    - U.S. corporate and real estate

4. CAPITAL MARKET

    - Derivatives

- currency and interest rate swaps
- options and futures

■ Product structuring

- Japan, U.S., Europe, Asia

5. MARKETING

■ Japanese products overseas

■ Overseas products in Japan

■ Deal origination

Additionally, many specialists areas could be subdivided into sections of further specialization, each requiring specific experience and focus to understand it.

The JFIs had an interest in most of these sectors. It was already clear that deregulation in Japan would eventually allow all of the JFIs to compete in money management and other areas. The overseas market was crucial in terms of actual business and in terms of learning how to compete in the Japanese market after restrictions were lifted.

Just as the JFIs were able to "rent" names of individuals or firms through joint ventures or acquisitions, it was assumed by Japanese and foreigners alike that individuals could be "purchased" to work for JFIs. It would be only a matter of price. In fact, they were able to hire many foreign specialists. As one commentator stated, "Experience could be bought. They (the JFIs) have recruited a succession of top traders and strategists, all of whom receive salaries far above those of their new (i.e., Japanese) bosses."[7] Talent and expertise usually does gravitate towards compensation.

Implicit in the assumption of hiring experience was the notion that a narrow technical or specific skill would provide a simple solution. For example, an American futures trader could be plugged into the JFI system to provide expertise to the necessary departments in New York and Tokyo. Baseball again provides an analogy. If a team needed a shortstop, it would find one in the free agent market and negotiate a contract for his services. He would immediately be productive and fit into the team.

---

7 Tasker, *Inside Japan,* p. 273.

How then did the specialist fit into the JFI structure? The possibilities could be viewed as a spectrum with degrees of interaction between the foreigner and the JFI.

NO INTERACTION——————TOTAL INTERACTION

1. *No interaction*—The JFI would provide capital and pay expenses. The foreign specialist would have a profit-sharing arrangement. This method was easiest to monitor. It was applicable for some traders, portfolio managers, salesmen, swap teams and leasing specialists. Their performance was easy to quantify, and they could be eliminated when necessary. (An example of how quickly a JFI can get rid of its staff is illustrated by the JFI that fired all the foreigners in its leasing department in one day, after the business had started to lose money. Interestingly, the JFI management had failed to heed the advice of its foreign staff when they warned of credit issues that later became problems.)

At this end of the spectrum, the JFI could advertise expertise and dream of osmosis. The foreign specialist would not be frustrated by communication difficulties because there was little need to interact with the JFI structure. The capital and expense requirements would be decided in advance. The person or team would function as an entity separate from the JFI. He might give information unilaterally to his colleagues but would not be organizationally dependent on them.

The foreign specialist or entity is outside the system. If the JFI picks the right specialist, a profitable association can exist. Daiwa Securities made such an arrangement with Andrew Stone, a mortgage specialist, in 1990. Stone was a Salomon Brother alumnus. Daiwa provided the capital and gave Stone 35 percent of the net revenues of his department. Stone was allowed to build a trading, distribution, and origination department. Stone was not controlled by Tokyo or the bureaucracy. In the fiscal year ending March, 1993, his department "split about $80 million of Daiwa's estimated $225 million from mortgages."[8]

2. *Moderate Interaction*—This relationship would specify a high salary for a number of years and discretionary bonus. It could apply

---

8 Jereski, Laura, "Street's New Stars Shine in Hazy Mortgage-Bond Sky," *The Wall Street Journal*, May 25, 1993, p. C-1.

to traders, swap specialists, salesmen, loan officers, portfolio managers, investment bankers, and merchant bankers—specialists who could function as part of the JFI, with performance criteria as the main objective. Communication would be necessary in terms of trading decisions, loan approvals, and involvement with JFI departments who contact Japanese clients. JFI managers would be in a general supervisory position.

3. *Total interaction*—In this situation, the foreign specialist would become a JFI employee. The foreigner would have a higher salary than the JFI scale and a detailed employment description. He would not be subject to the JFI rotation system. Most specialists fit into this category. The foreigner would have a Japanese manager. His performance would depend on interaction with the JFI structure, while his department and activities might be altered or his job terminated, if necessary.

If the foreign specialist fit into the non-integration category, there was little active interface with the JFI; hence, frustration deriving from lack of communication or miscommunication was not a factor. Performance criteria were straightforward so that each party understood the expectations of the relationship.

When there was a requirement for interaction between the JFI and the foreign specialist, the extensive amount of foreign personnel turnover and the general dissatisfaction on the part of the foreigner and the JFI indicated that there were significant problems. Foreigners proved to be relatively easy to hire in the 1980s, but the results were unsatisfactory. The foreigners who remained at the JFIs were either very young or passive types who generally could not get as good a job elsewhere. Instances of foreigners in substantive senior management positions are extremely rare. One JFI general manager noted that his foreign staff members were not productive and were reluctant to leave the firm if they made over $100,000 per year. They could not obtain comparable salaries elsewhere. Otherwise, though, turnover of foreign staff was quite high.

SALARYMEN RESENT FOREIGNERS' HIGH COMPENSATION

The compensation issue cannot be dismissed lightly. The JFI salaryman resented the higher compensation packages of the foreigners. It was wrongly assumed that the salaryman would view the foreigner's compensation as important for his company's progress. Under this scenario, the JFI salaryman was supposed to subordinate his natural feelings of envy and jealousy for the good of the JFI—yet another sacrifice by the individual Japanese. On the contrary, JFI salarymen were accustomed to order and hierarchy. The foreigners did not fit into this structure. They were hired to perform. If it could not be precisely determined that the foreigner had contributed to a certain amount of profits, the JFI salaryman thought that the foreigner was overpaid. Unless there was a trading book where exact profits and losses were tabulated, it was often difficult to discern exactly what an individual produced. The salaryman would generally consider any subjective contribution as deriving from Japanese personnel rather than from foreigners.

The salaryman was naturally competitive. A higher salary was interpreted negatively by a JFI employee who had been conditioned to accept uniform pay levels, dress codes and social traits. He could not understand how a colleague could be paid more than he was. If the foreigner was deemed to be structurally separate, the salaryman might have adjusted.

Many of the same traits were found at foreign firms in Tokyo where highly paid Japanese employees were also extremely competitive about compensation. The smallest differences in compensation might result in disappointment and controversy. The Japanese were no different than Westerners; if the measurement standard was compensation, the Japanese would focus on money. If the measurement standard was bureaucratic promotion, as in the JFIs, the salaryman would prioritize politics.

SALARYMEN AND FOREIGN COLLEAGUES GENERATE FRICTION

Where interaction was required between foreign employees and the JFIs' Japanese staff, communication usually proved to be a major source of friction. The differences in cultural and educational background were too great. The foreigner needed dialogue and informational feedback. He responded to clarity and precision, valued individual choice over group cohesion. He did not feel secure in an environment characterized by vagueness. He found strict adherence to hierarchy and intolerance of disagreement oppressive.

This was the exact opposite of the salaryman's ideal working environment, where order and security, bureaucratic hierarchy, superficial harmony, peer pressure, political orientation towards Tokyo, and a general lack of concern about the success of an overseas assignment, were the norm. Clarity frightened the salaryman because of the implications of accountability and individual responsibility.

Even if the foreigner showed patience and was accustomed to working in a large organization, the communication gap was a chasm. Sooner or later, the foreigner would sense that the JFI salaryman's concerns were, first and foremost, his political connections to Tokyo, where knowledge of local markets was absent.

" Clarity frightened the salaryman because of the implications of accountability and individual responsibility."

After a few months of working together, one foreign employee of a JFI described his relationship with his Japanese colleagues as one of frustration. The foreigner worked in an area that was supposed to generate fees, and the JFI was not employing its capital to make a transaction. The business was not price-sensitive, and required a high degree of coordination with other departments in order to be successful, which it most emphatically was not. The foreigner respected his Japanese colleagues' intelligence, and found them to be pleasant. There were no negative personal feelings. But he did not find their attitude constructive or positive. His colleagues were resigned to their three-year assignment as a sentence to be passively and stoically endured. Already, the foreigner knew that there was no point in devoting a significant effort to establishing relationships with his colleagues because they would be transferred and had no real interest in a serious mutual understanding. Nor had the salarymen focused on a business or plan. They were chasing isolated, mostly unrealistic transactions without energy. When the foreigner approached the JFI employees about examining a particular transaction or area, they responded with silence, and the foreigner knew that his idea was relegated to a black hole. When discussing a proposal, the foreigner observed that the salarymen seemed to be almost daydreaming.

A foreign employee who had a position requiring interaction with a JFI faced terrible isolation. The JFI salaryman's educational background prepared him to respect authority, avoid public confrontation, and absorb information, but discouraged an active exchange of ideas or any informational feedback. Salarymen might reject an idea or transaction with a negative response, or no response, but rarely with a qualified response. The emphasis was on absorption of information, not organization or critique. The "wet" approach dictated ambiguity, not clarity and rational behavior, even when dealing with Western employees. The salaryman knew that Tokyo personnel needed to be given information which confirmed the wisdom of its policies.

The JFI attitude towards language was another factor inhibiting communication. The typical JFI salaryman, as was the case with other Japanese, regarded a fellow Japanese colleague's fluency in English with suspicion. Despite the large demand for English courses in Japan, and despite the fact that Japanese students had, in theory, been exposed to English language courses in school, competence in English often had negative connotations of admiring *gaijin* (foreign) society.

If a JFI salaryman was fluent in English, he was sought after by foreigners because a conversation was possible (although conversation did not necessarily mean communication). Non-English speaking colleagues regarded this association with foreigners as potentially corrupting. JFI salarymen were quick to point out the English speakers because they were conspicuous. Often JFI salarymen would demean a colleague by saying that he speaks English well but had no power. Domestic departments were generally referred to as power bases as opposed to international departments, although there are exceptions such as IBJ. At senior levels, English-speaking ability could be a political liability as conformity and "Japaneseness" are somehow made less pure by frequent contact with foreigners or even the possibility of contact with foreigners. English-speaking salarymen were constantly trying to reaffirm their Japaneseness. In the 1980s, senior JFI officials who spoke English well were generally well-known to most foreign financial officials in Tokyo, as well as their JFI counterparts, because of their limited number. There were very few foreigners who made the effort to meet the non-English speaking officials of JFIs.

The Japanese language itself reflects the form and hierarchy present in Japanese society. English words, such as relationship, obligation, and friendship, usually have different meanings to Japanese and Americans. The Japanese may use these words as formal expressions in order to be polite. Relationship is a particularly over-used word by the Japanese. In general, a JFI employee means coincidence of interest, rather than relationship when he speaks about a foreign firm or individual. The Japanese translation of English adds to the complexity of communication. In the

1980s, even foreigners who spoke Japanese were confronted with communication—as distinguished from language—problems, since the lack of clarity and dialogue were still present. In some ways, it was easier for a Japanese to be direct in English rather than in his native tongue, because the formality of the Japanese language tends to soften expressions and create vagueness in the interests of correct behavior.

Feiler made a similar observation about the Japanese language:

> English . . . is perfect for confrontation. Not only does the language favor frankness, but children are taught to be as direct as possible. Even our idioms are different: Japanese are constantly reminded to be polite, considerate, and mannerly, while Americans are told to "talk straight," "get to the point," and "put it on the line."[9]

One curious feature of the JFIs was their occasional need to have a foreigner introduce an idea. The foreigner, in some cases, was not an employee. Politically, it would be less threatening to have an outsider present a new idea to a department to determine reaction before proceeding.

THE OUTSIDER: BETWIXT AND BETWEEN

The foreign employee of a JFI was in an ill-defined position if he had to interact with the JFI. The JFI salaryman did not know how to treat the foreigner since he was outside the structure. Outside the true JFI bureaucracy, he was, in a sense, irrelevant. His title within the organization was usually meaningless. There was no possibility of corporate irredentism. He probably had little managerial power. Any JFI salaryman who theoretically reported to a foreigner might show deference, but would, in reality, report to a Japanese. Thus, there would be two structures, one for the foreigners and one for the Japanese.

Liaison was another problem area for the JFIs doing overseas business. U.S. firms had recognized the need for coordination and communication between and among departments. The departments at U.S. firms, though,

---

9   Feiler, *Learning to Bow,* p. 281.

were separate profit centers and were reluctant to share profits with other departments. The situation existed in all firms, but the severity varied from firm to firm depending on degree of vertical integration. When taken to extremes, the profit center mentality was harmful in complex transactions where multiple departments were involved.

> " **The foreign employee of a JFI was in an ill-defined position if he had to interact with the JFI. The JFI salaryman did not know how to treat the foreigner since he was outside the structure. Outside the true JFI bureaucracy, he was, in a sense, irrelevant.** "

The JFI departmental fragmentation produced the same lack of coordination and cooperation as the extreme form of American profit center mentality. The lack of cooperation between JFI departments, however, occurred because of political and structural reasons rather than performance-related competition, or compensation as in the case, at times, with the Americans.

Business and transactions often involved several departments and more than one office within a JFI, as well as a foreign firm. The mixture of elements within a business and a transaction made the distinction between international and domestic divisions anachronistic and artificial. Trying to fit a business or transaction within a single domestic or international department could only foster cumbersome communication and increased complexity. The distribution of international assets to domestic institutional or individual investors, in particular, required a coordinated effort.

The JFIs usually tried to cope with these communication problems through their planning departments. The personnel in these departments were mainly interested in avoiding confrontation with other departments. They would not want to antagonize any department by infringing on its territory or appearing to take away any part of its vaguely-defined mandate. If the planning department's personnel could postpone decisions for two or three years, they would be rotated. They, therefore, tended to encourage political compromises which resulted in minor reorganizations, insignificant changes, and a lot of wasted time and energy. Whenever possible, fundamental issues were never addressed.

INTERNATIONAL NETWORKS UNDERMINED
BY PROVINCIALISM

As previously discussed, the JFIs preferred to associate with large, famous counterparties as intermediaries. This was politically acceptable partly because it was a direct transplant of a Japanese domestic practice. The JFIs equated bigness with power and stability, the objects of respect in Japanese society. It is not surprising, then, that JFIs started pursuing large, famous American companies as clients in addition to the Japanese companies with operations in America. The Japanese brokers tried to develop U.S. institutional investors as clients for a wide range of securities, including Japanese equities and bonds and U.S. equities and bonds. They attempted to transplant Japanese marketing techniques—persistence and braggadocio—without a meaningful effort to develop professional analytical support. The Japanese brokers imported the concept of market share, which did not provide the continuous business or destruction of the competition which had been achieved by Japanese manufacturers. Uneconomical market share business with American borrowers through expensive bond bids did not create any lasting impression.

Japanese banks followed the same pattern as the brokers. They pursued large U.S. borrowers with aggressive pricing and low margins. In addition, the domestic habit of following trends led them to the activity of glamour lending, without proper credit analysis, in the U.S. real estate and LBO markets. No network of clients was ever developed.

Since JFIs ran their overseas business activities from Tokyo, domestic information sources of information proved to be influential. A Tokyo-based JFI portfolio manager might make investment decisions based on a Japanese newspaper's article on a U.S. company or market. Japanese reporters generally reacted to trends, the appearance of activity, or information fed to them by companies. Such superficial gossip-type articles had a wide impact on the JFIs' overseas business. Negative reports, in particular, were difficult to overcome.

Such a Tokyo-focused approach, and the resulting provincial attitude, helped to foster a tendency towards speculation among Japanese institutional investors. Because of their size, these institutional investors were extremely powerful, with the post-war bull market in real estate and equities adding to the illusion of the invincibility of the Japanese system. The ultimate result, however, was rampant speculation by JFIs in overseas markets. They were accustomed to markets rising, as well as enormous hidden reserves in the form of Japanese equity and real estate holdings, to cover mistakes.

In the 1980s, one large Japanese bank had over $500 million invested in U.S. equities and convertible bonds in its own proprietary portfolio. In 1987, the bank purchased 20 percent to 25 percent of many new issues of Euroconvertible bonds. The Japanese portfolio manager indiscriminately bought these issues, driving the offering price to absurdly expensive levels. He had no idea about the value represented by the premium over conversion and the coupon of the bond. His knowledge of the underlying equity was scant and often non-existent. He and other Japanese institutional investors created an exclusive market for new issue convertible bonds because of their mindless, speculative purchases. He never took the time to evaluate the secondary market for convertible bonds. He was waiting for U.S. investment bankers to present him with fully packaged offerings. The U.S. investment bankers obliged willingly and concentrated on new issues because their fee was much larger in the primary (new issue), rather than secondary, market. The JFI portfolio was solely at the mercy of the market, without any strategy, basis, or analysis. In other words, it was pure speculation.

Another Japanese bank lent money to a Japanese real estate firm to speculate in the U.S. equity market. The real estate firm had a portfolio exceeding $500 million in U.S. equities. The real estate firm's Japanese portfolio manager, who bought and sold securities, did not speak or read English. His contact with the U.S. equity market was solely through a couple of securities salesmen, one of whom was a foreigner whose only qualification was his fluency in Japanese. The composition of the portfolio was exclusively determined by the size of the U.S. banker's fee on the purchase or sale of a security. The real estate firm was a captive client of the foreign broker, and its portfolio was an ill-conceived hodgepodge of securities—a dumping ground for the broker. The real estate firm was a major contributor to the profits of the firm's Tokyo equity division.

There were such numerous examples of this type of activity that it came to represent common practice in the domestic and foreign markets. A Japanese chemical company's speculation in Japanese government bond futures caused major losses and was the type of conduct that occurred regularly in the 1980s. The amounts involved were staggeringly large. The JFIs were allegedly conservative. The JFI salarymen, in their gray or blue suits, hardly resembled the loud crowd in the Chicago commodity pits, but they were full-fledged participants in the speculation. At least most of the Chicago crowd were professional speculators or hedgers. The JFIs took enormous risks often without the slightest understanding of either credit or market exposure.

Showa Shell Sekiyu KK reported a loss of 125 billion yen ($1.5 billion) in 1992 "because of a wrong bet on dollar futures contracts."[10] A company spokesman indicated that the loss resulted from a company employee exceeding his limits. The company did not really know "exactly what happened" or "whether this was part of the company's normal hedging activities." Showa Shell was actively engaged in financial investments.

JAPANESE INTUITION AND "WET" INSTINCTS

The JFI salaryman was also influenced by his "wet" instincts. There was a major emotional component to the Japanese salaryman's thought and decision making process. After a meeting, a JFI salaryman formed an impression which often related, not to the content of the meeting, but to his counterpart's demeanor or the physical surroundings. He would infer weakness from shyness, awkwardness, or coldness. Since the JFI employee had difficulty with dialogue and was programmed to focus on one subject, he did not see synergies or business connections easily. If the topic was general or did not pertain to the salaryman's particular limited interest at that time, he was distracted. Americans who frequently changed topics when speaking generated confusion. In those instances, the JFI would probably be more curious about the furnishings of the meeting room than the discussion. A day after one such meeting, a senior JFI official gave an extensive discussion about the prints of predatory birds in an American's office. He did not remember the business content of the meeting.

The salaryman's emotional reaction to a given person or transaction was significant in determining a course of action. Of course, his responses were cushioned by political safety. The ultimate decision by a salaryman might be whimsical or based on inspiration, as he was rarely called on to defend a decision, even one that had proven to be disastrous.

---

10 Hamilton, David P., and Williams, Michael, "Showa Shell Hit by a Big Loss on Futures Bet," *The Wall Street Journal*, February 22, 1993, p. A. A-6.

JAPANESE ENVISION HISTORICAL PROGRESSION

The success of the Japanese economy instilled a concept of historical progression. All events were interpreted as moving forward. The JFI officials saw themselves as part of the Japanese system and reasoned that their progress was inevitable. For example, a Nomura official, when describing Nomura's U.S. difficulties, said, "For a time, we had to build infrastructure rather than build revenues . . . But we now have to emphasize higher-margin businesses, to create some profits. To do that, we need a different mix of businesses."[11]

The statement implied that all is proceeding on schedule. The Nomura man indicated that the infrastructure was now properly built, and the next stage would concentrate on finding profitable, high-margin businesses. The logic is somewhat strange in that the businesses should have been considered before the infrastructure was built. Likewise, the Nomura official totally ignored the huge staff turnover and inability to develop a client base. He hinted that their previous business was based on muscle and aggressive bids, which did not lead to recurring activity. But this was unimportant in the context of a grand strategy, which was described as proceeding on schedule.

Sadly, he probably believed it true. The whole cultural and cognitive mindset of the Nomura man, like other JFI salarymen in the 1980s, created an overpowering logic which no one could, let alone wanted to, dispute.

Colonists in the true sense of the word, the salarymen, without thinking, attempted to transplant to overseas business a system they believed perfect and successful. That the system would not work in a deregulated environment only reinforced their commitment to it. Indeed, the reason it did not work in this alien setting was a lack of exactly what the JFIs most prized and dearly sought to bring with them—order and security.

---

[11] Sterngold, James, "Japan's Washout on Wall Street," *The New York Times*, June 11, 1989, p. 3-1.

CHAPTER 9

THE AMERICAN INVESTMENT BANK EXPERIENCE IN TOKYO DURING THE 1980S

The experience of U.S. and other foreign investment banks in Tokyo is important for two reasons. First, some were relatively successful. Second, in establishing offices in Japan, they had to grapple with the same organizational and cultural issues that the JFIs met in doing international business.

Japan's surplus cash is usually cited as the main reason for the rapid expansion of the American investment banking presence in Tokyo during the 1980s. Certainly, the sheer size of Japanese financial assets made the JFIs, both as investors and as intermediaries, critically important sources of business. Their impact on everything from U.S. Treasuries and corporate bonds to the Euromarkets was often enormous.

> " Some U.S. and other foreign firms found there were ample rewards in exploiting the market inefficiencies in the Japanese domestic financial system. This was done through proprietary trading—especially with the use of derivatives. "

But the fact that the bureaucratically-structured Japanese financial system was over-regulated, cumbersome, and antiquated provided other opportunities as well. Some U.S. and other foreign firms found there were ample rewards in exploiting the market inefficiencies in the Japanese domestic financial system. This was done through proprietary trading—especially with the use of derivatives.

MARKET INEFFICIENCIES ARE STRONG FACTOR

Japanese brokers sold securities to investors, but they did not—could not—look for relationships between securities for five main reasons:

1. Fragmentation of departments meant there was no communication between or among departments, about warrants, futures, convertibles, bonds, or equities.

2. The "new issue" or primary department did not concern itself with the secondary market.

3. Bureaucratic priorities dictated that selling the "identified" product was the exclusive goal. There was no interplay between client and broker, between primary and secondary departments, between quantitative, sales, or trading departments.

4. "Trading department" was a misnomer, as there was little positioning of securities. The firms did engage in market manipulation. A broker would accumulate shares of a particular company before recommending it to clients. This recommendation would cause the broker's own inventory to appreciate before selling it to clients and, ultimately, to sell to the market, leaving a profit for the firm and the favored clients who purchased the stock early in the exercise. This form of manipulation was widely practiced, in order to compensate favored clients for losses, before the demise of the Japanese equity market in 1990 made the technique impractical.

5. The rotation system ensured that personnel did not have enough knowledge to identify market discrepancies.

Although the Japanese banks and insurance firms looked with condescension upon the brokers, there were more similarities than differences between them in structural, attitude, priorities, and inexperience. The Japanese investors perpetuated and actually increased inefficiencies in both domestic and foreign markets. Thus, in many cases, domestic and foreign assets were purchased for non-economic reasons, such as:

1. *Political*—The Japanese life insurance company's yen-syndicated loans were made in the 1980s to generate publicity. Opportunities were created in currency and interest rate swaps for foreign firms.

2. *Momentum*—Japanese investors would purchase a category of assets, such as "country equity funds," e.g., Germany, Thailand, or Taiwan, because there was a lot of activity. The activity was actually promoted by the Japanese brokers who hoped to create a self-fulfilling prophesy, just as they often did in the Japanese equity market, by recommending a stock and marketing it so aggressively that the stock price rose regardless of the merits of the underlying company.

3. *Speculation*—The Japanese institutional investors became intoxicated with their power and made whimsical investment decisions.

4. *Regulatory*—Two examples will suffice. The inability to make distributions from capital gains made the purchase of fixed income securities attractive to life insurance companies. The life insurance companies made unwise investments based on their need for "current income." Individuals' purchase of zero coupon bonds in 1982 and 1983, because of no capital gains tax, was another example.

5. *Performance*—The absence of performance competition, criteria, or comparison led to major market distortions and perpetuated incompetence.

6. *Conformity*—The JFIs tended to follow one another into markets, thus exacerbating a trend and, again, creating temporary distortions. Foreigners were eager to find or anticipate the next market or market sector that would feel the impact of the stampeding JFIs.

All of this created opportunities for some of the foreign firms.

THE MOF INDIFFERENCE TO ABUSES

Some foreign (and domestic) firms were able to benefit from the overvalued or undervalued situations created by this system.

Where was the MOF? Unless there was negative publicity, the MOF was unconcerned about market manipulation, fraud, investor protection, poor performance and incompetence, despite its ubiquitous presence within the financial system. Practically speaking, the transaction flow would have been difficult to monitor under the existing Japanese regulatory system because of the sheer volume of business. Compounding this, the MOF's own rotation system produced generalists unfamiliar with the ever-changing market products, technology and environment. As a result, it was easier for the MOF personnel to ignore these issues and focus instead on the Ministry's internal political matters—after all, that was the road to promotion.

It is interesting to contrast the MOF's tolerance of market manipulation with the Securities and Exchange Commission's (SEC) quick response when it became aware that Salomon Brothers had attempted to rig several U.S. Treasury auctions in 1992. There was a full-scale investigation, the involved Salomon's senior officials were expunged from the firm, and a stiff $290 million fine was imposed.

The significant profits generated by some U.S. investment banks dramatically underscored the importance of Japanese capital and the market inefficiencies. Japanese business was extremely lucrative. The extent of the success for some American institutions operating in the Japanese market is not well-understood. Until recently, foreign observers vastly understated the profits made by some U. S. investment banks in Tokyo. One author, in a revised edition of a book dated 1990, stated that, "Over the past few years, Salomon has actually succeeded in showing a profit—$11 million in 1986-87."[1]

> **" Until recently, foreign observers vastly understated the profits made by some U. S. investment banks in Tokyo. "**

On the other hand, *The Economist* wrote that, "In the six months to March 31, 1986, success in bonds contributed to Salomon's revenues in Japan of 9.2 billion yen ($46 million), more than double that of any other foreign broker in Tokyo."[2] The numbers used were the publicly-reported figures given to the Japanese tax authorities to determine tax liability. These numbers were publicly available and were broadly disseminated by reporters in the 1980s as being representative of a firm's profits. Burstein used this paltry number to illustrate that even though "Salomon is perhaps

---

[1] Burstein, *Yen!*, p. 227.
[2] "Japanese Bonds: As Wise as Salomon," *The Economist*, June 14, 1986, pp. 75-76.

the most successful (of the U.S. investment banks in Tokyo), it (Salomon) had gained only a 'toehold in Tokyo.'"[3] (Burstein also contrasts the U.S. firms in Tokyo with the JFIs in the U. S., "The American presence in Tokyo is several orders of magnitude less significant than the Japanese presence in U.S. markets."[4] In fact, the JFIs were making no inroads or profits in America. The form was there, but the substance was lacking— and so, too, the profits.)

Even *The Economist's* use of Salomon's reports to the Japanese tax authorities was misleading. In fact, *The Economist* in 1990 revealed that foreign firms often wanted to find ways to avoid showing profits because Japanese tax rates were higher than elsewhere:

> Some "gaijin" (foreign) houses have been making handy profits for several years, but have sensibly chosen to book their profitable trades offshore where possible. Others have taken advantage of Japanese tax laws to load their Tokyo offices with costs from their operations elsewhere in the Pacific. Now most of the firms feel it is time to come clean by declaring profits and paying taxes in Japan. Even so, the declared profits of many foreign houses, including Salomon, considerably understate their recent success.[5]

Foreign firms, of course, did not suddenly start paying taxes because of guilt feelings. The increased volume of Japanese equity commissions with Japanese clients was visible and could not be hidden. Salomon's huge volume in Japanese government bonds and futures was extremely conspicuous.

Foreign firms were able to circumvent Japanese taxes by booking transactions offshore. There was nothing mysterious about this practice.

The trading profits of foreign securities sold to JFIs located in Japan were primarily booked in New York or London, depending on the venue of the trading desk involved. A transaction sold to a JFI might have an arbitrary, minuscule commission attached for purposes of Japanese taxes, but the transaction profit was retained by the trading desk. Fixed income securities, except for new issues, were traded without a commission. The profit or loss was determined by trading. This was true in all operations with

---

3 Burstein, *Yen!*, p. 228.
4 Burstein, *Yen!*, p. 228.
5 "Showing the Locals a Trick or Two," *The Economist*, July 14, 1990, p. 77.

profit centers and distribution outlets. For example, if a corporate bond was sold by an American broker's Los Angeles-based institutional salesman to a Los Angeles institutional account, the profit would be booked in New York, where the trading desk was located.

Tokyo offices of American firms operated as distribution centers, as well as trading centers, depending on the activity involved. Several firms, including Salomon, made tens of millions of dollars each year through the distribution of U.S. fixed income assets booked elsewhere. These profits never appeared on the tax returns.

There were a number of other reasons why profits might, quite legitimately, appear lower than they actually were. For example, Salomon New York might sell a security to Salomon Tokyo, which sold the security to a Japanese investor. This would occur because the Japanese client was only allowed to deal with a Japanese security firm, which Salomon Brothers Tokyo was. The transaction would be credited with a small commission for tax reporting purposes, but the profit was shown in New York or London.

In another example, the Japanese client might want to hold an asset in New York, London, or Hong Kong, in which case the transaction would take place outside of Japan for tax purposes, even though negotiations and discussions occurred in Japan. The business done with Japanese overseas offices probably in fact emanated from Tokyo but was never considered part of a firm's Tokyo office profits.

A third example would be that a foreign firm might want to hold an arbitrage position offshore in either Japanese equities or Japanese bonds, when the trading desk was in Tokyo, because of lack of capital available at the firm in Tokyo or the usual tax reasons.

Beyond these, there were many other possibilities, including the murky world of swaps.

During the early and mid-1980s, the major contributors to Salomon's Japanese business were distribution of fixed income related assets—both public securities and structured products as well as yen bond trading and yen bond arbitrage. The yen bond futures market began in October 1985, and Salomon immediately became one of the two largest dealers. The BOJ recognized Salomon's prowess in the yen bond market when it allowed Salomon to be the first foreign firm to deal directly with the BOJ in 1985. Salomon's Japanese equity effort began in late-1985, and the Japanese equity index futures began trading in 1988. The Japanese equity futures contract was yet another example of an inefficient market which the JFIs did not understand. Both Salomon and Morgan Stanley were able to capitalize on the mis-priced futures contracts.

As activity and opportunities increased throughout the decade and into the early 1990s, profits of Salomon's Tokyo office were between 49 percent and 83 percent of the entire firm's pretax income. This amounted to several hundred million dollars between 1989 and 1991.[6]

This article disputed the notion that all American firms were inconsequential in Japan. It attributed the major portion of these significant numbers to yen bond and equity trading and arbitrage. Again, the percentage of Tokyo source income might have been higher with foreign asset distribution included. Salomon Tokyo's profits throughout the 1980s were grossly understated. Those American firms that were properly focused and organized could do quite well in Tokyo and compare favorably with JFIs in the U.S.

After the Japanese fiscal reporting period ending September 1992, foreign press headlines read, "Foreign Firms Outperform Japanese Securities Firms"[7] and "Foreigners Profit in Tough Tokyo Market."[8] The articles mentioned that Morgan Stanley Inc. had reported profits of 12.66 billion yen ($101.9 million) in the period March-September, 1992, and noted that foreign securities firms had outperformed Japanese firms during this period. This was primarily due to trading in equity derivatives which presented an opportunity at this time. One should not extrapolate this success into the future, though, because of changing markets and the varying ability to adjust to different environments.

SALOMON TOKYO'S DEVELOPMENT

Salomon's growth in Tokyo began when it received a branch license, effective September 1, 1982. The firm immediately consolidated its Asian operation by closing its Hong Kong office and shifting its Asian headquarters to Tokyo. At the time, there were fewer than ten employees at Salomon Asia, Ltd. By mid-1986, there were around 170 employees, and Salomon's Japanese institutional client list numbered over 400.

---

6 "Solly's Man in Tokyo: 'He's a Money Machine,'" *Business Week*, March 16, 1992, p. 106.
7 *The Wall Street Journal*, November 12, 1992, p. D-12.
8 *The Wall Street Journal*, November 4, 1992, p. C-1.

U.S. investment banks operating offshore in the 1980s had to be selective in their choice of businesses. Flexibility and opportunity were necessary and the need to adapt to changing markets was essential. In light of the need for presence and profit, the amount of infrastructure and proper deployment of limited resources was constantly being re-evaluated. The investment banking world was not static, as the JFIs wanted to have it. Salomon, as well as other firms, might carry out an integral role in certain areas, but not in others, just as JFIs could not maintain a ubiquitous role in America. Clearly, some firms achieved degrees of success, and others did not.

In other words, focus was a prerequisite for success in Tokyo. From the outset, there was an attempt by Salomon to avoid the mistakes American investment banks had made in Europe during the 1970s and early 1980s. That was the time when American banks expanded rapidly overseas, often because other U.S. banks were there. Whether there was actual business for these offices was not considered thoroughly. Nor did banks focus on their individual strengths and weaknesses. There was no recognition of limits of communication, resources, management, and capital. Rather, there was simply the assumption that a global presence was essential for survival. Global growth, it was believed, bought economies-of-scale. These, too, were always interpreted as necessary, even when it was clear many activities—such as merchant banking—generated diseconomies-of-scale because of communication difficulties.

During the 1960s and 1970s, American commercial banks were simply trying to do too much overseas. They tried to be all things to all people despite too few resources, rushing pell-mell into activities that fit no clear strategy, matched no sure strength, and, consequently, generated no significant profit.

Publicity was important. In the 1970s, many U.S. commercial and investment banks tried to establish Eurobond trading and marketing operations in London. The commercial banks, in particular, were eager to gain credibility in the securities area offshore, as they were denied the opportunity by the Glass-Steagall Act that separated commercial and investment banking.

Like the JFIs in the 1980s, the Americans in Europe were fascinated by the volume of deals done and the publicity of the League Tables. As a result, the primary and secondary markets were extremely active as American banks had to compete by making aggressive bids to borrowers. No strategic advantage materialized. Interestingly, in many cases the offering price of the new issues of bonds purchased by firms from borrowers included no commission, so no revenue was generated.

If there were a special advantage, such as the JFIs enjoyed in bringing Japanese equity-related issues in the 1980s, it was possible to run profitable operations. When it became apparent that many of the London Eurobond operations were not making money, many of the American banks reduced the scope of their operations or closed them. By the mid-1980s, London was a graveyard of U.S. commercial banks' Eurobond areas. In the 1990s, as market conditions dictate, there have been significant opportunities in areas such as proprietary trading of bonds, currencies, and swaps.

Understanding the JFIs had to be a priority because they controlled the asset flow. But Japanese institutional investors were not simply standing on the street handing out money. Navigating through the labyrinth of bureaucratic approval—as distinct from the decision-making process—put a premium on understanding how the JFIs worked, rather than professional competence. Interfacing with the JFIs was often tedious and, invariably, time-consuming. Contact with Japanese institutional investors was usually a monologue by the Americans; there was no feedback, whether the subject was a transaction or general discussion. The rotation system added to the frustration, as it was impossible to establish long-term relationships in the Western sense, and the knowledge level increased at a glacial pace.

In some cases, the relationship between investment bankers and portfolio managers in the U.S. or Europe could be constructive and lasting; in others, it could be adversarial and unproductive. In Japan during the 1980s, the rotation system did not allow a portfolio manager system to develop except at Japanese broker's investment companies, which were often mired in conflicts of interests and certainly were no bastions of professionalism. Hence, it was structurally impossible to develop a level of confidence and familiarity to engage in an exchange of information or ideas. Contact with a JFI was a rather formal, unilateral flow.

PRODUCT: IMPORTANT ASPECT OF FOCUSED APPROACH

Initially, two primary business areas were the distribution of U.S. fixed income assets and yen bond trading. With the former, Salomon Tokyo brought to the market a progression of fixed income products such as U.S. utility bonds, mortgage securities, asset backed securities, yen hedged securities, and high yield bonds. Much emphasis was put on properly packaging these products and presenting them at the best time in terms of market need and acceptance.

Salomon had learned much from its experience with zero coupon bonds in January 1982. This was an extremely profitable venture for Salomon and prompted a great deal of cooperation within the firm in trying to determine what was suitable for the Japanese market rather than blindly marketing U.S. products without consideration of Japanese interests, needs, or priorities. Unfortunately, professional dialogue was not part of this process and influencing performance was less important than manipulating the system, because that is what the system dictated. In some cases, entirely new products were created with special cash flow characteristics. In other situations, existing products were modified or prioritized. The JFI's stubborn unwillingness to focus on technical matters such as call features was taken advantage of as well. In each case, the JFIs impacted the markets by paying higher prices than U.S. domestic investors. When the JFIs did not participate, the prices dropped and returned to normal market levels based on risk and reward.

" . . . the JFIs impacted the markets by paying higher prices than U.S. domestic investors. When the JFIs did not participate, the prices dropped and returned to normal market levels based on risk and reward."

Although relegated to historical obscurity, the zero coupon situation is worth reflecting upon. In December 1981, Salomon's Asian operation was based in Hong Kong. It was at that time that I noticed Japanese individual investors were purchasing small amounts of U.S. dollar zero coupon bonds through Japanese brokers. Upon investigation, I discovered that the securities firms were selling the bonds to individuals because the discount, which was considered capital gains, was tax-free income. This was very attractive in a country where marginal tax rates were quite high (above 75 percent) and tax-exempt vehicles were limited. Also, the Japanese securities firms used simple interest computations that grossly overstated the actual yield. Furthermore, there was no consideration of currency risk. The perceived benefits, unfortunately, far outweighed any concerns about currency exposure or the relative interest rate levels.

When I tried to explain that the bonds were less attractive than they thought, the Japanese securities firms did not care. Any attempts to disillusion the Japanese of the false premises of their calculations were fruitless. This was my first real lesson in Japanese finance. Performance and risk were not considered.

Salomon, then, contacted American "brand name" borrowers—such as General Motors Acceptance Corp. and Arco—who issued bonds through Salomon in January 1982. Salomon distributed the bonds by allowing Japanese brokers to underwrite the deals. Since the bonds were placed with individuals, Salomon (whose client base is institutional) had no interest in the actual distribution. The American borrowers enjoyed this exercise because their rates were more advantageous than in the U.S. The Japanese proved to be impervious to relative value.

Salomon made over ten million dollars on these risk-free transactions. My introduction to Japanese finance was both lucrative and instructive. This pattern was repeated over the years. The Japanese overpaid for assets. Japanese buying distorted the market. Well-known borrowers received cheap money. When the Japanese were no longer involved with the market, normal conditions and spread relations resumed.

This transaction reinforced Salomon's conclusion about the importance of understanding local market conditions. Although these bonds were merely the target of opportunity, not an ongoing business, Salomon showed flexibility and coordination among departments. Within weeks, other U.S. firms, as well as Japanese brokers, were contacting U.S. corporations and the market was saturated. Two years later, when Japanese tax authorities removed the tax advantage, the market vanished.

The Japanese market presented a myriad of opportunities for the fixed income market, if a U.S. investment banker carefully studied the local preferences, performance guidelines, and institutions. Among the interesting conditions were the following:

- Life insurance companies equated performance with current yield rather than with total rate of return.

- Life insurance companies, until 1992, could make distributions to policy holders from current income (interest or dividends), not from capital gains.

- Life insurance companies were generally near their limit of allowable foreign securities exposure so they had to find ways to increase their yield. One way was through foreign currency deposits with other Japanese firms who would invest the amount of the loan in foreign currency denominated assets.

- Japanese bond yields could not fulfill the income requirements of Japanese institutional investors.

- Japanese companies were willing to borrow money and reinvest at extremely low margins. There was no concept of either return on equity or risk reward in their investments.

- Japanese institutional investors were not making decisions about the relative value of particular assets or asset categories. They were diverting cash flows rather than choosing assets.

Salomon was particularly well-suited to create fixed income products with integrated research, trading, and capital markets support in New York and London. There was experience and a willingness to try new ideas. Even in the then-arcane area of fully hedged bonds, Salomon had been successful in the late 1970s when it hedged Japanese government bonds and bank debentures into U.S. dollars and sold the three- to five-year instruments to European banks, who funded these assets with recycled petrodollars.

Although it did not appear to be an obvious area in 1982 for foreigners to attempt to penetrate because of the dominance of the Japanese brokers, the yen bond market presented opportunities. The size of the market (fully two-thirds as large as the U.S. government bond market) the increasing financing needs, the ever-present inefficiencies, the anticipation of the opening of a futures market, and the clumsy nature of the Japanese brokers were all factors combining to create a potentially profitable environment.

One Salomon employee, Shigeru Myojin, was largely responsible for the recognition of these opportunities. Also, he had the ability to capitalize on them. Myojin joined Salomon in 1979 in London. Prior to that, he was at Yamaichi Securities. He started to do business with Salomon in London and developed close connections to the firm. (In 1979, it was so unusual for a Japanese to leave a Japanese firm that John Gutfreund, then head of Salomon, had to personally make amends to the president of Yamaichi Securities for hiring Myojin away.)

Myojin was given the sobriquet "Sugar" because one of his Salomon London contacts could not pronounce Shigeru correctly. In a very un-Japanese manner, Myojin would visit Salomon London to give informal seminars about the Japanese bond market, either at lunch or after work. The timing was appropriate because of the U.S. dollar demise which had reduced dollar bond portfolio holdings of European clients, forcing Salomon to adjust to a weak dollar environment. It was significant that a Japanese was conducting the seminar, not the Americans. The conversation was always spiced with Mojin's aggressive sense of humor. There was a dialogue between Myojin and the Salomon staff which resulted in mutual benefit.

That Myojin was conceptually brilliant was easy to recognize. His unusual features—individual thoughts and expression, risk-orientation, adaptability, extroverted personality, and entrepreneurial spirit—set him apart from other Japanese. On one occasion in 1986, he even erupted in a meeting with senior officials of the TSE and stormed out. *Very* un-Japanese. He had been quite upset about the leakage of information about his transactions on the TSE. He did not conform, therefore, to the stereotype of the salaryman. Myojin has been described as being able to absorb, which is true but misleading. He is, more often, the initiator.

" **Clearly, though, the education system and corporate environment have nurtured distinct behavioral patterns which are generally difficult to change. The longer a Japanese is exposed to the Japanese molding process, the harder it is for him to adjust to another system.** "

As a result of Myojin's effort and the support of the office, Salomon became a force in the yen bond market, with a good client base as well. In 1985, Salomon was the first foreign firm to be given an account at the Bank of Japan. Upon the opening of the bond futures market in 1985, Salomon immediately became one of the three top dealers in terms of volume. The experience was extremely rewarding.

It is interesting to note that sometimes Japanese who have worked for JFIs fit extremely well within Western firms. The example of Shigeru Myojin at Salomon, although highly unusual, indicates the possibilities for

Japanese who are removed from the rigid and ritualistic structure. Clearly, though, the education system and corporate environment have nurtured distinct behavioral patterns which are generally difficult to change. The longer a Japanese is exposed to the Japanese molding process, the harder it is for him to adjust to another system.

SEARCH FOR AN IDENTITY

There is always the identity question for a U.S. investment bank in Tokyo. Is the firm supposed to be American, Japanese, or a combination? The answer is clearly that the office should represent a blend of American and Japanese styles, attitudes, and substance. More importantly, there should be mutual respect, a willingness to exchange ideas, and a serious effort to promote communication. Through the 1980s, there was tension involved in this ongoing search for an identity as each nationality resorted to familiar practices.

In order to operate effectively, the Salomon Tokyo's structure had to include a number of characteristics:

■ An independent identity—not fully Japanese or American but a blend.

■ Coordination with New York and London.

■ Significant Japanese senior management.

■ Personnel assimilation.

At the outset, it was recognized that making the transition from the Japanese system to Salomon's was a drastic change for the Japanese in terms of culture, style, and communication. Because of these factors, the assimilation process needed to be orchestrated. The traders, salesmen, and research staff were contacted before a Japanese arrived in New York for training and familiarization with the firm. In order to gain the Japanese employees' cooperation, it was certainly in the best interests of Salomon's New York staff to treat the Japanese seriously and professionally, rather than in the hazing manner in which it normally dealt with younger people. Later, the New York trading and sales personnel generally developed genuine social and professional relationships with the Japanese. The initial experiment had to be somewhat regulated. Later, as more Japanese entered Salomon, there was less need to monitor the assimilation process.

The New York or London departments generally rated language skill as their top priority for Japanese personnel in the early 1980s. Especially in the beginning, it would have been an error to populate the office fully with bicultural Japanese because, at that time, many of the fluent English speakers had spent most of their lives outside of Japan, and were likely to be more comfortable with Americans than with salarymen. Over time, some of the bicultural Japanese made valuable contributions, but language did not become a touchstone for hiring.

Thus, in the early 1980s, Salomon set a clearly defined policy for hiring Japanese staff for the Tokyo office. At the outset it was essential to recruit a few middle managers who were familiar with domestic business practices and had extensive experience interfacing with Japanese clients. Salomon recognized that it was more important for middle managers to understand the structure of Japanese institutions rather than bring a long list of clients. Indeed, the rotation system precluded the establishment of a stable network of individuals within the Japanese institutions.

The middle managers were supposed to assist in the identification of U.S. practices, transactions, and businesses that could be transplanted and in which form they could be transplanted. They would also manage the process of hiring and organizing staff. They were immediately part of a team. Two of the managers, Toshiharu Kojima (1983) and Toshihide Sakamoto (1985) came from Japanese securities firms.[9]

During the 1980s, Salomon's fixed income area began hiring personnel directly from the Japanese universities and from other Japanese firms on a highly selective basis. Salomon was the first foreign investment bank to make a serious effort to recruit from the Japanese universities. The combination of experienced managers and a practical training program provided the basis for effective personnel growth. The fact that Japanese are loyal to their employer made a major commitment to training and development feasible. Japanese, even at foreign firms, rarely left for positive inducements, such as money and title. They normally left for negative reasons, such as personal problems. There was virtually no Japanese staff turnover at Salomon in the early and mid-1980s. The initial recruits' positive experience at Salomon made further efforts at hiring on campus routine.

All of the new Japanese employees, regardless of age, went to New York and were introduced to the firm and its products. This exercise was

---

9 Parts of Salomon's exercise have been described by Samuel L. Hayes, III and Philip Hubbard in their book, *Investment Banking*, Boston: HBS Press, 1990.

for both training and familiarization. In other firms, the Japanese employees thought of themselves as working for the Tokyo office, which was a separate company, or else they identified solely with a department.

The conduct of Salomon's Japanese trainees was described by Michael Lewis in *Liar's Poker*, his bitingly funny portrayal of Salomon in the 1980s. Lewis attended the Salomon training program in 1984. His observations were couched in sarcasm:

> All six of them sat in the front row and slept. Their heads rocked back and forth and occasionally fell over to one side, so that their cheeks ran parallel to the floor. So it was hard to argue that they were just listening with their eyes shut, as Japanese businessmen are inclined to do . . . The Japanese were a protected species and I think that they knew it . . . A great deal of money could be made shepherding . . . (the Japanese surplus) capital from Tokyo by employing experienced locals . . . The rare Japanese whom Salomon had been able to snatch away (from Japanese firms) were worth many times their weight in gold and treated like the family china . . . In addition, while Salomon was otherwise insensitive to foreign cultures, it was strangely aware that the Japanese were different.[10]

Lewis was probably correct in assuming that the Japanese were asleep. Judging by his account of the inane presentations which were given, the Japanese demonstrated good sense by sleeping. As a rule, when a Japanese businessman has his eyes closed, he is asleep and not concentrating. Westerners find this Japanese habit disconcerting. Generally, the Japanese are not particularly intellectually curious in a Western sense, as their educational background is mostly rote memory as opposed to lively dialogue and stimulating lectures. Conversation and interchange are often a ritualized affair, reflecting the need for form and hierarchy.

Salomon's trainees, however, a mixture of experienced and inexperienced people, returned to Tokyo with a firm grasp of the basics of Salomon's business, because the Japanese did seriously study the information which was given to them. Also, the fact that Salomon did not hire large numbers of people was a function of the disregard for the "body count" school of management and a recognition of the difficulty and time required

---

10 Lewis, Michael, *Liar's Poker*, New York: W.W. Norton, pp. 44-45.

for assimilation and proper building rather than an inability to snatch away Japanese from other firms. Contrary to Lewis' assessment, many people at Salomon were culturally sensitive in the early 1980s—in the sales, trading, research, and investment banking areas.

The hiring and assimilation process allowed the firm to build a solid base from which to access the clients and engage in profitable trading activities. The success of the policies is evidenced by the fact that Kojima and Myojin were named co-heads of the Tokyo office in 1992 and Myojin was named one of the Vice-Chairmen of Salomon Brothers. Of the nine managing directors at Salomon in 1992, six were hired by mid-1986.

Salomon deliberately did not try to recreate Nomura in terms of client contact. There was no attempt to emulate the hyper-aggressive, persistent Nomura salesman who was flogging whatever Nomura ordered him to sell. Nor was there any effort made to encourage the kind of "wet" relationships which would lead to requests for compensation for losses or sham transactions to hide losses or tax liability. Clients made these requests, and they were always refused. An attempt to instill professional handling of clients was made. To be sure, the rotation system, lack of performance criteria, and bureaucracy interfered. Being a foreigner exempted Salomon from the traditional Japanese methods. The Japanese institutional investors often respected this approach and, despite the Japanese brokers' growth overseas, they never represented consistent competition in the foreign fixed income area during the 1980s, save in price-sensitive situations.

It must be remembered that there are two types of clients—individuals and institutions. Salomon's clients were institutions. When academics or government officials try to explain *penetration* in a market, they sometimes do not understand that it is very difficult to quantify institutional business. This can lead to confusion, as academics can grossly understate the importance of institutional activity. In reality, a few clients—especially those as large as the JFIs—could be responsible for an enormous amount of business.

There were adjustment problems. There were inherent conflicts between the U.S. firm and its Japanese clients and between the Japanese and the Americans within the firm. The Americans sometimes pressed for over-specialization—a reflection of the desire to maximize their own short-term profits. Sometimes they did this without considering the relative priority of a business or the feasibility of engaging in an activity given available personnel resources or client interest. New York departments always wanted to put their own American specialist in Tokyo without considering timing or business priorities. The specialists in turn would want total call on the beleaguered Japanese salesforce and staff, so that each department, left to its druthers, would have demanded full attention for its own product. The JFIs, generalists to a man, required enormous amounts of time when new products were introduced.

It is not surprising, therefore, that one of the real difficulties facing American managers in Tokyo in the 1980s was trying to keep the flood of traffic from London and New York to a reasonable level. The Japanese investors would have been totally confused by a blitz of ideas, which were sometimes ill-prepared and ill-conceived. London and New York staff were willing to fly to Tokyo at the slightest hint of a deal, regardless of how many of their colleagues were in Tokyo on genuinely well-planned visits. Such traffic control, however, was fraught with danger. It was all too easy to antagonize the home office, where political intrigue, especially at Salomon, was rife and powerful.

In this, Salomon was not immune to the political jockeying which bothered the JFIs abroad. In the early years, New York had to remind Americans that they should be personally committed to the office before being stationed in Tokyo. If an American was coaxed to Tokyo, as many were to London, with promises of money and title, they usually succumbed to the "3-3-3 syndrome"—three months enthusiasm, three months frustration because of communication difficulties in the office and with clients, and three months pleading to go back to New York. American tendencies towards impatience and immediate attention had to be curbed.

There were many problems on the Japanese side as well. The Japanese managers sometimes tended to look for personal loyalty as a first consideration when adding staff. Employees who were not hired by a manager had good reason to feel insecure. The managers would slip into the hierarchical Japanese management style, with oppressive results. If left alone, managers from securities firms would subconsciously try to recreate Nomura or Daiwa. Ex-Nomura managers would attempt to hire only, or predominantly, Nomura people and, likewise, Daiwa, only Daiwa men. Orthodox Japanese style would require conformity, white shirts, and no vacations. The Japanese who joined Salomon and other firms had decided to leave the traditional environment and would not have been receptive to rigid Japanese conformity. But it is still a potentially dangerous problem for firms if Japanese managers revert to traditional practices of rigidity.

The penetration of the Japanese institutional client base was clearly successful using an approach that focused on professionalism and institutional relationships while eschewing the egregious forms of Japanese brokers' behavior. Despite the attempts to offer professional service, Salomon had minimal impact on the JFIs' level of sophistication because of the various structural weaknesses that have been discussed.

Salomon's personnel experience contradicted Burstein's sweeping generalization about Japanese working in foreign firms. He viewed them as unfit to interface with Japanese financial institutions, ". . . those (Japanese) individuals are perceived as mavericks and misfits by the business world to which they are supposed to provide liaison."[11] This certainly did not have to be the case and most assuredly was not at Salomon in the mid-1980s. If handled properly, the Japanese institutional investors found it refreshing to deal with professional foreign firms, for many on an individual basis were aware of some of the deficiencies of their own system. Moreover, they were curious about foreign firms. There was deference paid to establishing a relationship with a Japanese institutional investor, but Western influences were prevalent as well. Possibly because American institutions were foreign, JFIs did not expect Japanese treatment in its purest form. Also, relationships must be viewed within the context of the Japanese rotation system.

SALOMON ENTERS JAPANESE EQUITY MARKET

At about the same time Salomon New York's equity department made the decision to enter the Japanese equity market (in mid-1985), the Tokyo Stock Exchange (TSE) announced that it would allow six foreign firms to be admitted as members for the first time.

There were over twenty applications for the six memberships, so the MOF and TSE faced an awkward selection procedure. As usual, form prevailed. Without considering which foreign firms would actually become substantively important members, the TSE, with the MOF's complicity, used existing trading volume on the TSE to determine which Americans would be chosen. A table, published by the *Nikkei* in September, 1985 showed Salomon as having insignificant activity relative to other foreign firms. The activity by foreign firms was miniscule in general when compared to Japanese firms in 1985. Morgan Stanley had artificially inflated its

---

[11] Burstein, *Yen!*, p. 230.

value by 1,000 percent in 1984–1985 by trading for its own account. This was easy to do because its base was small. This was done to impress the Japanese authorities.

The TSE chose three American firms—Goldman Sachs, Morgan Stanley, and Merrill Lynch—and three British firms—Warburgs, Vickers da Costa (50 percent owned by Citicorp) and Jardine Fleming. Salomon was not selected as one of the six foreign firms admitted as members. The political division on national lines was obvious as the Japanese government had to protect its interests in London.

The U.K., and Europeans in general, dealt with the Japanese on a bilateral basis. If the Japanese did not include a U.K. bank, the U.K. would limit the Japanese in London. The American government did not negotiate in this *quid pro quo* manner with the Japanese because the overall relationship between the U.S. and Japan was more complex and multilayered than between the Europeans and the Japanese. The State Department and the Defense Department would not let the government take such a hard line on behalf of the business sector. The U.S. government tried to encourage a "level playing field" rather than issue specific threats during the 1980s in its attempt to open the Japanese financial markets to American firms.

All of the Americans selected had significant Japanese equity operations and businesses at the time of the original announcement in June, 1985. While Salomon had no Japanese equity business prior to the announcement, the TSE and the MOF had convenient reasons for excluding Salomon. The situation was politically delicate for the TSE, who leaped at the chance to use form to exclude Salomon. Senior officials of the TSE had emphasized this in their meeting with Salomon officials from New York in July 1985. In September of 1985, the *Nikkei* published a list of Japanese commissions paid to foreign brokers to indicate that Salomon was not in the Japanese equity business. One publication succinctly stated the situation in March 1986, "Salomon is not a member of the Tokyo Stock Exchange, mainly because it began to trade equities only last July (1985)."[12] As noted by Hayes, "Salomon (had) achieved pre-eminence among foreign firms in (Japanese) government bond and note underwriting in yen futures," but its "tardy entry into the Japanese equity market was the reason it was not selected in 1985, as a member of the TSE."[13]

---

[12] Ollard, William, "Stock Market Lets Foreigners Play," *Euromoney*, March 1986, p. 92.
[13] Hayes, & Hubbard, *Investment Banking,* pp. 255-256.

Although there was publicity attached to the TSE decision, Salomon's initial exclusion from the TSE proved to be insignificant. Once Salomon London, New York, and Tokyo decided to enter the Japanese equity market, a major effort was made to become a sizeable and recognizable force in the market. Salomon was admitted to the TSE in December 1987; it became an important factor in the Japanese equity futures market. In addition, by 1987, Salomon had developed a respected Japanese equity research product. The arbitrage profits from the Japanese futures market, influenced by JFI structural weaknesses, were enormous, especially for Salomon and Morgan Stanley. However, Morgan Stanley, as usual, did not go to great lengths to publicize its activity, as was the case with Salomon.

In its formative years, Salomon Tokyo established its own identity. It did not try to become a Japanese company, and it avoided the tendency to try to transplant an American firm to Tokyo intact. Japanese managers were intimately involved with every decision. A selective process assured that qualified people would matriculate through the firm. There was virtually no personnel turnover. There was rapid advancement of Japanese employees within the Salomon system, in contrast to the JFIs' overt attempts to exclude foreigners from their overseas business. Trading and sales areas had been focused in terms of domestic and international product.

An extensive Japanese institutional client base was cultivated. Clients were contacted by generalists who would use specialists when appropriate. The opportunities that the inefficient Japanese system created were recognized quickly. Salomon's strengths, weaknesses, and limitations were considered in determining the pace of expansion, as well as the businesses entered.

MORGAN STANLEY TOKYO, CIRCA 1987

Morgan Stanley represented a different case of a broad commitment to the Japanese market. Morgan Stanley was more vertically integrated than Salomon. This yielded both strengths and weaknesses. Organizationally, it was easier to control costs and monitor profit centers at Morgan. In the 1980s, Salomon exhibited better inter-departmental communication and cooperation in Tokyo than Morgan Stanley. There was no natural tendency in the 1980s, as there was at Salomon, for the Tokyo fixed income and equity departments to communicate. Salomon even combined the departments in Tokyo, with the divisions being made between sales and trading rather than between equities and bonds, in terms of overall management purposes.

In Tokyo in the 1980s, Morgan Stanley had to be evaluated by department because of the vertical integration. Morgan was able to set up a more
diverse group of businesses than Salomon, but the quality was not consistent. The foreign fixed-income department, for example, was very effective
in distributing existing products and in structuring assets for the Japanese
market. This resulted because of the efforts of the senior Japanese manager
Kenji Munemuro and his American colleagues in the capital markets area.

In Tokyo, the Morgan Stanley Japanese equity operation was quite
profitable because of Japanese warrant trading based in London (warrants
are a highly leveraged instrument which Morgan used to good effect in the
Japanese equity bull market), Japanese equity trading (again, there was always an inventory in a bull market), and in Japanese equity index arbitrage.

The management of the Tokyo Japanese equity operation was a problem. In this regard, the Japanese equity derivatives—futures and options—
was a different, highly successful department. The personnel situation, for
example, within the Japanese equity sales and trading area was generally
fraught with troubles. The New York international equity management controlled the strategy and was totally enamored of Nomura's style. Poor selection of personnel—at times it seemed random—and a Nomura-like
policy of aggressive sales contributed to a personnel turnover of fifty- to
sixty-percent for several years in the mid-1980s. In its attempt to recreate
Nomura, Morgan's New York managers fired the talented American Japanese equity research director, in the hopes of finding a research director
who could promote a theme-of-the-week sales promotion campaign.

The extremely profitable equity derivative products area, which included futures arbitrage, was headed by a very capable young American,
Kevin Parker, who became a managing director in 1992. Parker was well
grounded in equity options and futures before coming to Tokyo in 1986 to
trade U.S. equities. Parker has been recognized as "the driving force behind Morgan's leap to the number one spot (in terms of 1992 reported
profits). That makes him boss of the most profitable trading desk at the
most profitable trading house in Tokyo."[14]

There were problems with visibility. The Japanese, looking for a
scapegoat for the TSE collapse, blamed the derivatives markets introduced
by foreigners. The *Nikkei* reported that Morgan Stanley was "the root of all

14 Adrian, Jeremy, and Kelleher, Kevin, "Speed Drives Morgan Past Other Brokers in
Tokyo," *International Herald Tribune*, February 23, 1993, pp. 11, 13.

evil" because of its futures arbitrage which was managed by Parker.[15] Anonymous telefaxes conveying death threats were received at Morgan Stanley's Tokyo office. The fearful Parker purchased a bulletproof vest.

Nonetheless, Parker was a good example of the positive impact a knowledgeable foreigner with patience and commitment can have on an operation in Japan. Certainly, both foreigners and Japanese alike respected Parker's ability to discern value and make arbitrage profits, but he was also able to hire and train Japanese staff. He devoted time, before it was fashionable, to understanding the market and developing a department. The proper foreigner is an underestimated asset in the Tokyo office of a foreign firm, indeed, in any overseas operation.

> **" The Japanese, looking for a scapegoat for the TSE collapse, blamed the derivatives markets introduced by foreigners. The *Nikkei* reported that Morgan Stanley was 'the root of all evil' because of its futures arbitrage which was managed by Parker. Anonymous telefaxes conveying death threats were received at Morgan Stanley's Tokyo office. The fearful Parker purchased a bulletproof vest. "**

The experience of both Salomon and Morgan Stanley illustrated the range of possibilities available to foreign financial firms in Japan. Other foreign firms faced the same general issues of prioritization, identity, limits, staffing, presence, profit, and long-term strategy. The ability to evaluate these matters within the perspective of their own strengths and weaknesses determined the relative success or failure of their Japanese operations.

DYNAMIC PROCESS KEY TO MANAGING GROWTH

The process of managing the growth and business of a foreign financial firm in Tokyo, as in other overseas locations, is dynamic. Flexibility and

---

[15] Bloomberg, *Business News*, February 22, 1993.

focus are always conceptually important. There are important domestic considerations as well, but, overseas without the usual home advantages, planning assumes a special character. In essence, a structure dealing with change and problems and identifying opportunities is necessary, both domestically and internationally. Samuel L. Hayes and Philip M. Hubbard eloquently express this when describing the need to handle activities and people within a system. With respect to investment banking, they outline the potentially fragile environment created by competition, highly self-centered, entrepreneurial employees, market cycles, product cycles, and the need for control as a more important issue than capital.

> Managing the downside of any market cycle is clearly the more challenging part of the top executives' assignment in these kinds of financial services firms. If you can find a way to juggle the need for a relatively flat and decentralized organizational structure to encourage individual initiative and the countervailing need for controls, which can identify problems early on, then the required capital is likely to take care of itself.[16]

Most U.S. investment firms are highly volatile places with a component of energetic, self-centered entrepreneurs, capable of rebelling frequently. Because of the extraordinary compensation, investment bankers—whether at Salomon, Morgan Stanley, or elsewhere—can gain an excessive sense of independence, self-importance and feeling of indispensability. This situation frequently leads to arrogance and greed. In the 1980s, investment banks were capable of reinforcing an employee's sense of importance by huge compensation and adulation. The public structure of the major investment banks (except for Goldman Sachs) encouraged the largess because partnership equity was not a possibility. In their compensation decisions, investment banks sometimes failed to distinguish between true performance or production and the luck of the cycle—being in the right place at the right time.

The experience of Salomon and Morgan Stanley, and some of the other foreign firms in Tokyo, was profitable, but changing conditions in the 1990s will test the ability of management in the future. Market inefficiencies, absence of JFI competition, and Japanese asset needs were the condi-

---

16 Hayes, Samuel L. III, and Hubbard, Philip M., Investment Banking: A Tale of Three Cities, Cambridge: Harvard Business School Press, 1990, p. 264.

tions which presented opportunities in the 1980s. Already Salomon has had to cut its Tokyo workforce by ten percent.[17] Merrill Lynch closed half of its retail offices and twenty percent of its sales force in Japan.[18] NatWest had to give up its seat on the TSE because of lack of business.[19]

Maintaining the proper balance of Japanese and Western influence within Tokyo remains a delicate, but critical, issue. In the future, exactly the same circumstances will not be present. Although both Salomon and Morgan Stanley have the necessary structure to cope with changes in Tokyo, their management skills will be tested.

---

[17] "Salomon Seeks Cuts in Japan," *The New York Times*, March 9, 1993, p. D-5.
[18] "Merrill Lynch Plans to Close Half of Retail Sales Offices," *The Wall Street Journal*, January 25, 1993, p. C-11.
[19] Williams, Michael, "NatWest to Give Up Seat on Exchange in Tokyo Market," *The Wall Street Journal*, December 11, 1992, p. A-9D.

CHAPTER 10

THE JFIS' OVERSEAS "DOMINANCE" IN PERSPECTIVE

*"In 1988, I described my first book about US-Japan issues, **Yen!**, as a 'report from the front lines of a war' . . . I hope my readers will not be surprised to find that many of my own ideas have changed as conditions have changed."*[1]

—DANIEL BURSTEIN

"'I think (the Japanese) probably lost more money in American real estate than anybody in history,' said Donald Trump, . . . a man who knows a thing or two about such losses."[2]

WHAT HAPPENED?

The following facile interchange has occurred numerous times in the last few years:

Question: What is the reason for the poor performance of JFIs during the last decade in their activities overseas (and at home)?

---

1 Burstein, Daniel, *Turning the Tables: A Machiavellian Strategy for Dealing with Japan*, New York: Simon & Schuster, 1993.
2 Pollack, Andrew, "Japan Glimpses—Art of Tough Talk," *The New York Times*, August 19, 1993, p. D-4.

Japanese Salaryman Answer: The bubble economy. This is a temporary phenomenon caused by easy money. Judgment was suspended between 1982 and 1992. All will return to normal. We are very long-term oriented, and *gaijin* will never understand us. We are dedicated, cautious, and prudent. We trusted U.S. investment bankers, and they sold us bad assets.

Myths about Japanese corporate traits pervade our popular culture. Detective Connor, the *gaijin* expert on Japan, in the bestselling novel (and sensationalist movie), *Rising Sun*, lectures the crude American Lieutenant Graham:

> The Japanese have a saying: "Fix the problem, not the blame." In American organizations it's all about *who* fucked up. Whose head will roll. In Japanese organizations it's about *what's* fucked up, and how to fix it. Nobody gets blamed. Their way is better.[3]

It is doubtful that either Detective Connor or the book's author, Michael Crichton, has heard JFI salarymen blame anything or anybody for their problems overseas. But they do. The bubble economy is blamed. Then they blame U.S. investment bankers. They vilify their joint venture and acquisition partners who were only interested in money. Nothing is mentioned about the passive role of JFI salarymen in these undertakings. Frustration leads to accusations about the U.S. legal system, market conditions, and untrustworthy, materialistic Americans. As we have seen, American futures traders are blamed for the collapse of the TSE. The MOF says deregulation is to blame. MITI criticizes the MOF. JFI salarymen blame their colleagues.

One searches in vain for a serious consideration of Detective Connor's opinion. Crichton's novel is hardly an innocent escape, as he used a bibliography to show the reader that he had a point of view.

GETTING PERSPECTIVE ON JFIs IN 1980s

At this point, it becomes possible to step back and begin to view the entire JFI phenomenon in the 1980s in a broader, more realistic framework—a framework which considers not only the reality of the JFIs, but their his-

---

3 Crichton, Michael, *Rising Sun*, New York: Alfred A. Knopf, 1992, p. 72.

torical context and the reasons their sudden emergence in the world of international finance generated such a strong reaction.

During the 1980s, many observers portrayed the JFIs as a threat to the U.S. financial system and even to the global financial system. Indeed, only five years after he tried to frighten America about Japan's financial empire, in his recent book *Turning the Tables*, Daniel Burstein has indicated, as can be seen in the quote above, that "many of my own ideas have changed." He does not say he was wrong, simply that he had changed his mind. He does not even give the full title of his 1988 book; he refers to it as *Yen!* rather than its full title, *Yen! Japan's New Financial Empire and Its Threat to America.* Japan had no financial empire, and it surely was no threat to America.

> **" The bubble economy is blamed. Then they blame U.S. investment bankers. They vilify their joint venture and acquisition partners who were only interested in money. Nothing is mentioned about the passive role of JFI salarymen in these undertakings. "**

The only apology Burstein offers is a meek explanation that Japan's financial authorities could not control the process completely. But, he assures us:

> Japan's financial authorities certainly know what they are trying to do. Even in Japan, however, they can't control the process completely. The stock market crash in particular appears to have overshot their targets, and the mess caused by the bursting bubble may prove less containable than they originally thought. A huge mopping-up operation remains.[4]

I am not sure what that means. Burstein is merely avoiding a discussion of his misinterpretation of Japan's alleged financial empire, a myth which he helped to create.

---

4 Burstein, *Turning the Tables*, p. 40.

In *Yen!*, Burstein deifies the MOF officials who have "long historical memories."[5] He is awed by the "control which Japanese authorities have maintained over their nation's financial functions—even as they deregulate . . . (this) is a strategic advantage in an unstable world."[6] One now does not have to ask where was the MOF; we now know. It was were doing very little about building a proper financial system. Now, we hear Japanese pleading for reform of the MOF.

The JFIs were seen as an integral part of the expanding Japanese empire, an economic juggernaut which looked set to dominate the world. They frightened many—alien in culture, monolithic in structure, so suddenly successful. Commentators saw a familiar pattern in the JFIs' overseas expansion—the same simple, brutal pattern Japanese manufacturers followed in their conquest of the U.S. automobile, consumer electronics, and semiconductor industries. (The American semiconductor industry has staged a comeback within the last few years.) There was, indeed, only one weakness in this script—it told more about the loss of underlying self-confidence in the U.S. during the Reagan era than about the JFIs.

The fear of domination by JFIs was not a new theme. There have been many other examples throughout history of apprehension about foreign financial, industrial, political, or military influence over domestic affairs. In the nineteenth century, the Americans eagerly sought British capital, but politicians and journalists were able to create a potent political issue by raising fears of possible foreign domination and interference. Indeed, Japan's rush to modernize in the *Meiji Era* was a calculated response to avoid the humiliation and subjugation that characterized China's domination by Western powers in the nineteenth century.

More recently, U.S. hegemony after World War II was feared and resented, especially in Europe. William Emmott's book, *The Sun Also Sets* (New York: Times Books, Random House) (1992), captured the essence of this misplaced fear in its response to the book by a French journalist, *Le Defi American* (The American Challenge).[7] The Europeans were concerned during this period about American industry's encroachment on Europe: "The scare-mongering best-seller warned that Europe was being invaded by American multi-nationals and that, if it did not wake up to what was going on, European civilization would fade away, superseded on its own

5 Burstein, *Yen!*, p. 143.
6 Burstein, *Yen!*, p. 161.
7 Servan-Schreiber, Jean-Jacques, *The American Challenge*, New York: Atheneum, 1967.

soil by the United States."[8] Emmott described how Servan-Schreiber has "often been maligned and misquoted as a xenophobe." Emmott pointed out that the book, ". . . welcomed American investment while loathing what it implied about Europe's weakness and the state of its civilization. The American invasion was an effect, not a cause. The best response to it . . . was to remain open, to learn from the invader, and build a truly common market."[9]

It is fascinating to examine this book that caused such a stir in 1967. Servan-Schreiber offered the possibility that "Fifteen years from now (1982) . . . the world's third greatest industrial power, just after the United States and Russia, will not be Europe, but American industry in Europe."[10] Hardly on the mark. He discussed the "dynamic cumulative process that characterizes (how) today's (1967) American actually works." He wallowed in the cooperation between American government and business, and delights in the "vigor of American education."[11] He argued that "success of major operations depends on having firms big enough to be competitive. But that is not enough. An effective campaign requires sustained government aid."

This is so similar to the fears created by pundits about the Japanese in the 1980s! American government officials still seem to want to emulate aspects of Japanese society—just as Servan-Schreiber called for imitation of America.

Servan-Schreiber cites the commitment of IBM's French subsidiary to training and research. He adores bigness, government and business cooperation, and government subsidies. He rightly identifies software as critical.

Brink Lindsey unmercifully, but correctly, rebukes Servan-Schreiber for his analysis.[12] Servan-Schreiber would have been amazed, as Lindsey indicates, that "some government-backed colossus . . . (did not) beat IBM and other established leaders but entrepreneurial upstarts like Apple, Sun, and Dell."[13] As Lindsey points out, *The American Challenge* was "causing

---

[8] Emmott, William, *The Sun Also Sets*, New York: Times Books, Random House, 1992, p. 162.

[9] Emmott, *Sun*, p. 162.

[10] Servan-Schreiber, *American Challenge*, p. 3.

[11] Servan-Schreiber, *American Challenge,* p. 67.

[12] Lindsey, Brink, "The Has-Been Pundit and the Brand New President," *The Wall Street Journal*, February 25, 1993, p. A-14.

[13] Lindsey, Brink, *Has-Been Pundit*.

a sensation as a runaway bestseller on both sides of the Atlantic."[14] America did not take over Europe. Government intervention and bigness have not been a formula for success. American industry in Europe is not "the world's third greatest industrial power."

Interestingly, similar arguments were used by pundits, like Burstein, and are used by government officials. They have merely changed the title of their theme to the Japanese challenge rather than the American challenge. Both were sensationalist and misleading. Political conservatives in America will chuckle when they learn that Arthur Schlesinger, Jr. wrote the Foreword to the English edition of *The American Challenge*.

In retrospect, the U.S. in the 1980s was not in danger of being purchased by the Japanese, just as Europe was not threatened by American financial and industrial power in the 1960s. During the 1980s, the JFI accumulation of U.S. assets, which was encouraged and promoted by Americans, was viewed as threatening by journalists and politicians. The investments were made in a highly disorganized, superficial, unprofessional, publicity-driven, and speculative manner. The JFIs were mainly following fashionable trends, which they had helped to create. Usually, when investments are approved and accumulated through this process, the economic and strategic results are poor.

" The JFIs were mainly following fashionable trends, which they had helped to create."

The JFIs did assist the U.S. government fund its debt. They also enriched American financial intermediaries and American principals who sold assets. It is difficult to see what the Americans could learn from the JFIs in the 1980s except for the dangers of speculative investment and structural weakness. Another lesson is that misunderstanding and exaggerating the strength of the JFIs could have been avoided by a substantive examination of their behavior. Servan-Schreiber indicated that the Europeans could learn from the American "invader." There were probably valuable lessons to be learned from the Japanese manufacturing "invaders," but not from the JFIs.

---

14 Lindsey, Brink, *Has-Been Pundit.*

The JFIs could have benefitted from their contact with Americans and other foreigners and also from a proper and objective reflection on their misadventures in the American markets. The Americans' mistakes and successes should have been studied by the JFIs. The JFIs normally blame the market rather than themselves, so nothing is gained from their experiences.

SUCCESS IS WHERE YOU FIND IT

Observers and participants simultaneously used many of the same facts and statistics to support their interpretations:

- Relative size
  - Japanese bank assets and deposits
  - Japanese broker capital
  - Japanese life insurance premium income and asset size
  - Japanese surplus capital flows
  - Capitalization of the Tokyo Stock Exchange as larger than that of the NYSE
- NYSE volume
- Eurobond League Tables
- Acquisitions and joint ventures
  - Nippon Life/Shearson, Yasuda Life/Paine Webber, Sumitomo Bank/Goldman Sachs (participating loan)
  - Nomura/Wasserstein Perella, Nikko/Blackstone, Yamaichi/Lodestar
  - Nikko/Wells Fargo

The interpretation was almost uniform. Although this author, for example, expressed grave doubts about the Nippon Life/Shearson transaction,[15] the expansion of the JFIs was moving at such a rapid pace and seemed to be so carefully planned in Tokyo, few observers delved below the surface when analyzing the events of the 1980s.

---

15 Faber, Marc, *The Great Money Illusion*, Hong Kong: Longman Group, 1988, p. 84.

Domestic and foreign observers typically overestimated the competence of the JFIs. They did not see that Japan's ebullient economic conditions, regulatory protection, and bull markets provided a halcyon environment for the JFIs domestically, or that when they engaged in international business from Tokyo or overseas in unregulated markets, their organizational structure was an impediment. Indeed, at home, the flaws were only gradually being recognized when one of the JFIs' supporting pillars—the bull markets—faltered in 1990.

Until then, the Japanese media, like the JFIs themselves, put great faith in the invincibility of the Japanese and, therefore, in their own system. In the mid-1980s, most foreigners swallowed this dogma, reinforcing the JFIs' narcissism. Confident of the JFIs' overwhelming competitive strength, one writer reported glowingly of the vision of leading JFI officials:

> Useful as the protected financial environment had been for Japan's past growth, it now manacled the ambitious dreams of the large financial institutions. Men like Tabuchi of Nomura, Komatsu of Sumitomo Bank, and Kurosawa of IBJ recognized that Japan could now become a global financial power. Their companies could stand at the forefront of world finance, if only they could break down some of the regulatory walls . . .[16]

By 1992, Tabuchi and Komatsu were forced to resign. Kurosawa has been faulted.

DISSENT SUPPRESSED

There were those who dissented, especially among foreign equity analysts and portfolio managers, although the Japanese government, press, and business made it difficult for individuals or institutions to openly criticize events and practices. Ostracism was a real threat. Foreign bankers had to be cautious about their remarks as well.

Many foreign equity analysts, using Western standards, were uncomfortable with the seemingly extravagant valuation of Japanese equities. By the late 1980s, TSE prices and Japanese real estate prices appeared to be

---

[16] Burstein, *Yen!*, p. 132.

dangerously speculative and represented a tulip, mania-type bubble. Books such as *Unequal Equities* and *The Sun Also Sets* accurately described the potential risk of the Japanese market. Put options on the *Nikkei* index were actively traded on the American Stock Exchange as foreigners wanted to protect themselves against a decline in the Japanese market or wanted to vigorously bet that it would fall.

" The symptoms of a bubble were extremely visible—rampant speculation, leverage, or borrowing money with real estate as collateral to purchase stocks, arrogance, and the total absence of prudent analysis. "

The symptoms of a bubble were extremely visible—rampant speculation, leverage, or borrowing money with real estate as collateral to purchase stocks, arrogance, and the total absence of prudent analysis. The Nippon Telegraph and Telephone (NTT) Company, offering shares at a price/earnings ratio of 250, and IBJ's loan to Ms. Onoue indicated the pervasiveness of the bubble, as these Japanese establishments were not the peripheral players but major participants in the speculative game.

By the late 1980s, it was becoming apparent to some that the JFIs were less than formidable. Weaknesses had been exposed. There was a critical shortage of skills in many areas such as money management, research, technology, risk analysis, and merchant banking. Borrowers had responded to *kamikaze* bids, but an overseas client base had proven elusive. Strength had come from domestic sources of money. Simply put, all the JFIs had was money.

Even then, much of the old faith persisted. The JFIs saw the acquisition of skills as the next phase of a well-conceived strategy. The foreigners believed the JFIs could buy expertise easily. No one focused on the difficulties of grafting these specialists or special skills onto the JFI structure. Either by acquisition, joint venture, or employment of foreigners, the JFIs were supposed to obtain the missing ingredients for success. Deregulation was cited as hastening the process. An orderly transition was contemplated.

MARKET DEBACLE OF 1990 EXPOSES WEAKNESSES

Tight money policies of the late 1980s and the market debacle of 1990 exposed the problems of the Japanese financial system and significant difficulties for the JFIs at home and abroad. The market crisis and capital problems were symptoms of weakness; they did not cause it. The bubble economy helped make the flaws visible; it did not create the structural problems. The JFIs' underlying structure created the weakness which culminated in the market decline. The organizational issues were also responsible for the market inefficiencies domestically and the flawed attempts to invest overseas and build overseas businesses, both of which resulted in huge profit opportunities for foreign and, especially, American investment banks.

> **" The market crisis and capital problems were symptoms of weakness; they did not cause it. The bubble economy helped make the flaws visible; it did not create the structural problems. "**

When the Japanese equity market began its precipitous decline in 1990, a predictable set of problems arose:

- Loan losses for JFIs
- Real estate price deterioration
- Pressure on JFI earnings
- Bank capital ratio problems
- Low volume on the TSE
- Revelations of kickbacks and market manipulations
- Forced sales of equities in hidden reserve

The financial system was under great pressure. The deteriorating situation was forcing JFIs to sell shares which they held for relationship purposes.

There were several forecasts. One view held that there would be a crisis within the Japanese financial community. Already there had been several mergers—Mitsui Bank/Taiyo Kobe Bank and Kyowa/Saitama

Bank—during the debacle. These were prompted by vulnerability and weakness of one or both parties. There were rumors of a Bank of Tokyo merger as well. These mergers were handled smoothly with the MOF intimately involved. Whether the operations can be combined smoothly is open to question, especially if the Dai-Ichi Kangyo Bank is an example. The staffs of the former Dai-Ichi Bank and Kangyo Bank are still operating with many duplicate management positions even though the merger occurred in 1971.

Another prediction was that the market debacle would hasten deregulation of the financial area. In this case, the system would be cleansed and ultimately become more competitive. However, this view does not indicate how the fabric and structure of the JFIs would change.

Some thought the current problems in the financial system were an aberration caused by the bubble mentality of the 1980s and the stock and real estate market decline, and all would return to stability when conditions in these markets normalized. It was assumed that the MOF would intervene if the situation deteriorated.

ALL ACCORDING TO PLAN?

Observers, even those who gave harsh accounts of the realities of the JFIs, assumed that change was being carefully orchestrated. William Emmott wrote, "What (Japanese) fund managers had in common when the surplus (capital in the 1980s) flooded them was ignorance." He correctly portrayed "Japan (as) . . . a nation of speculators."[17] He accurately forecasted the problems which would ensue if the Tokyo market crashed.

Yet, when he spoke about the ignorance of fund managers, he implied that the problem had been identified, and a solution had been implemented:

> (Japanese) fund managers have learned fast because they have had to . . . The Japanese government hopes that domestic firms will learn from foreign firms, either through competition or tie-ups. More apparent than that have been investments in fund manager and investment banks overseas in order to gain training and experi-

---

17 Emmott, William, *The Sun Also Sets—The Limits to Japan's Economic Power*, New York: Times Books, 1989, pp. 113, 115.

ence for Japanese fund managers . . . All are buying brain power, not control.[18]

He cited Nippon Life/Shearson and Yasuda Life/Paine Webber, both of which were ill-fated. Yasuda Life sold part of its equity in Paine Webber in January, 1992 and Nippon Life would surely have liked to rid itself of Shearson. Emmott glossed over the structural issues when he indicated that JFI problems would be solved by acquiring foreign firms or hiring foreigners.

In his recent book, *Japan's Global Reach*,[19] Emmott does not refer to this prediction in *The Sun Also Sets* (1989)—that the JFIs would rectify their deficiencies in managing money. He asserted in *The Sun Also Sets* that the JFI fund managers "have learned fast" and were "buying brain power" from foreigners. This has not happened, and Emmott does not address his previous views.

> **" Another prediction was that the market debacle would hasten deregulation of the financial area. In this case, the system would be cleansed and ultimately become more competitive. However, this view does not indicate how the fabric and structure of the JFIs would change."**

He asserts that the JFIs' prominence lasted only as long as their pot of gold but qualifies his criticism by saying that there are few examples of success overseas—Salomon Brothers and Morgan Stanley in Tokyo. The difficulty, according to Emmott, is that "borrowers, investors, lenders: all are nationals of one particular market" and foreign financial intermediaries are precluded from "closeness to these customers," i.e., relationships. Thus, the Japanese securities houses were prevented "from building genuinely

---

18 Emmott, *Sun Also Sets,* p. 114.
19 Emmott, William, *Japan's Global Reach: The Influences, Strategies and Weaknesses of Japan's Multinational Companies*, London: Century, 1992, pp. 142-192; also published in different form as *Japanophobia—The Myth of the Invincable Japanese*, New York: Times Books, 1993.

domestic business in America (because of) their remoteness from the customer."[20] They were indeed remote from their customers, but as we have seen this resulted from structural reasons. Given their abundant capital, they had access to developing a customer base abroad.

The JFIs were supposed to be masterful planners. Why could they not determine which businesses to develop? Access to institutional fund managers, in many areas, is not restricted to domestic firms. Why did the Japanese not learn to select proper partners in fee businesses, proprietary trading, selection of assets, and money management? They certainly had distribution capability and assets under management in Japan.

Why were they not performance driven? Emmott resorts to the standard themes—bubble economy and arrogance. He is even optimistic about the JFIs. He is confident that "the (current) consolidation of Japan's banking industry will make it stronger." These are blind leaps of faith without any basis in past experience.

As the title indicates, another analysis of Japan's political and economic misadventures of the 1980s, Christopher Wood's *The Bubble Economy*, blames JFI problems on the bubble which was created by easy money.[21] Wood, like Emmott, writes for *The Economist* and has reported on Japan extensively as a journalist. His thesis is straightforward:

> The Bubble Economy inevitably spawned scandal in the banking and securities businesses, which had shocking consequences for the real economy.[22]

He uses separate chapters to describe banks, securities firms, and life insurance companies. In reality, these entities do not need distinct classifications, as their underlying structures and problems are the same. Wood has constructed a tidy sequence of events with a well-crafted explanation of land speculation and bubbles in perspective. He marches through banks, securities firms, and securities in order to get to the scandals, which are the really entertaining part of the book.

---

[20] Emmott, *Global Reach*, pp. 142–192.
[21] Wood, Christopher, *The Bubble Economy: Japan's Extraordinary Speculative Boom of the '80s and the Dramatic Bust of the '90s*, New York: The Atlantic Monthly Press, 1992.
[22] Wood, *Bubble Economy*, p. 2.

Wood only once mentions the evils of the rotation system. He quotes an American observer who blames JFI staff "either Japanese executives on a two-year rotation from Tokyo . . . or fourth-rate Americans" for poor JFI credit analyses.[23]

Nomura's "fall from grace is likely to prove strictly temporary," according to Wood. He cites its deep "financial resources" and ability to "transform" the way it does business as reasons for its returning to eminence and power. Wood argues that Nomura will grant its branches "autonomy" and introduce professional standards in terms of research, sales presentations and conduct. Wood does indicate that "this will take time" because of "cultural and regulatory obstacles."[24]

" The JFIs happen to be located in the second largest economy in the world. They will remain huge. Whether they move from primitive to professional is the question. "

Yet Wood attributes the underpinnings of Nomura's success to fixed (and high) commissions and its ability to operate "as a superbly disciplined army known for its aggressive, highly centralized management and quasi-militaristic culture."[25] Wood forecasts the end of fixed commissions and a move to negotiated (i.e., lower) commission rates and decentralization of branch management. This would imply the demise of the basis of Nomura's strength, rather than a reason for optimism. How Nomura will change its corporate culture and source of profit is not really discussed, other than a reference to cash accounts, similar to those of Merrill Lynch.

To be sure, Nomura and all large JFIs have the infrastructure, franchise, and client base to remain huge and powerful financial institutions by world standards. The JFIs happen to be located in the second largest economy in the world. They will remain huge. Whether they move from primitive to professional is the question. The reformation and reconstruction of the JFIs will be painful and difficult.

Wood makes a rather curious comment:

---

23 Wood, *Bubble Economy,* p. 32.
24 Wood, *Bubble Economy,* pp. 98-102.
25 Wood, *Bubble Economy,* p. 99.

> Loss compensation may be bad business practice because it is ulti-
> mately self-defeating, but it is hardly unique to Japan. Nor is it so
> terrible.[26]

By loss compensation, Wood is referring to the paybacks by JFIs to influential politicians, major corporations, and powerful businessmen for losses
that they incurred because of the TSE collapse. If the TSE had not col-
lapsed, the practice would still continue. America is hardly a financial uto-
pia, but one should be careful about making such comparisons between
Japanese and U.S. financial institutions.

In reality, loss compensation is at the heart of a system that has no
accountability or performance criteria. Obligation replaces fairness, professionalism, skill, and law. Wood's analogies to the U.S. are weak. Soft dollars (the use of commission dollars by money managers to pay for
equipment) is not illegal, is publicly known, and is minor relative to the
billions of dollars involved in Japan's scandals, which were not publicly
known and discriminatory. Adequate redress is available in the U.S. legal
system and regulations can be enacted if the public feels outraged. The fact
that individual investors pay more commissions is also spurious. The time
and effort needed to service individuals create cost issues for brokers. Also,
in America, if individuals do not want broker service, they can use discount brokerage firms which charge minuscule commissions for transaction
execution capability.

Wood conveniently blurs the distinction between Japanese manufacturers and financial institutions. He uses the car and electronics industries as
examples of *"growing anecdotal evidence of just such a change in corporate behavior."*[27] What about the JFIs?

It is useful to review these accounts of Japan in the 1980s. Both Emmott and Wood have valid and interesting observations. Some of their insights about JFIs need to be qualified, supplemented, or revised.

JAPANESE SOCIETY IN CONFLICT

Westerners generally refer to "the Japanese" and "the Japanese system"
without realizing that there is tension and competition within Japanese so-

---

[26] Wood, *Bubble Economy,* p. 127.
[27] Wood, *Bubble Economy,* p. 206.

ciety, as in all societies. Policies and practices of JFIs overseas in the 1980s have had a major negative impact on the Japanese economy, Japanese manufacturers, Japanese pensioners, and Japanese investors.

Various elements of Japanese society should respond to my observations according to their role within the drama of JFI activity overseas in the 1980s. The JFIs and the MOF could benefit greatly from this work, which is objective and hopefully will lead to constructive change. The majority of JFI and the MOF officials will probably react defensively to the study. Many JFI salarymen and the MOF officials will recognize the validity of my comments but will be prevented from expressing their opinions for fear of ostracism.

- *The Japanese Ministry of Finance (MOF)*. This is the group that tolerated fraud, market manipulation, major distortions of markets, and kickbacks to influential investors. It presided over a system which was intentionally unconcerned about performance. Its only real interest was control. Certainly, investor protection and the welfare of Japanese pensioners was not part of its agenda.

- *The Japanese Ministry of International Trade and Industry (MITI)*. It has engaged constantly in competition with the MOF and is blaming the MOF for many of the recent problems. It has even been expressing its views openly to the press.

- *The Japanese people*. They have entrusted their savings to the JFIs and have received poor returns and witnessed the JFIs becoming a drain on the entire economy. Their pension funds have been poorly managed with a total absence of performance criteria and publicly-available information within the stifling regulatory atmosphere. In return for their self-sacrifice and passivity, which are functions of societal peer pressure, they have had to endure substandard housing, two-hour commutes, discriminatory kickbacks to influential investors, and a scandal-infested government and financial system. They know the rules—power alone deserves respect. They are forced to absorb news through a carefully controlled media willing to manufacture truth.

- *The Japanese Financial Institutions (JFIs)*. They have enjoyed the privileges of a totally regulated franchise, the benefits of a 45-year bull market, and the cash generated by the manufacturing sector. They have burdened the Japanese people with poor results, both in terms of loan losses and under-performing assets. They have squandered the trade surpluses in their disastrous forays overseas in the 1980s. At times, they have serviced the *yakuza* quite well. They have evolved into ossified bureaucracies.

■ *The Japanese manufacturers.* This group has often viewed the financial sector as parasites. They have felt that the JFIs should play a secondary—often expressed as supporting—role in the economy. They often describe the activities of the JFIs as paper shuffling. They were (and still are) oblivious to the dangers of having a poorly-functioning financial system.

GRAND DESIGNS, GRAND EXCUSES

The JFIs never blamed themselves for their shortcomings. They cited the market or, better yet, excused everything as being part of a long-term plan. Thus, Hirohiko Okumura of Nomura Research Institute passed off the JFIs' lack of concern of currency risk in the U.S. investments in the 1980s as an initial phase of their "international financial expansion." By his logic, "Japanese banks and brokerage houses at first meeting wanted to build up substantial portfolios . . . no matter what the exchange rates."[28]

This prepared the way for the second stage where, Okumura explained, "They (JFIs) are managing and shifting those assets, rather increasing them sharply."[29] He added that "Japanese investors are getting more sophisticated and more cautious."[30]

It is easy to discern something more serious than a face-saving pattern of excuses. The JFIs did not really understand that their forays into overseas business were devoid of thought. They saw this as a phase. In no way did they question their basic organizational structure. Rather they assumed instead they had grown "more sophisticated." How? Since not by design, presumably by osmosis. Certainly they became more cautious. But this is a natural bureaucratic reaction, more akin to paralysis than prudence.

More to the point, perhaps, Okumura failed to ask the essential hard questions in his typology of overseas business. Why should a JFI build a

---

[28] *The New York Times,* March 22, 1992, p. 12.
[29] *New York Times,* March 22, 1992, p. 12.
[30] *New York Times,* March 22, 1992, p. 12.

portfolio that disregarded currency risk? Why emphasize size and prestige over quality and performance? What evidence was there to support his contention that the Japanese investor had grown "more sophisticated"?

> **" It is easy to discern something more serious than a face-saving pattern of excuses. The JFIs did not really understand that their forays into overseas business were devoid of thought. They saw this as a phase. In no way did they question their basic organizational structure. "**

The answer partly rests in the automatic assumption that a response to a problem represents progress—an attitude some foreigners have adopted in their analysis of the JFIs. When Tabuchi was forced to resign from Nomura in 1991, the new chief executive, Hideo Sakamaki, was described as representing, "A Marked Change in Style for Nomura's Leadership."[31] In the context of Sakamaki's career, this represented a remarkable turnabout. At a 1985 dinner in Tokyo, Sakamaki was asked what Nomura most respected. A true Nomura man, Sakamaki unhesitatingly answered: "Power!"

Whether by conversion or design, for *The New York Times*, Sakamaki clearly chose to present a gentler side. Picturing him as "thoughtful and soft-spoken," *The Times* stated Sakamaki had "devoted himself to strategic planning."[32]

The article did mention that the Japanese securities industry had "not yet achieved" what Sakamaki had "been prodding Nomura do to." That was "expand abroad, learn new businesses, and change its very culture." But the author, who is usually quite astute and seemed to know much about Sakamaki's past activities, did not press key questions. It has to be assumed that Sakamaki obtained Nomura's top slot because of political skill and aggressiveness. Tabuchi made similar statements about overseas expansion throughout the 1980s, and Nomura has remained dependent on

---

31 Sterngold, James, "A Marked Change in Style for Nomura's Leadership," *The New York Times*, June 26, 1991, p. D-1, 6.

32 Sterngold, James, "A Marked Change in Style for Nomura's Leadership," *The New York Times,* June 26, 1991, p. D-1, 6.

the domestic equity market and captive sources. Also, JFI senior management does not have the opportunity or authority to influence a company the way an aggressive, strong-willed American official might. The JFI official simply does not have the mandate.

The dynamics of change within the JFI's organization will be far more difficult than has been realized. The JFIs' recent use of phrases such as "return on equity," "high margin business," and "profit" does not mean that they can formulate strategies and implement policies to effect these changes within the existing organization. Structural issues require substantial effort to change. An ethnocentric attitude toward foreign employees cannot be erased by fiat. Assimilation with foreigners, by definition, is abhorrent within Japanese society. Communication problems, cultural gaps, and prioritization difficulties are not likely to be eliminated without structural change.

FROM PRIMITIVE TO DOMINANT TO PRIMITIVE

In any event, the symptoms of weakness appeared, and in 1990 the JFIs were being called "primitive" by the press. The impressive size of the JFIs, which had intrigued observers in the early and mid-1980s, could no longer be seen as deriving from sophistication, masterful planning, competence, and Japanese uniqueness. The JFIs of the 1980s now resembled Western financial institutions of the past.

This examination of JFIs' overseas activities in the 1980s has provided insights into structural weaknesses that have caused poor performance and blunders. Focusing on the JFIs' overseas operations indicated how the JFIs experienced difficulties when their protective regulatory environment was removed. The JFIs could not understand overseas markets and conditions as they tried to apply the investment and management techniques that they had become accustomed to in the post-war domestic bull market. Their habits and organizational structure could not be effectively transplanted. In many ways, the growth of JFIs were a function of a bull market they did not understand. Particular Japanese cultural and national traits were assigned as reasons for the explosive growth of the JFIs overseas.

In reality, the only basis of their "dominance" was money, which was an inheritance in some ways similar to Arab money—a fact neither the JFIs nor their admirers appreciated. The JFIs were not responsible for producing the capital surplus that they were recycling. The money was merely a product of the regulatory franchise granted by the MOF, bull markets, and a dynamic manufacturing sector.

The JFIs' movement from primitive to dominant and then back to primitive was the superficial interpretation of Western observers. The reality of the JFIs in the 1980s can be judged only through the complex interplay of bureaucracy, centralization, provincialism, and domestic business practices. Viewed from this perspective, the fallacies of the assumption of JFI overseas domination, competence, and strategic planning become clear.

PUTTING JFIs IN INDUSTRY CONTEXT

In terms of their foray into overseas business during the 1980s, therefore, the JFIs were not some new, strange, uniquely Japanese juggernaut. Like the Arabs in the 1970s—indeed, like most financial institutions that suddenly find themselves able to operate on a global scale—they were beneficiaries of their national economy.

In other words, it is imperative to keep in mind that many of the problems the JFIs encountered in their overseas businesses were the same as those foreign financial institutions encountered when they tried to do business across national boundaries, including lack of focus, insufficient rigor in analyzing business opportunities, staff transience, poor communications between headquarters and overseas branches, political in-fighting, the desire to transplant home office norms wholesale, difficulties in assimilating local staff into the organization, bureaucratization, publicity-seeking—the list is endless. The JFIs did not invent bureaucracy.

Moreover, the mere act of going overseas can create difficulties. When expanding across borders, there is an almost inevitable necessity, in certain businesses, of becoming superficial in terms of a country or market. For example, trying to make private equity investments, e.g., real estate, venture capital, private companies, and illiquid corporate situations—which have higher return characteristics—is hazardous in a large organization that does not use in-depth, reliable sources of information. Reliance on local brokers in these markets is treacherous. Some American banks were guilty of this in Europe in the 1970s and the JFIs followed this pattern in the U.S. in the 1980s. Establishing a useful network of information and transactions is time-consuming and requires a depth of commitment that is often lacking in large institutions overseas.

COMPARISONS WITH U.S. BANK EXPERIENCE

The JFIs' overseas expansion had many parallels with the American banks' experience. Growth was undertaken without proper training and for non-economic reasons in many cases. Having failed to prepare adequately, both have suffered unpleasant consequences and missed opportunities.

1. *Presence and profit*

American firms in the 1960s and 1970s, like the JFIs in the 1980s, frequently confused presence with profit. They justified any activity, project, or office by the need to have a presence. Engaging in the activity, completing the project, or establishing the office was, in and of itself, viewed as a success which could be published in the press, described in an annual report, or generally boasted about. Business journalists usually accommodated this exercise when they hastily and superficially prepared articles. Whether the presence was profitable, effective, well-conceived or substantively significant, short- or long-term was not relevant to many large financial institutions who blindly expanded overseas.

" **American firms in the 1960s and 1970s, like the JFIs in the 1980s, frequently confused presence with profit. They justified any activity, project, or office by the need to have a presence.** "

---

2. *Loan losses*

In the 1970s and 1980s, many American commercial banks experienced outrageous loses in their loans involving Third World countries, energy-related businesses, and U.S. real estate. In retrospect, it is difficult to imagine what kind of organizational structure would have encouraged, or even allowed, this to happen. Upon closer examination, it is possible to see that the various loan officers were evaluated by the volume and not quality of their loans. Performance criteria skewed priorities. The banks, like the JFIs, tended to follow fashionable trends and emphasize asset size over all else. Activity begat activity.

The U.S. investment banks' flirtation with bridge loans to LBO candidates in the 1980s was another illustration that American financial firms can be distracted by fees and publicity to make imprudent credit decisions. The JFIs were equally susceptible to this practice in other markets.

Also during the 1970s and 1980s, the American S&L industry became the most costly banking fiasco in U.S. financial history. Among the reasons were faulty government regulations, such as the provision for government insured deposits, which removed market discipline. The bipartisan acquiescence of U.S. government officials during this episode was partially the result of campaign contributions by several officials of the offending S&Ls.

Major U.S. insurance companies' improper investment in high yield securities and U.S. real estate led to critical situations at some of the large insurers.

3.   *Bureaucracy*

All large organizations require organizational infrastructure which is bureaucratic. There are limits to entrepreneurial activity, flexibility, and individual scope within any large organization; otherwise, chaos would ensue. American banks, insurance companies, and securities firms encounter some of the same bureaucratic issues that plague JFIs domestically and overseas in terms of decision-making, coordination, strategy, and communication.

Because Japan's financial system is already consolidated, the JFI bureaucratic problems are to some extent more acute because of their sheer size. There are fewer but larger institutions in Japan, as opposed to the U.S. For example, Japan has fewer than 100 commercial banks as compared to 13,000 in the U.S. Japanese life insurance companies number 21 versus 2,100 in the U.S. The Japanese brokerage industry is dominated by four firms. There is no concept of regional firms, discount firms, or specialty firms.

Bureaucratic procedures certainly helped to create problems within American institutions by distorting substantive credit examinations for investments and loans. Volume, publicity, and political safety were features of the large American financial institutions in the 1970s and 1980s. The JFIs did not have a monopoly on bureaucratic incompetence.

The JFIs' structure, to be sure, was more bureaucratized than the American system. In addition, it is difficult to look at the JFI bureaucracy in isolation. The faults of JFI bureaucracy were exacerbated by government protection and the absence of performance criteria. Generally, the American problems eventually came to the surface and had to be dealt with. The Japanese problems—whether loan losses, bad investment decisions, or excessive costs—have long been ignored. Even prior to the 1990 market debacle, poor performance and mistakes were not confronted. Even the vagueness with which the Japanese banks account for non-performing loans allowed them enormous scope for postponement of their day of reckoning. In a bureaucracy, the usual course of action is paralysis in recognizing and dealing with problems, and in these respects the JFIs represented an almost pure form of bureaucracy.

4. *Centralization*

American commercial and investment banks were not immune to problems deriving from home office meddling, myopia, and misinformation. American officials, like their Japanese counterparts, enjoyed the perquisites of international travel, and substantive business matters were not always a priority when they visited overseas offices. Shopping, sightseeing, and social interests were often higher on the agenda. When American officials received presentations at home or overseas, the discussions were likely to have a positive slant and to involve what home office people wanted to hear, as opposed to reality. The American profit center mentality and vertical integration meant that each area had significant autonomy to staff and build infrastructure without regard to office needs, resources, or opportunities. Americans were shipped to London and Tokyo with promises of promotions and extravagant housing allowances—in one case $30,000 per month in Tokyo—without thorough planning and without consideration of the impact on the overseas office.

Neither American institutions nor the Japanese fully understood or recognized the implications of the three categories of business and their interplay:

1. Domestic
2. International
3. Global

For U.S. and Japanese firms alike, centralization usually meant dealing with issues on a departmental basis from the home office. Centralized planning should have meant coordination and communication between departments to determine how to handle a situation overseas. Overlapping territories, products, clients, businesses, and time zones made departmental management from home office fraught with difficulty. The activity just did not fit into the domestic mold.

Both Japanese and American financial institutions encountered these issues. The lack of performance requirement, emphasis on form, failure to deal with mistakes, and an artificially profitable domestic environment allowed the JFIs to overlook their problems and reduced their flexibility. Americans were unable to overlook losses and costs and, therefore, were forced to adjust. After the initial adjustment process, some of the American firms established successful departments and businesses; some did not; and some retreated entirely. The process continues.

Centralization might imply strong individual leadership and management from New York for the Americans and from Tokyo for the JFIs. This certainly could be true with any American company, but it was unlikely with a JFI. The senior management of JFIs was often removed from the business and operated mainly in a ceremonial capacity. They were quite "busy" as there was an endless series of personnel meetings and social outings that senior officials are required to attend. They may have been involved with an acquisition or establishment of a new office, but the business activity was managed from the general manager and below. Also, the JFI consensus approach neutralized most major input or influence by the time approval of an idea was forthcoming. Similarly, the U.S. expected Japanese prime ministers to exert some authority, whereas they are actually the product of a political compromise that allowed them no autonomy, and also no accountability. A JFI senior official, such as Nomura's Tabuchi, IBJ's Kurosawa, or Sumitomo Bank's Komatsu, never could have exercised the independent power that strong-willed American executives might have.

5.   *Provincialism*

For the Japanese, American provincialism would imply short-term orientation, excessive individualism, job insecurity, total immediate preoccupation about money on a personal and corporate level, poor planning, and lack of commitment. Positive aspects of American provincialism would include better compensation, more responsibility for an employee at an earlier stage in a career, less pressure to conform, and absence of rigid office structure. These generalizations were valid to some extent in the 1980s, although there were important differences in strengths and weaknesses among American financial institutions. Competence, integrity, and attitude were qualities which should have been examined on an individual, departmental, and firm basis. By contrast, the JFIs' structure created a uniformity and mediocrity common to all firms within the system.

Another aspect of American provincialism was the tendency to try to convert foreigners to the American way. Often, this prevented the Americans from fully understanding foreign institutions and systems because the Americans were more comfortable talking than listening.

" Another aspect of American provincialism was the tendency to try to convert foreigners to the American way. Often, this prevented the Americans from fully understanding foreign institutions and systems because the Americans were more comfortable talking than listening. "

In the important area of assimilation, some American financial institutions were quite flexible and were able to attract qualified foreign nationals, integrate them into their operations, promote them, and reap the rewards of having local contacts, expertise, and knowledge. Their presence impacted not just local business, but international, global, and domestic operations as well. Some of the Americans have become multinational; others have global operations in particular businesses.

The JFIs were uniformly unsuccessful in assimilating foreign employees into their structure, thereby limiting their ability to transfer skills, technology, and knowledge, as well as hampering their efforts to build overseas businesses and local client relationships. Business in America, therefore, was purely a function of aggressive pricing, domestic capital, and naive trend-following. The JFIs even built up considerable ill will with their separatist approach to personnel management. It is fair to say that Americans who joined JFIs did not have other alternatives, and that the frustration level of people who worked for JFIs created a severe turnover and morale problem. The foreigners who remained with JFIs were often quite passive.

Certainly, major European financial institutions were provincial relative to U.S. institutions in terms of personnel assimilation, but they are not in the JFI category of separatism.

6.   *Transients*

The U.S. financial institutions had nothing comparable to the JFI personnel rotation system. People did have different jobs and responsibilities during their careers, but there was no attempt to move people on a programmed basis to gain familiarity in many areas. Employees could achieve a high level of compensation and responsibility quickly, probably too quickly, if their particular skill or department were experiencing the favorable part of a market cycle. Maturity and management skill development might have been better served had the employee been exposed to more responsible supervision and direction. These issues were constantly being reviewed at U.S. financial institutions, which suffered the problems of loose control and rapid advancement of young people in addition to enjoying the profits of allowing bright people to have initiative and responsibility at an early age.

In an extreme case, the Salomon Brothers' government bond trading scandal of 1991 was the direct result of lax supervision. Management ignored its responsibility to monitor its employees, even when it knew of illegal practices that were being used. The large profits of the youthful, government trading desk were combined with gamesmanship—a powerful combination for a management which had grown quite callous.

7. Personnel

It is difficult to compare personnel at American financial institutions with JFI staff in the 1980s. The personality, competence, and motivation of Americans varied considerably between institutions and between types of institutions such as an investment bank, insurance company, and commercial bank. Each job carried a different set of priorities. A partial list of the categories would include loan officer, research analyst, sales person, trader, support staff, manager, investment banker, portfolio manager, quantitative specialist, and capital market personnel. Then there are hybrid functions, such as the quantitative personnel who trade securities. The entire gamut of personality types and demeanors, from volatile to reflective, might be represented within a U.S. financial institution.

Management of such a diverse and highly motivated group requires flexibility and perspective. Compensation, responsibility, and advancement depend on performance.

Many investment and merchant banking activities are highly cyclical in nature. When investment banks became public companies in order to raise capital, compensation shifted towards cash payouts rather than equity (except for Goldman Sachs, the only remaining private partnership among the major U.S. investment banks). Bonuses were determined on a yearly basis and depended on fees or trading profits generated in one year. In its extreme form, this forced personnel to concentrate on generating as much profit as possible in one particular profit center without regard to ethical or professional behavior. Especially in the merchant banking and trading areas, there was often no concern for the performance of a transaction after its completion, because compensation was based solely on fees generated before the yearly compensation meetings. Although all firms were guilty of this to varying degrees, some firms (such as Drexel Burnham & Lambert) took this compensation system to its ultimate conclusion. In addition, employee turnover and *prima donna* attitudes were a constant feature of the highly charged environment of U.S. investment banks.

Interestingly, several publicly-held investment banks that specialize in wholesale or institutional business are moving back to employee equity ownership by awarding stock as part of the compensation package. Under this arrangement, the employee would benefit if the firm performed well over a period of time—as the stock price would reflect consistent earnings.

JFI personnel inhabited a different system. Compensation and promotion were linked to age. The JFI used the enforcement of conformity and peer pressure to create a standardized employee. The structure inhibits and retards development as presently constructed. Perceived general management skills were valued over specialist knowledge. Specialists were regarded with condescension and resentment. The thought of being able to quantify a result implied individual accountability—anathema within the Japanese system. Profit and performance criteria were noticeably absent from the JFIs.

THE MOF AND THE SEC

The U.S. regulatory body, the SEC, does not have the broad mandate or power of the MOF. The SEC concerns itself with investor protection, fraud, manipulative market practices, and standards of fairness. By contrast, in the 1980s the MOF allowed the JFIs to engage in speculative, often fraudulent, behavior and seemed totally uninterested in protecting the investor. Despite its power, information, and mandate, the MOF either did not know about the JFIs' business dealings with organized crime, or did not care. Rather, the MOF attempted to control and direct the Japanese financial system. But the Japanese financial system and the economy was already too large and complex to manage in the feudal manner in which the MOF operated. Trying to monitor a massive volume of transactions on an individual basis was folly. Attempting to control the activities of JFIs overseas was very difficult. The MOF's use of generalists made their supervision superficial. The rotation system was at work again. Rotation of personnel at the MOF was so widespread that an English language journal, the *Japan Financial Report* ("JFR") regularly published a list when changes were announced so that foreign firms had a reference. The MOF's main thrust was apparently the retention of its political power rather than proper supervision of the financial system.

The difference between the MOF and the SEC is poignantly demonstrated by the SEC's immediate reaction to Salomon Brother's manipulation of the U.S. Treasury market auction. Salomon's huge trading muscle allowed it to corner the auction market and distort prices by a few basis points. The billions of dollars involved meant that, although the price distortion was small—merely an abstraction to the American public—the impact was millions of dollars of profit for Salomon. More fundamentally, it was a direct assault on the integrity of the U.S. financial system. The investigation, new management at Salomon, and the huge fine are history. Although the SEC certainly is not perfect, its attitude and philosophy is clearly reflected in the 1991 Salomon scandal.

The MOF, on the other hand, routinely allowed enormous price distortions to occur without understanding them or dealing with them. Consequently, the JFIs were accustomed to operating in an artificial environment which ultimately corrected itself, as evidenced by the stock and real estate market declines of the 1990s. There is a direct linkage of the market debacle to the MOF's guidance. The MOF's and JFIs' attempt to blame the decline on foreigners is yet another example of passing the buck or no accountability.

Westerners are often impressed by the appearance of the MOF activity. When the MOF announced a new study group to investigate an issue, or when it developed "reform legislation" to deal with a problem, Westerners reacted with admiration and respect. They viewed this as yet another example of the Japanese government exercising its leadership role in its partnership with business. Americans, searching for a role model, were especially eager to praise Japan. The reality of the MOF's efforts are hardly commendable. Their professional knowledge of markets was highly suspect. They either did not understand the JFIs' distortion of markets or, possibly, they did not care. The MOF watched idly as Japanese money managers jeopardized the economic well-being of pensioners through inept and irresponsible behavior.

What Americans interpreted as activity by the MOF was often simply the appearance of dealing with a problem. The loosely-worded laws merely indicated administrative guidance. This was very different from detailed American legislation with specific terms, conditions, and punishments. Even allowing for confusion arising from interpretation of American laws by lawyers and courts, it is inappropriate to compare the MOF's broad degree of discretion with American practices. Again, there was extreme danger of misinterpretation of Japanese motivation and behavior when Westerners attempted to superimpose their vocabulary on Japanese situations without an awareness of the particular Japanese context. Even simple concepts such as the importance of form over substance must always be remembered in evaluating a Japanese situation.

> **" What Americans interpreted as activity by MOF was often simply the appearance of dealing with a problem. The loosely-worded laws merely indicated administrative guidance. This was very different from detailed American legislation with specific terms, conditions, and punishments. "**

Examples of Westerners' naive assumptions of the MOF's competence abound. Underestimating the pitfalls of administrative guidelines was a fertile source of miscomprehension. *The Wall Street Journal* pointed to the potentially direct connection between administrative guidance and corruption in an editorial:

Part of the reason for (Japanese) political corruption also lies in Japan's administrative guidance system which allows LDP-appointed bureaucrats to interpret deliberately fuzzy regulations. "Whenever we had to do anything, the first thing we had to do was to go to . . . (the MOF) and bow low" says Yoshio Terasawa, a former executive at Nomura Securities who is now a member of the upper house of the Diet for the Japan New Party. This provides a huge incentive for businesses to court goodwill through political donations.[33]

---

[33] "Democracy in Ferment," *The Wall Street Journal*, December 2, 1992, p. A-16.

Politicians, bureaucrats, and businesses had their own agendas that entailed power and control, rather than professionalism and competence. It was definitely a partnership. Yet, this arrangement was hardly a role model to be emulated.

The rhetoric of reform within the MOF and the MOF's position with the Japanese government are popular topics. The struggle between the politicians and the bureaucrats is the subject of one article entitled, "The Waning of the MOF."[34] This article, as well as others, do not grapple with the reality of the complex relationship between the MOF, JFIs, and the Japanese government viewed within the structure of Japanese society. Issues of political turf and the rhetoric of reform are visible. Change is hardly imminent.

ATTITUDES TOWARD CHANGE DIFFER

Conceptually, it is interesting to contemplate changing the structure of a JFI. However, this would entail a challenge to the Japanese system that JFI officials and employees have followed blindly for years. In their overseas business endeavors, unless compelled by crisis to do more, JFI officials are more likely to make insignificant changes on the periphery rather than question their structure or sink into paralysis and non-recognition of their problems.

With an American financial institution, change has to be dealt with on a daily basis. Losses cannot be hidden indefinitely. Although the managements of Citicorp and American Express were able to avoid responsibility for errors committed during the 1980s, they eventually had to perform adequately, or they were replaced. Change within the American financial institutions often occurred dramatically and cataclysmically during the 1980s. Firms went out of business or were merged, entire departments were eliminated. Firms charged into new areas and retreated from old ones. Some of the efforts were timely, well-planned, and well-executed, while others were badly conceived and poorly implemented. Firms were forced to react to losses and different circumstances. If profits were absent or could not be identified in the foreseeable future, firms were compelled to adjust in terms of personnel, structure, and activity.

---

[34] Michael Hirsh, "The Waning of the MOF," *Institutional Investor*, December 1993, pp. 45-51.

Many of the problems could have been foreseen, and the process often could have been handled in a smoother and more professional manner than actually occurred. The U.S. savings and loan crisis represented the most destructive of the events that could have been avoided.

The American banks, generally, lost significant assets to independent money managers who focused exclusively on managing assets. Money managers can be quite large (such as mutual funds like Fidelity) or small, so that they can take advantage of specialized skills or areas of the markets. The decentralization of money management was an issue that should have been studied by JFIs in terms of future strategy and separate structure. Since the Japanese banks will be allowed to pursue many areas within the securities industry, a significant examination would not be hypothetical, but real.

When viewed from the post-war perspective, it is difficult to imagine how the JFIs will make a major transition to allow them to be more competitive in a deregulated environment. Their structure has been developed to cope with a highly regulated, protected market. Its foundations were an ebullient market and a successful manufacturing sector. The JFIs have trouble even recognizing and admitting mistakes because of cultural, educational, and institutional traditions. The next steps involving the awareness of the need for change, formulating a strategy, and implementing a plan would be a move into uncharted territory. The Japanese pride themselves on adaptability within the system. This is justifiable, in many cases, but the JFI's background does not lend itself to adjusting the system itself.

" Ironically, the Japanese personnel rotation system has a most un-Japanese consequence—short-term orientation. "

Many aspects of the financial markets require specialized skills and continuity of contact, which is impossible under the Japanese rotation system. Ironically, the Japanese personnel rotation system has a most un-Japanese consequence—short-term orientation. The JFI salaryman is only concerned with his three-year stint within a department. His major priority is negative—avoiding a mistake. (He is allowed to make politically acceptable mistakes.) His other focus is loyalty. The result of this practice is a system that resembles a government bureaucracy in its inefficiency and lack of intensity. Again, it is necessary to delve below the surface to qualify the myth of the hardworking JFI salaryman. If hours expended at the job and entertaining colleagues defines hard work, the JFI salaryman is a very hard worker. If productivity, efficiency, results, and intensity are goals, most JFI salarymen would be considered unfavorably. However, it is the structure that is responsible for the inefficiency, not the individual salaryman.

The personnel rotation system does have positive attributes, but there need to be accommodations made to operating in specialist areas and overseas markets. This does not mean that JFI employees should become specialists because this would mean that the entire JFI structure would have to be modified. It does mean that a way to access skills, knowledge, contacts, and clients has to be found, or certain overseas businesses cannot be undertaken effectively.

LINEAR VIEW OF PROGRESS

By the 1980s, if not sooner, American financial institutions had lost the illusion that progress could be taken for granted. They were constantly under pressure to evaluate and examine businesses. There were successful, as well as unsuccessful, attempts in this regard.

The JFIs still had a naive view that was tantamount to a rationalization of past activity. No matter how egregious the error or how ineffective the business, the JFI officials could place the mistake in the context of a precondition—a necessary phase that would be followed by another phase in which the JFI would move further along the imaginary strategic plan. The Nomura Research Institute official who spoke of establishing a portfolio in the first phase, and managing it in the second phase, is typical of this faith in progress. He did not dwell on the problems of the first portfolio, or how they would be corrected in the second phase. It is difficult to see how the Nomura Research Institute official could automatically assume progress, given rotating Japanese personnel and inadequate U.S. staff. But a JFI official could always hide behind the 50-year horizon or retreat into paralysis.

Still, we find it difficult to believe that the JFIs cannot adapt. *The New York Times* reported that:

> . . . there is much more competition in the Japanese financial markets than ever before, as American and European securities firms bring in sophisticated new tools and products, like program trading

and derivative securities, that the Japanese have been surprisingly slow to develop.[35]

It should no longer be surprising that JFIs cannot assimilate technology.

ABSENCE OF ROLE MODEL

The comparison with U.S. financial institutions indicates the fundamental problem facing JFIs in the 1980s. There was no perfect role model for the JFIs to study. Theoretically, they ought to have been able to examine and learn from the mistakes and successes of foreign institutions. But that was not their mindset. Multi-layered conceptual thinking was not the JFIs' forte. They wanted a "black box" for overseas business and there was none.

To be sure, the fact that Salomon and Morgan Stanley made huge profits in derivatives should have provided the JFIs with valuable conceptual insights. The successful penetration by some foreign institutions of the domestic Japanese institutional client base in the foreign-fixed income and equity markets, and later in the domestic equity market, ought to have been signposts for the JFIs. The same is true of Salomon's extensive domestic client base in Japanese government bonds. Those foreign activities took place in the 1980s in the backyard of the Japanese securities firms, yet they do not appear to have learned from them.

> **" In many areas, the preference for foreign contact by Japanese institutional investors could now be interpreted as a interest for more objective and professional sources of information. "**

---

[35] Sterngold, James, "For Tokyo Brokers, Time of Pain," *The New York Times*, October 7, 1992, pp. D-1, D-6.

In many areas, the preference for foreign contact by Japanese institutional investors could now be interpreted as a interest for more objective and professional sources of information. This is relative because the quality and motives of foreigners are not consistent, but theirs were certainly better than those of the Japanese brokers. Obviously, this was relative, because it is dangerous to generalize about the objectivity, integrity, or professionalism of foreign investment banks. This is only to say that these firms compared favorably to their Japanese counterparts.

Rather than learn from the foreign firms' experience, the JFIs focused on their domestic competition. They attempted to find simple solutions in terms of creating products, thereby underscoring the fragmentation of their approach. A senior official of Yamaichi Securities, for example, told *The New York Times*, "The traditional ways of doing business are just not profitable . . . We are constantly trying to think of new ideas we can introduce. Everything depends on new ideas."[36]

This was not the reasoned judgment of a far-sighted financier outlining a strategy. It was the desperate reaction of someone venting his frustration because the JFIs were not able to compete. The Yamaichi official's notion of the process of finding "new ideas" neglected the integration necessary for an effective process. Information flow from investors to salesmen, and active interchange among salesmen, traders, capital markets personnel, and research staff within the systematic structure were totally alien to the JFI. The JFI official usually thought that a specialist or designated person sits in an isolation booth creating an idea. The JFI desperately wanted to find that "black box" to replace the need for decision, interaction and communication. The Japanese brokers have been conditioned to sell products to investors. They are told what to sell and how much to sell. They are discouraged from thinking.

In other words, the pursuit of new ideas was more a matter of chasing the tail end of other people's fads. There was no innovation. Given the system, there could be no innovation unless, of course, the system changed, or the faults of the system were recognized and truly complementary features were created outside the system to supplement it.

---

[36] Sterngold, James, "Japan's Washout on Wall Street," *The New York Times*, June 11, 1989, p. 6.

STRAWS IN THE WIND, OR STRAW HOUSES?

In March 1992, Nomura made headlines in the foreign press by announcing that it would issue negative research reports about companies when their prospects warranted such an opinion. This was a major policy departure from the past, when Nomura would never issue sell recommendations for fear of antagonizing a corporate client. Prior business was done by only recommending stocks to purchase. Nomura's reputation for power within the market was enough to gain an investor following. After the market debacle in 1990, Nomura's loss of credibility and the enhanced reputation of foreign brokers' research in the Japanese market presented the Japanese brokers with a dilemma. Nomura's reaction was actually a minor concession done with great publicity. The substance of changing the way business is done will require more than form for all the JFIs.

But is this possible? A JFI's self-analysis would have to include the methods of foreign firms, and it would have to involve a critique of itself as well as of other JFIs. This would be difficult to do because of the unwillingness to admit, much less analyze, mistakes. The rotation system would interfere by making information and responsibility impossible to trace.

Presently, the JFIs prefer to deal with peripheral issues. They want to eliminate a few minor expenses. Even as late as 1992, one senior JFI official in New York identified his main goal as approving New York-related expenses in New York rather than in Tokyo. This did not pertain to budget considerations, merely to routine expenses such as client dinners. The bureaucrat thrives on these details, as matters of control. In one such incident, a JFI manager disallowed a six-dollar hotel laundry bill for a foreign guest who was conducting an expense-paid seminar for his institution. JFI officials indicate an awareness of the problems of personnel rotation, and defensively assert that many people are staying an extra year or more in a position—as if that made a difference.

Without modification of other aspects of the structure, though, the salaryman—even if he spends more time in a given job—will lack intensity and commitment. The performance criteria will remain political, and the salaryman will view his career as more managerial than specialist. Also, by the time a JFI salaryman has been employed for a few years, he has become somewhat influenced by the bureaucracy, and his tendency towards conformity, risk aversion, and paralysis has been reinforced to such an extent that change is difficult.

During the 1980s, the JFIs' search for immediate solutions and publicity led them into acquisitions, joint ventures, hiring specialists, and the quest for "black box" technology. After the initial pursuit, the JFIs, in general, adopted a passive approach to understanding the dynamics of these projects and making them work effectively—characterized by a brittleness devoid of communication.

> " Without modification of other aspects of the structure, though, the salaryman—even if he spends more time in a given job—will lack intensity and commitment."

The issue of assimilation has to be addressed. As indicated, JFIs have an almost insurmountable problem in terms of integration of foreign employees or joint ventures within their structure. The only areas where foreigners have seemed to fit were those which did not depend on interaction with the JFI, such as research or independently-financed profit centers. Conversely, the Japanese activities of both Salomon and Morgan Stanley would have been impaired without being able to assimilate Japanese and foreigners. The case of Shigeru Myojin at Salomon and Kevin Parker at Morgan Stanley indicated the positive influence of a Japanese on foreigners and a foreigner on Japanese.

The rigid conformity of the Japanese system has to be viewed in terms of the diversity of skills and personalities which are necessary to succeed in the financial services area. The various types of jobs—trading, sales, research (both quantitative and fundamental), investment banking, systems and support, and management—do not inherently require specific personality types. However, people tend to represent a wide assortment of characteristics—individualistic, volatile, introverted, extroverted, leader, follower, passive, active, reflective, reactive, self-centered, entrepreneurial, and supportive. The ability to manage a diverse group is critical to the success of a particular operation. The JFI tendency to impose conformity has constituted a barrier in terms of accessing different skills outside its organization. Within the JFI, conformity stifled creativity and production by distorting substantive priorities.

How will the JFIs have to change in order to compete in the deregulated world? How will their foreign trading partners need to change? These questions will be discussed in Chapter 11.

CHAPTER 11

COMPETING IN A DEREGULATED WORLD—THE CHALLENGE OF THE JFIS IN THE 1990S

" 'Japan's current recession was engineered deliberately by its government to strengthen financial institutions,' he (Chalmers Johnson) said '. . . Soon a group of large powerful (Japanese) banks will emerge that will be better suited than U.S. banks to deal with a rapidly changing post-Cold War world . . .' "[1]

On July 18, 1993, the Japanese voters did not give the Liberal Democratic Party (LDP) its usual majority of representatives in the Japanese Diet. For the first time in 38 years, a coalition of parties that consisted of former LDP members and Socialists was numerically slightly greater than the LDP. The former LDP members called themselves reformists. It remains to be seen what this fragile majority can accomplish. On January 28, 1994, the Japanese government passed a reform measure involving electoral re-alignment and campaign contributions. It is not within the scope of this book to predict the impact of the new government's policies on Japan's financial system, but one can safely say that the structural issues which have been outlined here are not understood by the Japanese political and financial establishment.

---

[1] Johnson, Chalmers, as quoted by Martin Rosenberg, "Academics Disagree on Future of Japan," *The Japan Times*, April 21, 1993, p. 7.

The collapse of Japan's bull markets in both equities and real estate in 1990 exposed the JFIs' vulnerability. As the markets tumbled lower, capital adequacy ratio problems, bad loans, and declining earnings all surfaced. By 1992, some JFIs were clearly liquidating their hidden reserves—their portfolio of closely-held equities, putting yet more pressure on Japan's beleaguered stock markets.

The JFIs' dreams for overseas business also suffered as their profitable business lines, such as credit enhancement guarantees, suddenly became uneconomic. Losses at home meant less money to invest overseas, curtailing both asset growth and infrastructure expansion plans. Indeed, today it is difficult to reconcile the JFIs' apparent retreat from, and more obvious paralysis in, the overseas business area with their oft-stated ambition to become world-class financial institutions.

WHAT DID JFIs LEARN FROM 1980s?

The obvious question is, whether the current pause in the JFIs' overseas advance is only a temporary phenomenon caused by a correction in Japan's markets, or a more fundamental change of course. The answer to that question, however, depends on another: What did the JFIs learn from the 1980s?

During the 1980s, the JFIs came face-to-face with the harsh reality of doing business in overseas deregulated markets and were found wanting—in terms of profit, performance, business and client development, deal flow, due diligence and asset screening, internal and external communication, organization, and corporate culture. What did the JFIs glean from this experience?

Based on their reactions, the answer seems to be—not much. The JFIs still view the 1980s as a phase in their development and, having completed this one phase, they are ready for the next. Largely unwilling to recognize mistakes and unable to take significant corrective action, they talk and tinker. JFI rhetoric now includes phrases like "return on assets," but a 50-year investment horizon and the lack of accountability make such phrases meaningless. The Japanese still believe in their system, their idea of change encompasses slight modifications in the rotation system, caution, and the continuation of current policies. Yet, reality dictates that the JFIs should explore the weaknesses of their own structure and institute basic reforms.

IS THERE A WAY? A WILL?

The list of changes needed in the Japanese system is already long. In 1991, one of Japan's most visible business consultants, Kenichi Ohmae, called the MOF a "dinosaur":

> To reduce the potential for conflicts of interests, the ministry must be broken apart into a number of smaller regulatory agencies. And the ministry's mandate must shift from protecting financial firms to defending investors, depositors, and all other users of financial services . . . a first step would be to break the ministry into several offices according to function. Industry development should be taken away from the central government and, if done at all, go to local authorities . . . The remaining functions of the ministry— taxation, budget, planning, financial market regulation and so on— should have their own unique office . . . This necessary change has been slow to come because of the unsavory relationship that the bureaucrats of the Ministry of Finance have established with the financial firms.[2]

" This, by the way, is the same MOF that was given credit for creating and supervising the Japanese financial system and the JFIs, and the same MOF that was held in awe by the foreign press for its wisdom, dedication, power, and achievement during the 1980s."

This, by the way, is the same MOF that was given credit for creating and supervising the Japanese financial system and the JFIs, and the same MOF that was held in awe by the foreign press for its wisdom, dedication, power, and achievement during the 1980s.

Ohmae recommended drastic, fundamental, structural changes for the MOF. He questioned its mandate and competence. Such a sweeping reform

---

2 Ohmae, Kenichi, "The Scandal Behind Japan's Financial Scandals," *The Wall Street Journal,* August 6, 1991, p.76.

would not be possible within Japanese society without extensive discussion and dire circumstances. Also, it is doubtful that the MOF would want such a reform, so the process of political compromise would make changes an even more remote possibility. The MOF derives power from the breadth and vagueness of its mandate, so it has a vested interest in maintaining the status quo.

What would provoke this major political reform, with such major entrenched interests, which the JFIs, the politicians and the MOF opposed? Reform should be distinguished from political change prompted by the desire for increased power. The docile electorate shows a virtually limitless potential for self-sacrifice and self-denial. The Japanese people and the Japanese manufacturers, in effect, subsidize the financial system, which itself was a burden on the Japanese economy. The reform would call into question the alleged superiority of the Japanese system. Where does the drive for reform emanate from in a land of conformity? How does a Japanese citizen express his frustration?

The JFIs were responsible for frittering away much of the Japanese trade surplus with their unwise investments and poor performance. In a sense, the JFIs were responsible for the economic problems that led to the government's embarrassment and subsequent downfall. Would the Japanese economy have deteriorated so dramatically if financial resources had been allocated efficiently? The government's embarrassment and subsequent downfall were directly connected to the JFIs' inability to recycle the trade surplus and invest professionally domestically and abroad. A properly functioning stock market and real estate market would certainly have provided the underpinnings for a sound economy. Loss compensation could not have existed in such an environment. Market forces and fairness would predominate.

One Japanese Diet member and former Nomura Securities executive recommends "an overhaul of the bureaucratic structure."[3] His target is the MOF. He wants to "create an autonomous Securities and Exchange Commission on the U.S. model." This would mean publicly available information and full disclosure. He calls for liberalization "of stock brokers' commission rates," i.e., negotiated rates. Weaker firms would not survive. He applauds the discipline that this would foster. He then cites the need to "establish fairer practices and guidelines within the ministry."

---

3 Terasawa, Yoshio, "Break Japan's Finance Bureaucracy," *The Wall Street Journal*, July 14, 1993, p. A-12.

Without a doubt, this sounds reasonable to *The Wall Street Journal* and its readers. The free market advocates view this as a vindication of its quasi-religious tenets. Is it feasible? Can an autonomous commission be superimposed on the Japanese system? What about all those vested interests? What would prevent the commission from being co-opted by the establishment? Would this not become a Japanese Securities and Exchange Commission which existed for the sake of form and control, not investor protection and professionalism? A facile how-to-do-it solution is appealing, but not appropriate.

The Japanese would be tempted to find a scapegoat, such as foreign brokers who have been active trading the index futures contract. It is conceivable that the government would want to restrict the activities of foreigners. They have even resurrected their fabrication of a conspiracy of "international Jewish bankers." (In the past, the Japanese have identified J.P. Morgan, John D. Rockefeller, and Franklin Roosevelt as part of the "international Jewish conspiracy.")

One well-known foreign observer, Chalmers Johnson, even appears to retain his faith in the Japanese system:

> "Japan's current recession was engineered deliberately by its government to strengthen financial institutions," he (Chalmers Johnson) said ". . . Soon a group of large powerful (Japanese) banks will emerge that will be better suited than U.S. banks to deal with a rapidly changing post-Cold War world . . ."[4]

This scenario is highly improbable. Yet, it is interesting, as an example of the continued acceptance of the omnipotent planning capacity of the Japanese government.

On a practical level, how does change take place in a specific case, such as a Japanese pension fund which is being poorly managed by a JFI? How does a JFI fire its manager? The person in charge of the pension fund is likely to be a rotating salaryman who is not concerned with performance. The company is likely to have several layers of interaction with the JFI, including that of borrower. The overall set of obligations between the parties would reduce the possibility of changing managers.

---

4   Johnson, Chalmers, as quoted by Martin Rosenberg, "Academics Disagree on Future of Japan," *The Japan Times*, April 21, 1993, p. 7.

MISPLACED PRIORITIES RESPONSIBLE FOR FAILURE

The list of changes needed in the Japanese system and at the JFIs is already long.

In 1992, an article in *The New York Times*, about "Japan's Rigged Casino, The Tokyo Stock Market,"[5] suggested that the weakness of the financial system was caused by the failure of government and brokers to prioritize financial matters. The article then went on to identify the Japanese brokers as the real culprits. In a more recent article, the same author cites "The $6 Trillion Hole in Japan's Pocket" as an estimate of Japan's stock market and real estate losses.[6] This time he focused on the banks rather than the brokers. No specific group can be isolated in terms of blame. The system itself is at fault.

In reality, brokers, banks, and insurance companies all share the blame for creating the 1990s market debacle, as well as an often corrupt and definitely flawed financial system. The article's obvious faith in the ability of the Japanese government—for which read the MOF Ohmae excoriated—and business to prioritize financial matters and correct abuses is just as obviously misplaced. Interestingly, implicit in both cases is the assumption that the MOF had not guided the system properly in the past.

Somewhat closer to the mark are calls for specific reforms in the domestic equity market. Knowledgeable foreigners call for such measures as increased emphasis on competitive performance in the money management area. Some foreigners, for example, call for remedial action such as:

- Lowering the ceiling on corporate holdings from the present 5 percent

- Outlawing tokkin funds

- Forcing fund managers to compete

- Permitting share buy-backs[7]

---

5 Sterngold, James, "Japan's Rigged Casino," *New York Times Magazine*, April 24, 1992, p. 24.
6 Sterngold, James, "The $6 Trillion Hole in Japan's Pocket," *The New York Times*, January 21, 1994, p. D-1, 2.
7 Zielinski and Holloway, *Unequal Equities*, pp. 223-228 and Viner, *Inside Financial Markets* p. 285.

Although such reforms nominally apply only to the domestic market, they are relevant to overseas operations, if only because they highlight lack of performance. Yet, in another sense, such measures—whether at home or overseas—are meaningless. They fail to recognize, let alone address, the main structural weakness of the JFIs.

WHO SPONSORS REFORM?

Not attacking the structural flaws in the JFIs, of course, is a popular course. Japan's financial establishment and government have a major vested interest in the maintenance of the status quo. The MOF wants to keep control. The JFIs want to enjoy their franchise. The salaryman wants to avoid accountability. Stability is always preferred over change.

Japanese society suppresses dissent by ostracizing the offender. The Japanese people are restrained by peer pressure and conformity. Shareholders are docile.

In doing overseas business, however, the JFIs' problems have been exposed and can easily be related to weaknesses in the Japanese financial system itself—bureaucracy, rotation, provincialism, excessive conformity, politicization, the absence of accountability, and the dearth of innovation. The entire system needs to be questioned; performance cannot be mandated within the present structure. The JFIs must develop a mindset which does not include total dependence on the MOF.

" Japanese society suppresses dissent by ostracizing the offender. The Japanese people are restrained by peer pressure and conformity. Shareholders are docile . . . The entire system needs to be questioned; performance cannot be mandated within the present structure. "

By 1993, reform was topical, even fashionable, in Japan. Attempts to distill reform to easy how-to-do-it blueprints appeared in the press, on television and radio, and in books. Ichiro Ozawa, one of the new reform politicians and co-founder of the Japan Renewal Party, capitalized on this theme in his book, *Blueprint for Building a New Japan*, which became a bestseller.[8] Ozawa, as any casual observer of Japanese politics knows, was the protege of Shin Kanemaru, the disgraced LDP boss who was the epitome of Japanese corruption and powerbrokering. Despite the possibility that he may have experienced a moral, social, and political conversion, one should be a little suspect of Ozawa's motives, sincerity, and intentions.

The attempt to find easy, specific answers to JFI structural problems is doomed to failure. There are no instant-cure approaches with five easy steps for rectifying weaknesses, identifying future opportunities, or reforming the MOF. Consulting firms charged millions of dollars to create studies for JFI activities overseas. JFIs were looking for the formula, a plan to copy. It did not exist. It does not exist. The answer lies imbedded in Japanese assumptions and society.

" Full disclosure, performance orientation, and accountability are limited in a society where stability is paramount "

The strengths, as well as the weaknesses, can be found in the structure of Japanese society. General characteristics associated with Japan—diligence, conformity, hierarchy, and other traits mentioned in this study—are well-known. An understanding of these traits is fundamental to prescribing a future course of action. Practical issues of regulation and performance cannot be viewed in isolation.

Full disclosure, performance orientation, and accountability are limited in a society where stability is paramount. Redress through the courts is restricted. Group lawsuits brought by shareholders against companies are increasing. However, if shareholders sue a board of directors and prevail, the money that they receive goes back to the company.[9] Not very punitive. This would have dubious deterrent effect in terms of corporate behavior. In this setting, confrontation must be avoided and change carefully orchestrated. Even the issue of assimilation in a Japanese context is hardly comprehensible to foreigners. Surely, the Japanese point to America's

---

8   Schlesinger, Jacob M., "In Japan, the Torch Has Been Passed to a New In-Group," *The Wall Street Journal*, August 10, 1993, p. A-4.
9   Hardy, Quentin, "Japan Toughens Financial Disclosure," *The Wall Street Journal*, August 10, 1993, p. C-10.

assimilation failures, but the magnitude and qualitative differences between American and Japanese make analogies hazardous.

It is not necessary to make a detailed behavioral study of the Japanese educational system, the Japanese government, or the JFIs to recognize the salient issues. There are ample secondary sources that have sufficiently identified characteristics. Anyone who interacts with JFIs should become aware of these societal traits.

JFIs NEED TO MAKE BUSINESS CHOICES

Rather than talk about structural change in the abstract, it is more efficient to consider what the JFIs must do to become effective in their overseas business operations. This begins with making their own independent evaluation of business opportunities, prioritizing these opportunities in terms of risk/return and the available expertise, and allocating resources accordingly. Thus, the JFIs must determine which businesses to pursue and what priority to assign to each. They must recognize that capital, resources, and management are not available to do everything.

Above all, perhaps, they must develop a clear sense of why they are entering a business and, therefore, establish what they expect to get out of that business. This requires the discipline to identify and pursue realistic business objectives. JFIs must ask whether the business needs infrastructure or whether it should be conducted with an outside partner.

Essentially, as has been mentioned, there are four main goals which would be a valid rationale for a JFI's overseas business operation:

1. Profit/Performance
2. Transfer of technology, knowledge, and skills
3. Publicity, presence or market share
4. Servicing Japanese clients at home and abroad

Through the 1980s, the JFIs usually muddied these goals. Form prevailed over substance, excuses over reason, and businesses were justified by whichever rationale seemed most convenient. As a result, little was accomplished except for costly, and sometimes embarrassing, publicity.

Implicit in any assessment of business goals is an appraisal of both realistic business expectations—what will the transaction or enterprise actually yield?—and what results can be achieved within the JFI's current structure. If the projected results cannot be achieved within the existing structure, obviously, the JFI must ask whether it can change its structure or create a new external entity. In other words, any practical discussion of what businesses are best for JFIs ought to lead the institution to a reappraisal of its own structure and operational order as it impinges on overseas business.

"... any practical discussion of what businesses are best for JFIs ought to lead the institution to a reappraisal of its own structure and operational order as it impinges on overseas business."

FITTING STRUCTURE TO BUSINESS AND VICE VERSA

Having advanced this far, the JFI needs to raise a number of hard questions:

- What is the importance of the particular business?

- Where and how does the business fit within the JFIs' organizational structure?

- To what extent does the business require foreigners, and is that dependence temporary or permanent?

- How will communications with foreigners be handled?

- If an outside entity is needed, in what form should it be?

- Is the business supposed to represent a good investment for the JFI, create a product in which the JFI can invest, create a product for the JFI to distribute to its Japanese client base, or generate fee income?

As is evident, these questions apply to activities as diverse as commercial or investment banking, securities brokering, or passive investment as well as in the context of domestic, international, or global markets. In the past, for example, the JFIs generally tried to become active in M&A. In America, JFIs formed joint ventures, made acquisitions, and hired expensive Americans to pursue cross-border M&A business without fully understanding the cyclical nature of the activity, without perceiving how to use the operation in a purely domestic M&A situation and without knowing how to integrate the M&A entity into the JFI organization. These entities created publicity value in a period of over-confidence.

After these questions are dealt with, the JFI still must contend with implementation and coordination within the bureaucracy. The autonomous departments and fragmented approach, combined with a lack of accountability and remote senior management, make this task organizationally complex and politically difficult. The elaborate organizational charts that JFIs construct look impressive, but are not effective. It may seem that these concerns and recommendations are elementary, but the JFIs' activity in the 1980s was devoid of these rather basic considerations.

JFIs MUST FOCUS ON STRENGTHS

In setting priorities for potential overseas businesses, the JFIs must focus on their various strengths as well as weaknesses. These strengths include:

1. *The Japanese economy*—The industrial sector and the growing consumer area will continue to provide the JFIs with a strong base from which to operate. This will provide cash and profitable opportunities for the JFIs. The JFIs will benefit substantially when the Japanese economy improves. The BOJ's policy of lowering interest rates in 1992 will positively impact the JFIs as well. The Japanese economy and the manufacturers are, in effect, subsidizing the JFIs. Although the Japanese financial system has decoupled from the manufacturing sector, it is still the recipient of the manufacturer's success.

2. *Franchise*—Although the financial sector is undergoing deregulation, the pace of regulatory change is slow and there is a residual regulatory franchise which will be difficult and uneconomical for foreigners to try to duplicate in many cases.

3. *Client and Asset Base*

   a. *Investors*—The individual and institutional investor client base is vast and represents a huge potential source of revenue. The JFIs have an extensive distribution network in place. In some cases, such as cross-shareholding arrangements, the client can still be considered as captive to a particular JFI. The massive amounts of money under management represent an extraordinary opportunity.

b. *Borrowers*—The JFIs occupy a significant advantage in their relationship with potential borrowers.

c. *Financial Services*—The JFIs have access to individual and corporate clients for providing a various assortment of services, such as M&A, swaps, and planning—both domestically and internationally.

In order to maximize these and other strengths, the JFIs have to be properly directed and organized in order to reestablish credibility.

ASSET MANAGEMENT MUST BE REFORMED

One area of business in which reform is absolutely unavoidable for the JFIs is the management of assets. In terms of overseas and domestic business, the ability to select asset categories and individual assets in a systematic manner is critical for performance. The JFIs must learn how to evaluate international as well as domestic assets. The JFIs have to be able to respond to opportunities, whether they be in the domestic or overseas markets. Asset types would vary for the different activities of the JFIs.

1. *Banking*—Loans, equity-related investments, credit enhancement, asset-backed loans, etc.

2. *Securities*—Portfolio management, either as principal or agent

   a. Domestic—Equity and fixed-income, hybrid securities, indexes, and derivatives

   b. Foreign:
      - Public—Equity and fixed-income, hybrid securities
      - Private—Equity, LBO, venture capital, real estate, and fixed-income

During the 1980s, the JFIs used an overly-simplistic process in selecting assets. The purchase of U.S. Treasury securities and other U.S. dollar-denominated fixed-income assets provides a cogent example. The JFIs were compelled to look at higher yielding bond markets because of (a) low Japanese interest rates, (b) implicit return guarantees to clients, (c) the inability of insurance companies to pay distributions to policy holders out of capital gains and only dividends and interest, (d) performance measurement often equated to current yield rather than total rate of return, and (e) significantly higher yields in foreign bond markets (primarily U.S., Canadian, Australian, and British).

The JFI portfolio manager reasoned that a three- to four-percent rate advantage in the U.S. market was enough protection against currency risk. If U.S. Treasuries yielded 8 percent in a seven-year maturity, and Japanese bonds yielded 4 percent, the portfolio manager thought that the dollar would have to fall more than 4 percent each year in seven years before he would "lose" money. In the interim, he could earn extra yield. In any event, he thought that currency losses could easily be offset by selling assets. There were also means of delaying disclosure of the currency losses. Needless to say, the volatile currency movements exposed the naivete of the JFI fund managers as they lost billions during the 1980s by not understanding currency risk.

Occasionally, the MOF may have suggested that the JFIs participate in a U.S. Treasury auction in order to support their enfeebled and profligate American ally, but this was infrequent and not the driving force behind the JFIs' massive purchase of U.S. Treasuries in the 1980s. In a broader sense, there was no attempt to systematize the asset allocation process. The procedure was *ad hoc*. Individual ideas were approved without the slightest understanding about the impact on the portfolio. On-the-job-training for young employees who were managed by equally unknowledgeable middle managers was the norm.

It is difficult to see how the process of asset management can be improved without internal structural reform and adequate performance criteria for portfolio managers, as well as asset selection. Because of the need for special knowledge and skill, many categories of assets cannot be professionally managed within the present structure. The ambitions, basic needs, and general performance also cannot be accommodated under the present JFI organization and attitude. In other words, a practical assessment of business should raise questions about the JFIs' internal structure.

MAKIN' MONEY

During the 1980s, the provocative American money manager, Jim Rogers, taught two courses at Columbia Business School. One dealt with various market-related crises, and the other with security analysis, which Rogers said was about "makin' money." The JFI staff should have taken both courses because they were about to experience a crisis, and they need to understand substantive analysis before they will be profitable in the U.S. markets.

During the JFI expansion overseas in the 1980s, performance was a vague concept. Costs and profits were ignored; infrastructure build-up, speculation, market share, and publicity characterized their activity abroad and at home. Performance criteria were never applied to individuals. Nor was performance in terms of portfolios compared to market indexes or absolute goals. Comparison was made to other institutions within the same regulatory classification, trust banks with trust banks, and so forth. American money managers also competed within categories, but JFIs resorted to carefully orchestrated and unrealistic comparisons.

I remember my surprise when I first saw lists of Japanese life insurance companies purportedly ranked by performance, only to discover that performance meant *current yield*. Current yield can be easily manipulated internally. The numbers were closely correlated so that all seemed to perform similarly.

" The JFIs were so averse to risk that the aphorism 'he who makes the fewest mistakes wins' was accepted as conventional wisdom. Again, risk meant 'political risk' or the 'risk of being different' as opposed to a 'prudent risk.'"

The JFIs did not want to perform significantly better or significantly worse than their peers for that would cause negative attention in a conformist society. The JFIs were so averse to risk that the aphorism "he who makes the fewest mistakes wins" was accepted as conventional wisdom. Again, risk meant "political risk" or the "risk of being different" as opposed to a "prudent risk." The ability to survive was synonymous with staying power. Under the guise of orderly continuity and orderly change, the JFIs have hidden their problems in terms of structure and earnings.

At the opposite end of the spectrum is the U.S., where sudden change was the norm in the 1980s. The occasional "bail-out," such as Continental Bank, was far outnumbered by the abruptness of mergers in Texas, the Bank of America/Security Pacific, Chemical/Manufacturers Hanover and others. In the securities industry, Drexel Burnham and E.F. Hutton fell without grace. Thousands of people were fired, entire departments such as

Salomon's municipal and commercial paper departments were eliminated, and billions of dollars were written off. This procedure is hardly suitable for Japan, and is so extreme that it is destructive even for a purported *laissez-faire* economy such as the U.S.'s. However, by these drastic measures, bad loans and inadequate performance, profit, and earnings are effectually dealt with, and the resulting structures are competitive.

The short-term mentality of American industry is often cited as a negative feature, but the JFI failure to recognize problems in a deregulated environment is certainly not the epitome of long-term strategic planning. Indeed, the American financial system had developed excesses and was dangerously short-term oriented. Profit and performance are essential goals, but the system was also characterized at times by greed and immorality. The U.S. economy was impaired and threatened by the excesses. Nevertheless, the absence of performance and profit motivation on the part of the JFIs within their particular environment allowed very harmful structural defects to develop. Even with all its faults, there is a self-correcting mechanism, although imperfect, at work within the American financial system.

Proper performance and profit motivation for JFI employees will be a serious challenge for the JFIs and represents another example of the need for reform. If the JFI deems management as the highest goal, then its managers must be judged by their ability to produce profits, either from their own staff or from outside partners. JFI officials have the utmost confidence in their managerial capabilities. Since the current structure for handling external partners is substantively ineffective, a new system is required.

Because of the JFIs structural deficiencies, the importance of outside partners and counterparties cannot be overstated. The partnerships could be informal or formal such as acquisitions, joint ventures, or profit-sharing arrangements. The time required to identify, select, and monitor partners could be substantial; certainly it could easily extend past a staff rotation. In areas where there is substantial interaction between foreigner and JFI, the JFI must assume the responsibility of accounting for its structural weaknesses in terms of assimilation, bureaucracy, rotation system, and overcentralization. During the 1980s, the JFIs were ambivalent about whether their involvement with their partnerships should be active or passive. The JFI salaryman will protest that the relationship was always active. The nature of the communication usually indicated that it was passive and ineffectual. If the JFI does not correct these communication problems or provide for alternative solutions, the JFI will be doomed to repeating the disastrous experience of the 1980s. Dealing with this issue is fraught with problems, but is not impossible to solve.

> **" During the 1980s, the JFIs were
> ambivalent about whether their involvement
> with their partnerships should be active
> or passive. The JFI salaryman will protest
> that the relationship was always active.
> The nature of the communication
> usually indicated that it was passive
> and ineffectual. "**

Similarly, it is only necessary to mention that the vital access to foreign markets and clients was severely restricted within the JFIs because of the inability to assimilate foreign employees. Currently a professional American, in a job which required interaction, would choose to work for a JFI only as a last resort. If he were to work for a foreign institution, Deutsche Bank would be preferable to IBJ, Sumitomo Bank or the Bank of Tokyo.

FINDING OVERSEAS PARTNERS

Japanese, American, or European financial institutions must consider which overseas opportunities require local partners. A JFI might be focusing on North America or China. An American financial institution could be looking at Japan or Europe. A European entity might be looking at Asia or North America. These businesses might relate to fee business, trading, or asset management. At times, these institutions may want their own presence, infrastructure, or skill base. Often it is not practical or economical to be self-sufficient. Many profitable opportunities are situational and fleeting. Prompt action is required. Others might be too costly to undertake independently. A JFI might have an asset base or a client without the skill or network to operate effectively in America. An American financial institution might have a product that would be beneficial to a JFI or its client base.

Does this mean that IBJ should seek an alliance with Morgan Bank or that Nomura and Fidelity Management should discuss joint ventures? Should IBJ look for smaller specialized firms with whom it might associate? Does Nomura need to search for smaller asset managers in America to provide product? Should a JFI be involved exclusively as a source of capital in certain situations? How should the association be organized and structured? How should the JFI communicate with the partner? How does it monitor and evaluate results? How does the JFI identify its goals and prioritize businesses? What can the JFI do alone?

For any financial institution—but especially for JFIs—these are critical questions. In fact, they must be answered within the context of the institution's strengths and weaknesses. True reform begins with these issues—not with the MOF. The JFI's dependence on the MOF must be questioned before reform can be discussed.

RETREATING FROM RETREAT

The JFIs describe their existing situation as resulting from the "current difficult market conditions." Many JFI officials would like to retreat to the protection of the Japanese equity, bond, and real estate market; however, these markets offer little comfort. Next, the JFIs look to increase their presence in Asia, where they think they understand the Oriental mind better than they comprehend "Western ways." They can also follow Japanese manufacturers there as a natural client base. Unfortunately, if the JFIs follow the same pattern as they have in the U.S. in terms of information, deal flow, and contacts, they will repeat their mistakes. In some ways, Asia will actually be more difficult than the U.S. because of the lack of publicly-available information, obstacles in developing a reliable network of business contacts and controls, and legal structure.

In reality, overseas Chinese—and often mainland Chinese—businessmen can communicate more easily with Westerners, especially Americans, than with a Japanese salaryman. Many overseas Chinese have been educated in America and the U.K. They relate to directness and individuals. Also, Chinese memories of Japanese occupation linger.

The domestic Japanese market is too restrictive for institutions with the size, needs, and ambitions of the JFIs. The JFIs do not have the option of retreating to the domestic market in the hopes that it will recover and solve all of their asset requirements and business needs.

In an interview with the *Asian Wall Street Journal Weekly*, the articulate former Vice-Minister of Finance and current chairman of Bank of Tokyo, Toyoo Gyohten, "dismissed earlier speculation" that Japanese banks would retreat from North America because of their lending follies. In perfect political-speak and obfuscation, he said:

It's true that Japanese banks have been less active in the U.S. than before, but there are specific factors that can explain this. In the latter half of the 1980s, the increase of their exposure in the U.S. had been just extraordinary. Such growth isn't sustainable; it can't be justified as a long-term trend. What we are going through right now is a normalization process.[10]

There is no particular reason why Gyohten, who received wide exposure in the foreign press in the 1980s, should have been frank with *The Wall Street Journal*, but completely overlooking the incompetence of Japanese banks strains credulity.

HOW JFIs DEAL WITH STRUCTURAL WEAKNESSES

Any JFI that has successfully raised the kinds of hard questions discussed here will have identified significant weaknesses in its organizational structure. It will also have recognized that its options in dealing with weaknesses is limited.

- *Domestic practices*—It can be assumed that there will be no substantial modification in the rotation system. Even if it was feasible to alter the rotation system, the other structural issues remain and would prevent any serious change. The rotation system needs to be supplemented. Currently, it takes a great deal of effort to even track the frequent personnel changes which are a product of the rotation system.

- *Overcentralization*—At the present time, there is only the pretense of localization. If Tokyo is going to retain absolute control, the organizational inferences and unintended consequences have to be discussed.

- *Bureaucracy*—The interoffice and inter-departmental communication and coordination issues have created inefficiency and lack of concern about performance. Performance criteria, accountability, and profit orientation have to be incorporated into the system. The JFIs have to find a means of motivating management to become

---

[10] Lachica, Eduardo, "Japan's Banks Won't Retreat from the U.S., Gyohten Says," *The Wall Street Journal*, September 28, p. A-1.

conscious of performance and willing to accept responsibility. In order to accomplish this, the JFIs have to institute some method of staff evaluation which can be partially objective. Also, they have to reorganize the functions of personnel to better suit actual business conditions, rather than artificial institutional hierarchy.

■ *Provincialism*—The negative experience of the 1980s, in terms of the failure of localization of overseas offices and the inability to assimilate foreign employees or partners, should provide a warning to the JFIs. Transfer of technology or knowledge was impaired because of the emphasis on form as opposed to dialogue and integration. The JFIs' reliance on vagueness and ambiguity in order to avoid accountability and create political acceptability prevented any possibility of effective strategic planning. Japanese conformity and inability to deal with clarity or mistakes produced JFI salarymen with a risk-averse mentality. The JFI officials could hardly be expected to admit, recognize or understand the implications of their provincialism. Yet their overseas activities were crippled by the problems of provincialism. An awareness of this issue would be the first step towards dealing with it.

SOME JAPANESE TRAITS HINDER REFORM

In addition to the structural weaknesses, several Japanese societal traits which have been instilled by government, schools, family and corporations, make reform and change difficult.

■ *Form over substance*—The Japanese emphasis on form over substance dominated the JFI salaryman's efforts overseas. Form has a rightful place, but not to the exclusion of substance.

■ *"Wet" over "dry"*—The tendency to evaluate matters with a heavy component of emotion and personal feeling led to a de-emphasis of rational criteria. The obligations which arose from this attitude were harmful, as in the case of the compensation for losses given to influential clients. The superiority which this fosters has been destructive, as in the arrogance which led to the excesses in the Japanese equity and real estate markets.

■ *Japanese uniqueness*—The notion of Japanese uniqueness has further impaired the difficult task of assimilating people into JFIs. It has also been partially responsible for the failure to succeed in foreign markets because Japanese have applied their own concepts to overseas business and possible opportunities, rather than seeking to understand them.

■ *Contextual truth*—Among other characteristics, the idea of contextual truth allowed the JFIs to avoid dealing with mistakes and accountability.

■ *Independence versus dependence*—The JFI employee was conditioned to believe that his institution should be self-sufficient and should not be dependent on foreign personnel or expertise. Yet, the JFI developed a dependency on large foreign and domestic intermediaries for financial products, clients, and information to the exclusion of potentially long-term, substantive, complementary relationships with firms, such as professional foreign money managers, or principal investors.

■ *Yumei na kaisha syndrome*—The Japanese emphasis on dealing with large institutions amounted to blind faith at times. This was confining and counterproductive.

■ *Conformity, peer pressure, and hierarchy*—All these related characteristics have been nurtured through family, education and corporation. Their existence is well-known. The consequences are not immediately discernible.

■ *Stability*—The above traits reinforce the absolute need for stability to the exclusion of change. All must be orchestrated. Ideas must be introduced such that the system is not challenged.

JFIs' CHALLENGE IN 1990s

The JFIs have begun the 1990s in a state of fear and confusion because of the domestic market debacle. The market crash and the capital problems of Japanese banks are only a symptom of the problem. The real issues are the structural weaknesses. The JFIs have described their new policy as cautious and sophisticated, when it is more accurately characterized by uncertainty and paralysis.

The JFIs must learn how to utilize, in an efficient manner, their loyal and competent staff, which is trained to work within a system. This means that they must develop a proper system of performance measurement, accountability, and motivation for individuals and businesses.

As we have seen, there are no blueprints for JFIs. In a sense, my observations are intended to provoke discussion and debate. The search for immediate and easy solutions will be superficial and yield no benefit. Institutional change is difficult.

> " The JFIs have described their new policy as cautious and sophisticated, when it is more accurately characterized by uncertainty and paralysis. "

American financial institutions represent many different strategies. Merrill Lynch, Morgan Stanley, Salomon Brothers, Goldman Sachs, Morgan Guaranty, Bankers Trust, Citibank, Republic Bank, Bank One, Wachovia, and Fidelity are constantly evolving and can not be copied by the JFIs. JFIs must learn to adapt, focus, and use their strengths effectively. They must learn how to permit experimentation.

The JFIs must recognize that the present structure for overseas business needs change and is leading nowhere. The JFIs must find ways to communicate internally and externally. They must find ways to complement the rotation system with reliable individuals and firms. They should create long-term strategies that survive rotating personnel. The JFIs should identify goals, be selective in what they undertake, and not try to do all things. During the 1980s, the Japanese institutional investors were diverting cash flow; during the 1990s, a more thoughtful approach to making quality investments with adequate returns and proper consideration of risks is warranted. Without higher returns, it is difficult to justify current market valuations of Japanese banks and securities firms relative to the overall Japanese market.

The success of the JFIs domestically was the result of external factors, such as regulation, bull markets, and the manufacturing sector. The strength of the JFIs was a function of these favorable domestic circumstances. To date, they have squandered an opportunity to build successful overseas operations in terms of recycling investments or establishing businesses. Instead, they have created a bottleneck for investments, cost structures, and unprofitable activities overseas.

The process of change is likely to take longer and be more difficult than is generally anticipated. The strengths of Japanese society have become weaknesses in the overseas financial area. Even when the domestic market stabilizes, the JFI system will be badly in need of reform. Reliance on the "convoy system," whereby all entities will proceed together, retards reform. The announced plans for deregulation in Japan make the changes even more relevant.

The lesson of the 1980s for the JFIs is that they cannot compete successfully in overseas business, whether in Japan or abroad, without significant change. The lesson for the 1990s for Japan is that its financial institutions, in a sense, became decoupled from the rest of the economy. Unless they change, they will become an increasingly heavy burden for the rest of the economy.

This does not mean that the Japanese financial system is in imminent danger of collapse should the JFIs fail to change themselves. These remain powerful institutions and retain a valuable franchise in the second largest economy in the world. Should a shakeout cause some JFIs to disappear through merger and absorption, those remaining might be better placed. The real question here, therefore, is one of momentum—will the JFIs be a positive or negative influence on Japan's and, by implication, the world's economic growth?

BIBLIOGRAPHY

Alletzhauser, Al, *The House of Nomura, The Rise to Supremacy of the World's Most Powerful Company, The Inside Story of a Legendary Dynasty.* New York: Bloomsbury, 1990.

Burstein, David, *Yen! Japan's New Financial Empire And Its Threat to America.* New York: A Fawcett Columbine Book, 1990.

Burstein, Daniel, *Turning the Tables: A Machiavellian Strategy for Dealing with Japan.* New York: Simon & Schuster, 1993.

Buruma, Ian, *God's Dust, A Modern Asian Journey.* New York: Vintage, 1991.

Chapman, William, *Inventing Japan, The Making of a Post-War Civilization.* Englewood Cliffs, NJ: Prentice Hall, 1991.

Crichton, Michael, *Rising Sun.* New York: Alfred A. Knopf, 1992.

Emmott, William, *The Sun Also Sets, The Limits to Japan's Economic Power.* New York: Times Books, Random House, 1989.

Emmott, William, *Japan's Global Reach: The Influences, Strategies and Weaknesses of Japan's Multinational Companies.* New York: Century, 1992.

Feiler, Bruce, *Learning to Bow.* New York: Ticknor and Fields, 1991.

Genji, Kieta, *The Lucky One And Other Humorous Stories.* Translated by Hugh Cortazzi. Tokyo: The Japan Times, Ltd., 1980.

Hayes, Samuel L. III; Hubbard, Philip M., *Investment Banking, A Tale of Three Cities.* Cambridge, MA: Harvard Business School Press, 1990.

Kennedy, Paul, *The Rise and Fall of the Great Powers, Economic Change and Military Conflict From 1500 to 2000.* New York: Random House, 1987.

Kennedy, Paul, *Preparing for the Twenty-First Century.* New York: Random House, 1993.

Lewis, Michael, *Liar's Poker.* New York: W.W. Norton & Company, 1989.

Prestowitz, Clyde V. Jr., *Trading Places. How We Allowed Japan to Take the Lead.* New York: Basic Books, Inc. 1988.

Sevan-Schreiber, Jean-Jacques, *The American Challenge.* New York: Atheneum, 1968.

Smith, Roy C., *Comeback: The Restoration of American Banking Power in the New World Economy.* Cambridge, MA: Harvard Business School Press, 1993.

Tasker, Peter, *Inside Japan: Wealth, Work and Power in the Japanese Empire.* London: Sidgwick & Jackson, 1987.

van Wolferen, Karel, *The Enigma of Japanese Power.* New York: Alfred A. Knopf, 1989.

Viner, Aron, *Inside Japan's Financial Markets.* Homewood, IL: Dow Jones-Irwin, 1988.

Viner, Aron, *The Emerging Power of Japanese Mercy.* Tokyo: The Japan Times, 1988.

Wood, Christopher, *The Bubble Economy: Japan's Extraordinary Boom of the '80s and the Dramatic Bust of the '90s.* New York: The Atlantic Monthly Press, 1992.

Zielinski, Robert and Holloway, Nigel, *Unequal Equities, Power and Risk in Japan's Stock Market.* Toyko: Kodansha Intern, 1991.

INDEX